Devotion to Truth
The Life of
Rt. Rev. Sylvester H. Rosecrans, D.D.
First Bishop of Columbus

Devotion to Truth
The Life of
Rt. Rev. Sylvester H. Rosecrans, D.D.
First Bishop of Columbus

by Donald M. Schlegel

Catholic Record Society-Diocese of Columbus

Devotion to Truth
The Life of Rt. Rev. Sylvester H. Rosecrans, D.D., First Bishop of Columbus
All Rights Reserved.
Copyright © 2018 Donald M. Schlegel
v2.0 r1.0

The opinions expressed in this manuscript are solely the opinions of the author and do not represent the opinions or thoughts of the publisher. The author has represented and warranted full ownership and/or legal right to publish all the materials in this book.

This book may not be reproduced, transmitted, or stored in whole or in part by any means, including graphic, electronic, or mechanical without the express written consent of the publisher except in the case of brief quotations embodied in critical articles and reviews.

Outskirts Press, Inc.
http://www.outskirtspress.com

ISBN: 978-1-4787-4781-9

Cover Photo © 2018 Lydia R. Curtis. All rights reserved - used with permission.

Outskirts Press and the "OP" logo are trademarks belonging to Outskirts Press, Inc.

PRINTED IN THE UNITED STATES OF AMERICA

Contents

I	Youth, Conversion, and Education, 1827-1852	1
II	Cincinnati Clergyman, 1852-1868	17
III	Auxiliary Bishop, 1862-1868	31
IV	New Diocesan Ordinary, 1866-1873	49
V	Clergy, Journeys, and Family Vocations, 1868-1878	65
VI	Academies for Young Women, 1862-1878	83
VII	Institutions and New Parishes, 1868-1878	97
VIII	St. Joseph Cathedral, 1866-1878	115
IX	This Life's End, 1877-1878	135

Tables:
1	Episcopal Acts as Auxiliary Bishop	43
2	Clergy Inherited from Cincinnati	67
3	Clergy Ordained for Columbus	68
4	Churches, Stations, and Pastors, March 3, 1868	109

Sources and Notes	143
Selected Public Words	161
Index	209

Selected Public Words

Charity and the Last Judgment Sermon	161
The Sifting of the Wheat Editorial, October 29, 1853	173
May Editorial, May 1, 1875	175
The Catholic Church a Kingdom Sermon, 1877	176
The Pope's Mission Editorial, Oct. 2, 1875	182
The Decoration of Our Churches	
Editorial, Sept. 11, 1875	183
The Necessity of True Faith Editorial, July 10, 1875	183
Devotion to the Sacred Heart	
Editorial, January 23, 1875	184
A Career for Catholic Young Men	
Editorial, Sept. 11, 1875	185
Conversion a Gift of God	
Editorial, December 25, 1858	186
Gallileo Editorial, February 13, 1875	188
Revolutionizing the Government	
Editorial, Feb. 23, 1861	188
Reforming by Law Editorial, July 9, 1853	190
Equality of Men Before God Editorial, June 6, 1878	192
Men are Not Equal Editorial, July 15, 1876	193
Socialist Unbelievers Editorial, August 19, 1876	193
Liberalism in Religion Editorial, Sept. 25, 1875	194
Religion and Progress Lecture, March, 1866	197
Promulgation of the Decree on Papal Infallibility	
Pastoral Letter, Aug. 30, 1870	205
The Editor-Bishop is Found Out	
Editorial, January 29, 1876	208

Acknowledgements

This work has been accomplished largely using the resources of the Catholic Record Society-Diocese of Columbus. The society was founded in 1974 by Msgr. Herman E. Mattingly in his retirement. He also worked assiduously in the diocesan archives, my second most important resource. Msgr. Mattingly, born in 1902, knew many persons who had known Bishop Rosecrans. He devoted some of his time in the archives to collecting the letters of the bishop and he published portions of the bishop's student journal in the pages of the Society's monthly *Bulletin*. Of special importance to this work, the Society holds microfilms of *The Catholic Telegraph and Advocate* from the bishop's lifetime as well as a useful collection of books and other printed works.

As always, one hesitates to name individuals who were of assistance in this work, because of the risk of omitting some. But those well remembered include Sister Debbie Lloyd, archivist of the Ursulines of Brown County, who provided photographs. Kathleen Washy, archivist of the Sisters of St. Joseph, Baden, provided information on that congregation's early work in Columbus and on Father Christy. The Ohio Province Archives, Sisters of Notre Dame de Namur, provided the earliest known photograph of Bishop Rosecrans. Other valuable resources were the University of Notre Dame Archives; the UCLA Library Special Collections, William S. Rosecrans Papers; and the A. T. Wehrle Library of the Pontifical College Josephinum.

Lydia R. Curtis photographed the Record Society's portrait of the bishop for the cover. Kate S. Ortega of Brooklyn kindly read the manuscript and made corrections and helpful suggestions. Kimberly Woodruff provided technical advice, always with a smile.

My thanks to you all.

Introduction

The life of Sylvester Horton Rosecrans, first Bishop of Columbus, was filled with accomplishments.

He was a pastor, an educator, a journalist, and a bishop. What he did in any one of those fields would have been enough to merit a book in its own right.

But perhaps the most remarkable of all his achievements was that Bishop Rosecrans was able to accomplish so much in the short span of 51 years. And he did so with a humble spirit.

Shortly after his death, his humility was described in this way by *The Catholic Columbian*, the diocesan weekly newspaper which he founded and for which he served as the first editor: "Vested with one of the highest offices of the Church, he aspired to no distinction as a prelate, but delighted in the simplicity of a humble priest." When he died, his possessions consisted of a watch, a few pictures, and "other trifles."

Bishop Rosecrans arrived in Columbus with no fanfare, getting off a train from Cincinnati in early 1867 and walking alone from the railroad station to St. Patrick Church with a tattered carpetbag in his hand. He didn't like the city at first, perhaps because, even though it was the state capital, it was much smaller than Cincinnati in those days, and the Catholics who did live there didn't seem to be that enthusiastic about the Church.

But he quickly came to love Columbus, so much so that he asked for and received permission from the Vatican to skip the First Vatican Council in 1869 and 1870 because he was too busy getting his new diocese established and overseeing his crowning achievement, the building of St. Joseph Cathedral.

That magnificent edifice in the heart of downtown was a 12-year project. Planning for its construction began in 1866 before the diocese was formed. Work got under way in 1868, the first Mass there was celebrated on Christmas Day of 1872, and the consecration ceremony was on Oct. 20, 1878.

It's well-known that Bishop Rosecrans died the day after the dedication and is buried in the cathedral undercroft, and it can fairly be said that the effort of getting it completed cost him his life. He suffered hemorrhages on many occasions when he became excited. Those hemorrhages became especially acute in the last two years of his life, with four attacks coming on the evening of the dedication and ultimately killing him.

The bishop was part of a remarkable family from the tiny Licking County town of Homer. Long before I had ever heard of him, I was familiar with the exploits of his brother, Gen. William Rosecrans, in Tennessee during the Civil War. This book tells Sylvester's story, but William plays a significant part in it because the older brother's conversion to Catholicism in 1845 led to the younger brother following in William's footsteps.

As Bishop Rosecrans said after visiting his brother on the front lines, "While the General is wielding 'the sword of the flesh,' I trust that I am using 'the sword of the Spirit.' He is fighting the rebels, and I am fighting the spirits of darkness." Bishop Rosecrans' mentor, Archbishop John Purcell, described the brothers in this way: "It looks as though the General would have made a good Bishop—and the Bishop a good General."

William Rosecrans also served as what today might be termed a consulting architect on construction of the cathedral.

The bishop always will be remembered for his efforts in building the Diocese of Columbus spiritually and the cathedral physically, but he had his share of disappointments and controversies. He had problems with Archbishop Purcell and didn't get along well with the Dominican Sisters of St. Mary of the Springs, now the Dominican Sisters of Peace, who have been an important part of the diocese since its earliest days.

This book celebrates the sesquicentennial of the founding of the Diocese of Columbus, providing a thorough look at the times and the persons who were deeply involved in its beginnings, especially our first bishop.

Tim Puet

Reporter, *Catholic Times*, Columbus, O.

Chapter I
Youth, Conversion, and Education, 1827-1852

Youth

Sylvester Rosecrans was born with a father "of religious feeling who affiliated with no particular church and a grandmother who was a Methodist of intense convictions." In the nursery he heard of "the horror and bloody tortures of Popery," dungeons, chains, and the rack.[1] He was born and grew up in northern Licking County, Ohio, a region then noted for its anti-Catholic sentiments. But he followed the path traced for him by the finger of God, by which he became a Catholic, a priest, and the saintly first Bishop of Columbus.

Sylvester's father, Crandall Rosecrans, had been born in Wilkes-Barre, Pennsylvania, and had come to Delaware County, Ohio, with his parents, Dr. Daniel and Thankful (Wilcox) Rosecrans, in 1808. Dr. Daniel Rosecrans was a son of Captain Daniel Rosecrans, a soldier in the War for American Independence. His earliest American ancestor had arrived in New Amsterdam from Holland in 1651, where the name was spelled Rosenkrantz. The name was pronounced with three syllables and in later times the Bishop's closest brother, General William Rosecrans, insisted upon using all three. Crandall proved his patriotism by enlisting in the Light Horse Battalion that went to the relief of Detroit during the War of 1812. He returned home a Captain. In 1816 he married Jemima, a daughter of Timothy Hopkins. The family pointed with pride to Stephen Hopkins, a signer of the Declaration of Independence, as a relative. This patriotic ancestry reinforced the speeches full of warmth and toasts full of hope that young Sylvester heard at Independence Day celebrations in the groves of Licking County; it gave him confidence in the ultimate success of the country's great experiment in freedom—an experiment he would defend as a young priest in the pages of Cincinnati's *Catholic Telegraph*.

Crandall Rosecrans moved the family from Delaware County to the small village of Burlington, now named Homer, in northern Licking County, about 1820. There he owned several lots on the northeast corner of the town's single intersection, where he built a home in 1825. He opened a tavern and store, acquired additional lots and houses, and had a garden and a potash factory. At one time he commanded the militia of the area and from time to time he was engaged in the construction of public works. He also had a farm south of the village.[2]

General Rosecrans wrote of Crandall that he was strong-willed, self-reliant, was popular and well respected, despite his well-known iron will and hot temper. The mother Jemima he described as gentle, deeply religious, and insistent on everyone speaking the truth. Sylvester described their mother as "humble and yielding, always preferring the will of others before her own....She concealed her own grief and thought only of my advantages and comfort." Grandmother Thankful (Wilcox) Rosecrans was a Methodist, quick, small, dark and peppery. Grandma Phoebe (Nesbit) Hopkins had large blue eyes, a pale face, and, in her late years, a bald head. She was very charitable and openhanded.[3]

The older children of Crandall and Jemima were Chauncey (born 1817, died very young); William Starke (1819-1898) the famous engineer and general; Charles Wesley (1822-1865) who moved to Keokuk County, Iowa, and had one daughter; and Henry Crandall (1824-1904) who also lived in Keokuk County and had six children. Sylvester Horton, the youngest child, was born in Homer on February 5, 1827, in his parents' house, which still stands today.

Sylvester did not experience the secluded childhood in rural Ohio that one might imagine. He remembered being on the streets of New York City at the age of three, in the charge of a servant, and seeing a procession that never left his memory: a hearse topped with sable ostrich plumes, drawn by white horses draped in black; long files of soldiers with muskets reversed; societies in rank; countless citizens; the sad roll of muffled drum and the wail of the dead march from musical instruments. This, he was told, was the funeral of James Monroe.[4]

It is not known where the Rosecrans boys received their early education. It was said that young Sylvester manifested evidences of a powerful mind and the advantages of a collegiate education were placed at his disposal.[5] He was sent for secondary education to Kenyon College near Gambier in Knox County, Ohio, an Episcopalian institution.

Kenyon College

At Kenyon College, Rosecrans "was easily the outstanding scholar of his class," and his scholastic record was almost perfect.[6] His intellectual growth gave great hope to the professors at Kenyon and he ranked first in his class in physics and mathematics.[7] But he later realized that his attitude during these three years had been seriously wanting. He concentrated on music, the friendship of a few, worldly hopes, and expectations of advancement, "with but a rare chance thought upon my salvation." He had determined to live among the refined and to astonish men by showing what he could and would do for power and advancement. He had hopes of political advancement; of a life of proud and stern voluptuousness; of living as first among the refined.[8]

On the intellectual side, he was captivated by a desire to find out the abstract truths, "Whence are we?" and "Why are we?" He scorned the common lot, loathing to be one of the multitude. He believed then that greatness was the true end of his being; and accordingly he enquired, "What is it to be great?" This was the subject of his Junior Oration, "What is Greatness?" which he wrote in the winter of 1846. "I saw, moreover, that to preserve the dignity of human nature, this greatness must be independent of material circumstances. I began then to have a fair glimpse of the colossal proportions of the Christian, and began to 'respect not a little' the white-robed army of martyrs, though it was Protestant respect. From this time I thought with more intensity than before.

I was to do something more, to stretch myself beyond the common measure."

About this time he was given his first Catholic book, one of the many works of Richard Challoner (1691-1781), who had been Vicar Apostolic of the London District. (No doubt the book had been sent by William.) He would hide the book in his drawer and not read it when anyone would see him. By this time he had chosen religion for his "life plan," concluding that it was the true greatness.

Sylvester's brother William had won a congressional appointment to West Point, where he was admitted in 1838. He was graduated in 1842 and remained at the military academy as assistant professor of engineering. While still a cadet he had "obtained a few books treating of the Catholic Church from an old Irishman, who was in the habit of paying periodical visits to the institution to sell books and papers" and the peddler "in his own original way told him what the Church was." He became interested in the claims of the Church and it was not long until his logical mind was convinced. In 1844 he was received into the Church with conditional baptism, there having been a vague tradition that, in accord with his grandmother's wishes, he had been baptized in infancy by a Methodist minister. He wrote a letter to Sylvester, announcing his conversion and giving his reasons for this grave step.[9]

Thanks to William, the proofs of the truth of the Catholic Religion multiplied upon Sylvester until finally he believed in its authority before he was instructed in its doctrines. Finding such a frightful conclusion staring him in the face, he began to back out of his project of being earnest. To avoid a commitment to the true religion, he began to delight in sensual gratifications more, to suit his companions more. He received William's letters "with a pang, read them hastily, answered them with labor and forgot them as soon as possible." Old Rector Smith "nailed" him one evening when at his house, asking if Sylvester did not want to be baptized and confirmed the next Sunday. "His address froze me. I revolted from the thought, especially of being confirmed," so he refused flatly. Argument followed. "Finally, on my blunt refusal he said, 'very well my blood might be on my own head,' and left me. I was cut and stunned. I wanted Old Smith to think well of me, and my quarrel with him made me feel very unhappy." But the incident raised in him the intense question, "Here I have waited a year; am I going to wait until my death? I sat up very late that night and felt very unhappy."[10]

Conversion

That April of 1846 Sylvester was at home, at the family farm south of Homer, becoming re-grounded in the real world. "Here from the window I can look out upon our sheep and colts gathered together and basking in the sun down by the woods. Father and I have been making a garden last week. We have perpetrated a gravel walk from the front door to the road.... An old ill-looking fence surrounds the house.... Mother is well and blessed with excellent health...."[11]

William sent him a letter with $50 and an order to come east. He left home, half glad but half sorry, and made his way to Cleveland. As he departed from Cleveland on Lake Erie, he "left the sight of all I then in the bonds of worldly affection had linked to my heart. A new world then dawned upon me—and slowly afterwards my eyes were accustomed to its light. My old hopes, my old dreams, my old fears, then began to pass away. Oh! God of infinite mercy how tenderly Thou didst lead me along. If Thou hadst shown me before I left home the breaking of these ties of love, the passing from a circle of gay and generous friends; if Thou hadst shown me all I would have resisted Thy inspirations and stayed at home! But Thou didst lead me tenderly. Thou didst bear me on Thy shoulders, and while I thought I was following my own will, I was carried by Thee. Blessed forever be Thy name!"

He met William in New York City and the next day they sailed up the Hudson. That Sunday he went to the Episcopal Church for the last time, not paying much attention to the sermon.[12]

Father F. W. Gockeln, president of St. John's College, told a New York correspondent a story that, if not fully accurate, seems at least to truly present the concern that William and his wife Annie felt for Sylvester. ..."at the time young Sylvester

H. Rosecrans first visited his brother's family at West Point, in 1846, he was excessively fond of all out-door sports and passtimes, and was passionately fond of rowing and boating on the Hudson. On one occasion, Sylvester remained away from his brother's house until about eleven o'clock at night. On his return the family expressed their anxiety in strong terms, and the Lieutenant [William] admonished him to return at more seasonable hours. Mrs. Rosecrans was more disturbed than her husband and feeling a warm, sisterly, almost maternal interest in her young, handsome, happy-hearted brother-in-law, she exclaimed, 'How could you stay out on the river so late, when the water is so boisterous and there is such danger of your being drowned? Suppose you were to drown, and you not a Catholic? It would be terrible.' All this, and much more to the same effect, was said with an energetic emphasis that must have set the most thoughtless to thinking; and the younger Rosecrans was not a thoughtless youth."[13] (The story continues, erroneously, that Sylvester stayed out even later the next evening and, upon being similarly admonished, surprised the family with the fact that he had been baptized that day.)

That week Sylvester read Spalding's Review of *D'Aubigni* and some of Cobbett's *English Reformation*. "My old conviction of the catholicity of the Catholic Church was strong upon me. But still it did not guide me. The next Sunday William asked me if I would go to Mass. I have but a dim recollection of my impressions there. Poor Father Villanies sweat and I recollect feeling sorry that he was obliged to bundle himself up so."

"Time passed, I went to Mass again. I continued to read Catholic books a little. William and I had been bathing and were on the rocks in Washington's Valley talking. I had thought myself drawing away from Church and was secretly determined to put it off for many years, if not forever. God, however, pursued me. He might have left me. All at once William turned to me and said: 'My dear brother, I think you are sufficiently prepared to receive Baptism, are you not?' I was stunned, shocked, bewildered. The thing was come to a point. There was no escape. God helped me and spoke—by my mouth. He made me think, 'Well, if I have got to choose now between Religion and no Religion, I will take Religion.'

I answered 'Yes.' I had not even prayed. I did not know how to pray. William told me, 'What ever other prayers you say, I would like to have you say the Hail Mary.' I accordingly got on my knees and said the Hail Mary, and afterwards I said some other prayers, at least stayed on my knees awhile. That day I went to Mass, and Father Villanies asked me some eight or nine questions. I was not baptised, as I expected, at Mass, but in the afternoon. Afternoon came and we went over in the boat, landing at Mr. Kimble's boat-house and walking from there to the little church. We went in. There were only four or five there. Father Villanies had provided a Godfather and Godmother. Good Mr. Phalen and Mrs. Lawson."[14]

He was baptized at Cold Spring, opposite West Point, by Rev. Felix Vilanis, who was pastor of the Catholic Church there and was in charge of the station at West Point, on May 10, 1846.[15]

Crandall and Jemima showed considerable opposition to the new faith of their sons, so Sylvester, on William's advice, left Kenyon College in 1846 and enrolled at the Jesuits' St. John's College at Fordham, N.Y.

St. John's College

Sylvester had decided to study philosophy and elocution preparatory to studying law, to which he was inclined.[16] He went to St. John's despite already knowing that everything there would be totally different from what he had been accustomed to at Kenyon: "no private rooms for sleep or study; no roaming off solitary and alone, or in parties of twos and threes—stated hours for retiring and rising."[17]

On his arrival at St. John's, he had not yet made his first Communion nor received Confirmation. But, he wrote to William, he felt at home in the Church. Within just a few years of this time he had become very critical of his spiritual attitude during these first months at St. John's. "There I remained with all my pride and sloth. I revolted from the discipline. I did not like to be mixed up with little fellows. I had never heard Vespers. I was too proud to ask to have them explained to me. But human respect I had. I did as others. And how many times did I bow before the Adorable

Host without a single sentiment of my own or a single act of adoration, just as a monkey would have bowed his head had he been in my place." "I was exceedingly disgusted with my companions. They were so young and so boyish. So I gazed out the prison-house of my baptismal vows, and of my pledged word, and longed to run and riot in the deceitful brightness of all that is in this world. And cowardly that I was, I feared the brightness of truth."[18] One night Father Thomas Legouais called Sylvester up to his room. The student talked a great deal, but it was only about the emptiness of Protestantism. The priest did not seem pleased with Sylvester's volubility.

Sylvester also later noted in his journal that instead of making his first Communion so late and afterwards instead of going to Communion so seldom, he should have gone more often and with better preparation.[19] However, once during this period it occurred to him that he might perhaps one day be a priest.

On the academic front he was doing well. In October he was "elected" to give a speech on November 22. He did so and wrote out a copy of the speech for "my Society," which he did not name in his letter describing the incident.

He began to progress in the spiritual life and otherwise. "The luxurious habits I had at Kenyon were with utmost difficulty broken in upon; and continually feeling discomfort and continually fearing it, I suffered a great deal in the winter months..." Once when walking out towards the sound, he vehemently threw away his tobacco, never to use it again.[20] He made his first Communion on Christmas Day, 1846, in the little chapel at West Point. He had been to Confession three days earlier. On New Year's Day, 1847, William gave him an example he would never forget. He had promised to walk out with the old professor of French to make calls. But when he heard that there was to be Mass at the falls he wrote a note to the latter that there was going to be Mass and that therefore he was compelled to forgo the pleasure he had anticipated in making those calls.[21]

That winter or spring Sylvester and William made a retreat together. Sylvester thought he made it well, but could have done better had he consulted his confessor more, and with greater simplicity. It was about this time that he decided he was called to be a priest. During spring vacation William and he were walking on the banks of the Hudson. "I remember the place, the grey rocks that laid around us, the little weed I held in my hand. William approached me cautiously saying by way of preamble that the time was now fast approaching when I would be obliged to choose a state of life, etc. I then told him I had already chosen as far as I was concerned, that I had written to Father and Mother to ask their consent [to become a priest]. My good brother, how glad he was! Even then I hoped that Father would make some opposition and even the feeblest would have been sufficient. I told him also that I would go, I thought, to Ohio in which he freely acquiesced." His father wrote back, giving his consent in most loving terms. Sylvester considered, in May, whether "speedily being ordained is desirable," but by late June learned that he could not be ordained until reaching the age of twenty-five.

Meanwhile, he was preparing for Confirmation and graduation. He wrote to William, the only indication that we have, that he was to be confirmed at St. John's College on the feast of Corpus Christi, which that year was on Thursday, June 3.

Sylvester was not examined in his classes and did not need go to recitations after June 10, but he had a speech to prepare for the graduation ceremony, to be held on July 15. He was one of four graduates who received the Bachelor of Arts degree. (The other graduates were Thomas Dolan, Andrew J. Smith, and P. McCarron.) "The exercises were conducted in a large tent erected on the beautiful lawn in front of the college buildings, where, after the passengers from the last train had taken their places, there were present about two thousand persons, among whom we observed members of the City Legislature, officers of the army and other public persons, besides hundreds of pretty girls, beautiful young ladies and good looking matrons." Five speeches were given by students, that of Rosecrans, judged the best, being saved for last. It was printed in *The New York Herald*; the *Truth Teller*; and *The Freeman's Journal and Catholic Register*. It was titled

"Nothing Original" and was described by the *Freeman's Journal* as "counteracting the idolatrous 'Hero-Worship' of our age." It was "vastly more moral in its conclusions, than logical in its premises," but "it was well delivered and gave evidence that its author, both in writing and delivery, is capable of much more."[22] Sylvester later wrote disgustedly, "How intoxicated with vanity was I at the plaudits I received, and the publication and the night after."

Sylvester and William made another retreat together, apparently that summer. "How William did stride forward and how I lagged. He had a mind to seize upon the vast principles of Religion to penetrate its sublime maxims, and the strength and steadiness of nerve to apply them unflinchingly to himself, more necessary for me perhaps than it was for him. At any rate it was very necessary for me." Rev. Augustus J. Thebaud, president of St. John's College, thought the next retreat would be better, because Sylvester had not concluded at this time to be a Jesuit. "At any rate one of my resolutions then was to accede to any grade of perfection to which God was pleased to call me, to which Dr. T. acquiesced. I suppose the reason he made us the retreat so easily was he hoped to make me a Jesuit, and those hopes were not at all concealed from what I heard of that wild eyed man who had had the brain fever. I certainly had a very great repugnance to remaining in N.Y. and to becoming a Jesuit also. And whether this repugnance had anything to do for my refusal and how much had to do I shall see, of course in the day of Judgment. God help me help me then. Be that as it may, I then concluded anew to become a priest, and then for the first time began to conceive somewhat of the immeasurable privileges of that high vocation. I did not fear on the other hand. I scarcely cast a thought that direction. But passed—trusting in God? or in myself? We shall see the day of Judgment."[23]

He returned home via Albany, Syracuse, a packet boat to Oswego, and the Ontario Lake boat *Niagara* to Niagara Falls, thence to Cleveland and on to Homer by September 1. Sylvester now threw himself wholeheartedly into the practice of his faith. "He was intensely Catholic in all his feelings as

Youth, Conversion, and Education

well as his thoughts; a Papist to the core of his heart, as his former co-religionists would say."[24] He often walked the eight miles to Mt. Vernon, fasting, so that he could receive Holy Communion at Mass offered by Father Lamy in the temporary quarters then being used as a church. At this time he also encountered Rev. Matthew A. O'Brien, O.P., of St. Joseph's near Somerset, whom he recruited to explore the possibility of his parents' conversion to the Catholic Church. Father O'Brien visited them in Homer on September 20 and gave them some Catholic books. The next day Sylvester went with him to visit the Postlewaites, one of the few Catholic families in the neighborhood, and on the way back they stopped at Sylvester's Aunt Betsey's, where Father O'Brien left a catechism with her. His mother, he knew, wanted to know the truth and Father O'Brien promised to visit again in the new year. Sylvester remembered his own discussions with his parents on the subject: "God help me! If I had had the strength of character which William had they would have been converted without difficulty. But I was feeble; I wavered; now I was here, now there; now on one side, now on the other."[25] He took them to Somerset early in October. Sylvester reported the journey to William and said that Father O'Brien would stop at Homer again near Christmas on his way to Mt. Vernon and would baptize their mother if she were sufficiently instructed by then, and on his return he would give her Communion. But this was delayed.[26] Crandall never became a Catholic and died in August, 1848 while Sylvester was in Rome. After Crandall's death, Jemima did join the Church.

Meanwhile Sylvester, or perhaps his pastor, Father Lamy, had contacted Bishop Purcell in Cincinnati about his budding religious vocation. The Bishop wrote to him to be in Cincinnati by November 1. Someone had raised the possibility of studying theology in Rome, but the Bishop thought that Rome was no place to study just then because of the political upheavals in Europe.

Sylvester was in Cincinnati by October 22 and was kindly received by the Bishop's brother, Rev. Edward Purcell. He was given a room in the episcopal residence attached to the Cathedral; it had been last occupied by the pioneer missionary Father Stephen Badin, *Protosacerdos* of the United States, as he styled himself.[27] Sylvester later noted, "I entered upon my new quarters. I was half wild. Then I did not appreciate where I was or what I was doing. I went to see Uncle Parmenus [Rosecrans]."

Bishop Purcell immediately took Rosecrans with him to Vincennes, Indiana, for the consecration of Bishop Stephen Bazin for that see, on October 24, for whom Purcell was a co-consecrator.[28] Then, having become convinced of his merit, the bishop decided to send Rosecrans to Rome, after all, "Having an eye on what you will be in a few years." Purcell thought the discipline of the College of the Propaganda would take the kinks out of him.[29] A biographer many years later ascribed the Bishop's decision to seeing in Sylvester "every sign of a true vocation to the priesthood—piety, talents, prudence and generosity."[30]

His journey started on the dark, dreary night of December 11, 1847. The Bishop came down to the wharf to see him off. As the riverboat steamed downriver between Indiana and Kentucky, the lights in the farmhouses vividly reminded him of home, but he did not feel discouraged. He reached New Orleans ten days later.

Roman Seminary Days

Sylvester was in Lafayette and New Orleans from December 19, 1847, to January 10, 1848. He visited with Bishop Blanc, checked on vessels for Marseilles, was called upon by Father Peter Anderson, a Dominican who had been stationed at Zanesville whom he had met on the steamboat, wrote letters, read, and saw to his religious duties.

At 9 p.m. on Tuesday, January 11, his chosen vessel cast off and started down the river for the Gulf. Aboard ship he discussed religion with the captain, wrote a hymn to the Blessed Virgin, and weathered storms. They passed through the Straits of Gibraltar on Feb. 25 and landed in Marseilles on March 3. After Mass at the Cathedral on Sunday, March 5, he took a steamboat for Genoa. He arrived at Rome after dark on March 8 and was enrolled in the college the following day.

Youth, Conversion, and Education

The college Rosecrans entered was the Urban College, named for its founder, Pope Urban VIII. This pontiff had seen that the seminaries established in accordance with the decrees of the Council of Trent had produced excellent results in the various national colleges that had been established in Rome. But he found it necessary to establish a central seminary especially for countries that did not have their own national college there. "It seemed very desirable to have, in every country, priests educated in an international college where they could acquire a larger personal acquaintance, and establish in youth relations that might be mutually helpful in after life." He founded the seminary of the Congregation of the Propaganda known as the Collegium Urbanum in 1627, so that it was a venerable institution of over two hundred years when young Rosecrans arrived.

In Rome, Sylvester became aware of the true catholicity of the Church and the many persecutions and trials it faced around the world, for example Greek Catholics who faced repression by the Orthodox and their British rulers on Adriatic islands; Syrian Christians who faced poverty and persecution in the Levant; and the Negro priest from Guinea who stood and knelt next to him at ordination, headed for a difficult life on the missions in Africa.[31]

Rosecans's first sixteen months in Rome[32] were colored by events of Italian national significance. "Red Republican" radicals, anti-Catholic and anti-papal, wanted to unite Italy, including the Papal States, into a single, secular government. Their riotous actions and threats caused Pope Pius to leave Rome for exile in Gaeta in the Kingdom of Naples on November 24, 1848. A radical assembly proclaimed the Papal States to be a republic on February 9, 1849, and nine days later the Pope asked the Catholic powers to drive the radicals from Rome. On April 21 French troops arrived at Civitavecchia and within a few days had reached the gates of Rome. Garibaldi's revolutionary forces arrived, the firing of cannon began on April 30, and the French retired on May 1. The French returned towards the city in force on May 11. After negotiations failed, hostilities broke out again, with the French handing the radicals a defeat on June 3 but not finally taking Rome until July 3.

Rosecrans did not live through these events in isolation in the college. He heard of the convents, including that named for his patron, St. Sylvester, being cleared of nuns to make way for radical troops. "On many a sweet and starry night" he heard "Death to Jesus Christ!" ring out horribly. On May 2, 1849 came the first reports of priests being shot and shortly thereafter he considered leaving Rome, except that he had no money of his own and he already had "tried the temper" of his superiors on this. In June the radicals threatened to evict the students, in order to use their quarters for poor residents bombed out of Trastevere, but in the end they took only the part of the building that had been a museum.[33] From the end of April until early July the students and professors could hardly go outside and food had to be conserved.

During the days of radical power in Rome, Sylvester saw "a triumphant procession in honor of a cold-blooded murderer, and the glare of torches falling on a dagger borne aloft, red with gore." He saw "inoffensive men and women insulted, pelted, imprisoned, murdered, simply because they were dedicated to God." He heard from eye-witnesses the pandemonium that was made of the Pope's Quirnal palace, which had been turned into a hospital. There the last sacraments were mocked by lewd ceremonies carried out over expiring soldiers, suggesting "to the fast fleeting souls words of indecency and blasphemy," and "instead of holding the crucifix, or a picture of the Virgin before the failing eyes of their patients, they exhibited to that last gaze images and objects of loathsome impurity."[34] Throughout, Sylvester prayed for the radicals who were dying excommunicated from the Church, that God have mercy on them and convert those still living.

On July 4, 1849, the students were released from their confinement and Sylvester wrote a long letter to Bishop Purcell describing the events in Rome. It was published in the *Catholic Telegraph* on August 30 and again on September 7. His experiences taught him much about the anti-Catholic "Red Republicans" that later made its way into his editorials in the *Catholic Telegraph*. This knowledge also allowed him to accurately interpret the biased news accounts offered to America by the liberal European newspapers.

Youth, Conversion, and Education

Studies were taken up again in the fall of 1849, beginning of course with a retreat. Things went well. As of February 26, 1850, Sylvester was expecting to receive minor orders on the feast of St. Joseph, March 19.[35] Because his parents were not Catholics, on February 23 a dispensation had been granted for this ordination.[36]

Young Rosecrans distinguished himself in the philosophy course. He set an example of devotion and was prudent, and was esteemed for observing the rules. He held the post of Prefect of various dormitories for as long as he lived in the college, and governed wisely.[37] He "day by day showed more the signs of his noble vocation. He was gentle, kind, studious, and pious." An earlier student from Cincinnati at the college had been James Wood, who would become Archbishop of Philadelphia. It later was written of both Rosecrans and Wood, "by their zeal, talents and piety, they made an honored name for themselves in the Eternal City."

Archbishop Purcell (who was raised to that rank in 1850) visited Rome in the spring of 1851 and "had the happiness of seeing him [Rosecrans] in the Eternal City while he was yet a student, and heard his professors speak of him in highest terms."[38] Rosecrans described the ceremonies on Palm Sunday, April 6:

> I rose in the morning at half past five and left the college at six. From the Irish College to St. Peter's in vinculis where the Bishop said Mass and I made Communion. Returned to the Irish College. We found the carriage waiting and after making our repast we went to St. Peter's, Bishop Murphy, Archbishop Purcell and myself. Arrived there, we were stowed away by a good canon in a suite very near the Papal throne, just behind a row of Bishops and Archbishops dressed in Copes and Chasubles. After we had been there about half an hour we saw the procession coming with the Pope borne on the shoulders of about sixteen men. The choir struck up *"Tu es Petrus"* and *"Ecce Sacerdos Magnus"* away down near the door, and the procession moved slowly on with the waving of plumes, and diamonds flashing on the mitres and vestments of Arch-bishops, Bishops,

Patriarchs, Abbots. The Pope was finally conducted to his throne and intoned the *Dominus* &c, and sang the prayers for the Benediction of Palms.[39]

While in Rome the Archbishop expressed a wish that Rosecrans prepare for the examination for the Doctorate in Theology. He expected this would detain him in Rome an extra three months, until July of 1852.[40]

At the solemn distribution of premiums at the Propaganda on Sept. 4, 1851, Rosecrans obtained a premium in the class of Sacred Scripture, two accessits in Dogmatic Theology, a second premium in Ecclesiastical History, and an award in the second class of Gregorian Music.[41]

He continued through rounds of classes and retreats and on Wednesday, May 26, 1852 was ordained a subdeacon. The date of his subsequent ordination to the diaconate is not known. On Saturday, June 5 he was ordained to the priesthood by Constantino Cardinal Patriz, Bishop of Albano and Vicar of the Pope. Accompanying him were Rev. John C. Albrinck of the Cincinnati archdiocese, who was ordained a subdeacon, and 216 others (including 33 priests, 25 deacons, and 63 subdeacons).[42] He defended his thesis on July 13, before an appointed commission, and was awarded the degree of Doctor of Theology on July 28.[43] In the United States this was called the degree of Doctor of Divinity.[44]

Chapter II
Cincinnati Clergyman, 1852-1868

After receiving his doctorate and being ordained, Father Rosecrans toured Italy, France, England, and Ireland before returning to America. His travel expenses were covered by Cardinal Wiseman, Archbishop of Winchester, and charged to the Propaganda Fide account.[1]

He landed at New York City on August 23 from the ship *Atlantic*. Returning to Cincinnati, he made himself useful to the Archbishop as a pastor, theology professor, newspaper editor, and college president. Besides these major efforts, he also handled lesser ones, such as being clerical director of the Young Men's Catholic Literary Institute in 1853.[2]

His first assignment was to assist at the Cathedral. By November, the Archbishop was considering naming him pastor of St. Augustine's, a new church being built next to the Ursuline convent in Cincinnati[3] and the 1853 annual directory lists him as such, but it does not seem that the appointment was effective. He soon was appointed pastor of St. Thomas Church in Cincinnati. This building, on Sycamore Street between Fifth and Sixth, was purchased by the Archbishop towards the end of 1852 from a Methodist organization and was blessed on January 2, 1853. In February a newly ordained priest, Rev. William Barrett, was sent to him as assistant.[4] This pastorate was short; by August of 1854 he had returned to the Cathedral.[5]

That autumn of 1854 the Archbishop assigned him to teach Dogmatic Theology at Mt. St. Mary's Seminary of the West, the new diocesan seminary on Price Hill. This was some three miles from the archepiscopal residence at the Cathedral and often Rosecrans was the only passenger on the old omnibus that then accommodated the traveling public on the western hills, and on wintry mornings, when the bus failed to arrive, he walked to the seminary. Including travel time, teaching took four or five hours of his day.[6] "In theological erudition, for which his mind was peculiarly fitted, he had in this country few equals and no superiors. No heresy in philosophy or theology could escape the searching, analytical power of his naturally strong and admirably trained mind. His healthy, matured intellect discerned instantly the faintest shadow of error that crossed the domain of Catholic dogma....And his soul loved the faith in all the fullness and accuracy with which his calm, probing intellect grasped its far reaching truths."[7]

Another priest wrote of a different side of Rosecrans as a teacher: "He seemed to be a born teacher—in theology his clear philosophical mind made his lectures most entertaining and instructive for the students. By little familiar stories he could clear up all the difficulties of the students and enable them to see answers to objections. Thus the theology classes were a real treat to the students. While he could rise to the heights of theology, he could go into the classes of boys just beginning to encounter the difficulties of xyz of algebra and reach down to the boyish mind and teach it to master mathematical problems. His clear mind made him an adept in condensation."[8] Teaching from fifteen to twenty-five talented students was the most enjoyable of his tasks.

The Catholic Telegraph

In October of 1852 Father Rosecrans joined the editorial staff of *The Catholic Telegraph and Advocate*, the diocesan newspaper that was read across the country. Until that time it had been edited by V. Rev. Edward Purcell, brother of the Archbishop. The issue of December 11 already shows Father Rosecrans's name above that of Father Purcell as editor, but he always referred to Purcell as the "senior editor." He spent ten or twelve hours each week in this occupation.[9] Expectations were high for his work. Remarked Father Purcell when Rosecrans joined the effort, "If anything particularly good should hereafter appear in our columns, the reader will please attribute it to the pen of our young friend." A long editorial

Father Rosecrans wrote in December about the influence of the Church on America's republican form of government was immediately picked up and republished by the *Cincinnati Enquirer*. Father Rosecrans did an extraordinary amount of work for the *Telegraph* in 1853, writing at least thirty-eight editorials that year, during at least part of which Father Purcell was in Europe.[10]

It was Father Purcell, apparently, who wrote of the job of Catholic editor, "We do not believe, with one our Protestant exchanges, that the office of an editor is more onerous and responsible than that of a bishop, but it is onerous and responsible enough to make a man think twice before he undertakes it, and when he has undertaken it to labor to discharge its duties zealously and conscientiously."[11] After some years on the job, Rosecrans himself, apparently, wrote of Catholic editors, "...we can reach many a spiritual want, and apply to it its remedy by laboring humbly in our vocation. We can refute many a calumny, remove many a doubt, banish many an evil thought, by one little effort of brain and movement of pen. And each one of these efforts counts in the great aggregate of work to be done by Catholics."[12]

Rosecrans served on the staff of the *Telegraph* until March 1862. However, a letter written in June of 1868 implies that he continued to write at least occasionally, anonymously, for the *Telegraph* until that time.[13] Towards the end of his time on the staff, the New York *Metropolitan Record* had the following to say of the *Telegraph*, which obviously reflected the abilities of Father Rosecrans:

> It is with no ordinary feelings of pleasure that we observe the greatly improved appearance presented by the last issue of our much-esteemed and able cotemporary, the CATHOLIC TELEGRAPH of Cincinnati, and Official of the Most Rev. Archbishop of that diocese. The TELEGRAPH is one of the oldest Catholic papers published in this country, and deservedly occupies a high position in the rank of American newspapers. Its editorial department is conducted with rare ability and with great force of argument on theological questions. The general reading matter is selected with a nice discrimination...[14]

Years later one of his former students wrote of Father Rosecrans's work on the *Telegraph* and, later as Bishop, his work on the *Catholic Columbian*, "His journalistic work could never be mistaken. It bore always the stamp of a mind original in thought and of crystal clearness. He always wrote with enviable freshness and vigor. The faith never had in this country a more able editorial defender."[15]

The Bedini Incident

In 1853 Pope Pius IX. asked Archbishop Cajetan Bedini, papal nuncio to Brazil, to visit the United States on his way to Brazil, to investigate several parish trustee controversies. Monsignor Bedini had been secretary to the Papal Nuncio at the imperial court in Vienna and then internuncio in Brazil, where he defended the rights of German Catholic immigrants. The Holy Father had then appointed him to govern the city of Bologna, "where scenes of blood had been enacted by rebels and anarchists which we shudder to think of," but where he soon established peace and prosperity. Father Rosecrans had enjoyed Bedini's hospitality there and had seen him revered there as a law-giver and loved as a father. Rosecrans announced his hopes for a visit of the Archbishop to Cincinnati in the *Telegraph* on July 9, 1853.

The Nuncio arrived in New York City on June 30, but his visit to this country was not a peaceful one. He was attacked from two sides: the nativist American press misrepresented the mission as a scheme to establish the inquisition in the U.S. and to promote secret societies that would subvert the country's democratic institutions, while the radical Red Republican immigrants from Germany opposed him from the other side, accusing him of cruelty in pacifying Bologna and in other ways opposing them in 1848 and 1849. In Boston a mob burned his effigy and threatened the home of Bishop Fitzgerald, where he was staying. In Wheeling he had to be rescued from a mob by a band of Catholic Irishmen. He was jostled and bullied in Pittsburgh. Guns were shot into his room in Baltimore. He spent the Christmas holidays in Cincinnati, staying at the archepiscopal residence next to the cathedral. On Christmas night a crowd of between 500 and 1,200, mostly German members of secret societies, marched toward the Archbishop's residence carrying the nuncio's effigy, a gallows, clubs, pistols, and banners proclaiming, "Down with the Priests" and "No Pope! no Bishop!" The police, led by Captain Luken, stopped them a block away. In the ensuing melee one was killed, 15 wounded, and 65 arrested. The "sound Protestant population" of Cincinnati looked on the riot with reprobation as a movement of voluntary aliens (they refused to take the oath of allegiance) trying to dupe the community into acts of violence.[16]

Despite the riot, Archbishop Bedini made a pleasant tour of the Catholic institutions of the city and, it is clear, Father Rosecrans accompanied him and possibly wrote the glowing account of it for the *Telegraph*, including both the abilities and character shown by the students at the various colleges and schools, and the kindness and appreciation of the Archbishop.[17]

Archbishop Bedini left Cincinnati on January 3 but another demonstration was staged on the night of Saturday, January 14. About two thousand men marched through nearly all the city, "in wild confusion," carrying banners declaring "Down with Bedini!" "No Priests!" and the like. "Arrived opposite the Cathedral they saluted it with uproarious yells, causing the poor people who were still in the church preparing for Confession, or beseeching God to make them ready for Communion the following morning, to shudder over their prayers." Near the city buildings they set fire to the effigy of Bedini and threw it against the watchhouse door. They injured the city marshal and a sheriff. They dispersed about 10:30, but scattered divisions continued to make the night hideous with occasional yells until after one o'clock on Sunday morning.[18]

In 1878, shortly after the death of Bishop Rosecrans, a Columbus seminarian (very likely James Hartley, who later would become the fourth Bishop of Columbus) was walking around the grounds of Mt. St. Mary's Seminary when Archbishop Purcell, who was visiting, invited him to sit beside him on an old bench beneath a large shade tree. Finding that the seminarian was from Columbus, he began to talk of the conversion of General Rosecrans to the faith, his great piety and devotion to the Church, and through him the conversion of his brother. Referring to the visit of Bedini, then a quarter-century in the past, he told of the prejudice that had been stirred up against him and the hostile demonstrations. When the mob gathered around the archbishop's house at night, smashing windows with stones and making violent threats, "Rev. Doctor Rosecrans, who was assistant priest at the cathedral, and who had lately returned from Rome where he was ordained, bravely came down the stairs, faced the mob and helped to disperse them.

"The old Archbishop recalled the scene in a most vivid manner—and having the two distinguished brothers in his mind—the General was still living, and the Bishop had just died a few months before—he made this remark, 'It looks as though the General would have made a good Bishop—and the Bishop a good General.'"[19]

In July 1855 Father Rosecrans journeyed to St. Joseph's College near Somerset to deliver a lecture on Independence Day, "History, Why and How it Should be Studied." From Somerset he went to Lancaster and visited the Ewing family. He wrote to his brother William that the patriarch Tom Ewing was "inconsolable" that William was leaving the state for the East. He reached Cincinnati again on July 14 and on Monday, July 16 departed for the Ursuline convent and academy at St. Martin's in Brown County. It was a two-hour ride on the railroad to Hillsboro, then a few miles farther on the omnibus to the pleasant campus, a place of cool breezes and pleasant sights, in comparison with summer in Cincinnati. There he attended the distribution of premiums, at which the Archbishop presided.[20] This was his first visit to Brown County that we know of, where he formed friendships that lasted the rest of his life. Mother Julia Chatfield, foundress of the academy, though nearly twenty years older than Rosecrans, became one of his dearest friends. He often made retreats there, came for the distributions of premiums, attended the professions of novices and sisters, and, after becoming a bishop, administered Confirmation. In the spring of 1857 he happened to be visiting when Johanna Purcell, mother of the Archbishop, passed away, and he gave her the last absolution and indulgence.[21] At the distribution of premiums in 1858 the students put on a play "by the skillful and racy pen of Dr. Rosecrans."[22]

*Mother Julia Chatfield, O.S.U.
(Courtesy of the Ursulines of Brown County)*

Mt. St. Mary's College

In 1856 Archbishop Purcell opened a college for Catholic youth in connection with the seminary. It was announced in *The Catholic Telegraph and Advocate* on September 13:

Mt. St. Mary's College, near Cincinnati.

Our Catholic readers are requested to read the Prospectus of this new institution, which we publish today. The demand for a college in this vicinity has become so pressing, that the Most Rev. Archbishop determined to have the institution opened for the reception of pupils this month, though the buildings are not yet completed. When finished, which will be about the first of November, the College and Seminary will not be surpassed in the solidity of the work and beauty of design.

We may here state that no efforts will be spared to make this College of Mt. St. Mary's a first-class scientific and literary institution. Many of the professors are graduates of the College at Emmitsburg, and the course of studies, discipline, and rules, introduced by the sainted founders of that distinguished school, will be adopted, with such improvements as the times may require, by Mt. St. Mary's of the West. We invite our Catholic brethren, priests and people, to unite heartily with the Archbishop in establishing on a solid basis this new College, which is destined, we believe, to occupy a pre-eminent position amongst the literary establishments of the Church.

Rosecrans was appointed its first President and moved his residence to rooms at the college. His endeavors placed it on an equal footing with the best colleges in the West. It was chartered to confer degrees the first year of its existence. The staff of the college was quite impressive:

- Rev. John Quinlan, who was rector of the seminary and professor of liturgy and moral theology; he later was named Bishop of Mobile
- William Barry, who was ordained for the Archdiocese in 1857
- Father Francis Pabisch, professor of ecclesiastical history in the seminary, replaced Father Barry in 1858; he was principal of the German Department of the college.
- Xavier Donald MacLeod was the author of several works, including *Blood Stone, Life of Sir Walter Scott,* and *Life of Mary, Queen of Scots.* Formerly a Presbyterian, he had been taught the Catholic Faith and received into the Church by Rosecrans, and was principal of the Department of Rhetoric and Belle Letters for the college. He was ordained for the Archdiocese in 1861.
- Charles O'Leary, A.M., author of *O'Leary's Greek Grammar,* formerly a professor of Mt. St. Mary's, Emmitsburg, was principal of the Classical Department and professor of chemistry and geology for the college. He became a doctor and served in the army.
- Ezekiel P. J. Scammon, A.M., principal of the Mathematics

The faculty of Mt. St. Mary's College: standing, Rev. W. J. Barry, X. D. MacLeod, Charles O'Leary, M.D., and E. P. J. Scammon; seated: Rt. Rev. John Quinlan and Rev. S. H. Rosecrans, D.D.

Department, was an 1837 graduate of West Point and for seven years had been assistant professor there. He became a Catholic in 1846, perhaps under the influence of William Rosecrans. After retiring from the military he came to Cincinnati to teach at the college. He served in the armies of the Union during the war and rose to the rank of General.

- Henry Sofge, organist at the cathedral, taught music.[23]

Seminary students were the lesser teachers in the college.

The college had both Classical and Commercial courses. The Classical course comprised Greek, Latin, modern languages, rhetoric, logic, and mathematics with surveying, astronomy, natural philosophy, and chemistry. The Commercial course comprised lower mathematics, surveying, civil engineering, book keeping, and business. French and German also were offered.

The college opened with ten students, while the seminary had twenty-five.[24] Its graduates went into both the ministry and secular walks of life.

Typical of the college graduations of the time was that of June 24, 1858. On this Thursday morning the commencement began with a procession, led by an excellent band, from the college to the grove where the guests were seated in a semicircle around the platform where the president, professors, and visiting clergy sat. The lay professors wore cap and gown, and it was said the officers of the college intended to make the cap and gown the uniform of all their matriculated pupils. The exercises were closed by a few appropriate remarks from the President, Rev. Dr. Rosecrans, and the procession returned, in the order in which it had come to the grove.[25]

By the autumn of 1858 the college had attracted favorable attention. Even the Cincinnati *Daily Commercial*, with whom Fathers Rosecrans and Purcell on many occasions contended in their editorial columns in the *Telegraph*, printed positive comments. "Though yet in its infancy, it has progressed much under the able Professors who preside over the different branches of science and literature which are taught in this college, and which embrace as wide a range as in any similar institution in the United States. During the vacation, means have been taken to supply the college with a complete set of Chemical apparatus, so that the students may be enabled to make themselves acquainted with that science," useful for both industry and agriculture. The *Commercial* praised the college's provision of both commercial and classical studies.[26]

Early in 1862 Bishop Rosecrans's new duties compelled him to give up the presidency of the college, which position was assumed by the rector of the seminary[27] for a few months, until the college was closed in June. The college granted the bachelor of arts degree to twenty-one graduates during its six years of existence.[28] Bishop Rosecrans continued teaching theology at the seminary.

Among the students taught by Bishop Rosecrans at Mt. St. Mary's several were ordained for the Archdiocese of Cincinnati but came into the Diocese of Columbus as young priests upon its erection in 1868. These included Revs. M. J. Ahern, William Bigelow, H. Mayrose, Michael J. D. Ryan, Charles Schelhamer, F. X. Specht, and B. Wismann. Another student was Rev. Joseph Dwenger, later Bishop of Fort Wayne. Yet another of his students was Rev. John Lancaster Spalding, who spent one year at the college and graduated in 1859, who later was Bishop of Peoria.[29] Younger men who were ordained for the Diocese of Columbus, having been taught by Rosecrans at Mt. St. Mary's, were Nicholas A. Gallagher, Edward Fladung, and Daniel B. Cull.

Consecration as Auxiliary Bishop

Archbishop Purcell in 1856 asked the Vatican for a coadjutor bishop and proposed a *terna* of Fathers J. F. Wood, S. H. Rosecrans, and Edward Purcell. Nothing was done at this time. In 1859 Rosecrans's name came up again in regard to a position of great responsibility, that of rector of the American College in Rome. Bishop Martin Spalding of Louisville thought Rosecrans the most fitting for this post. Most Rev. Francis P. Kenrick, Archbishop of Baltimore, proposed the names of W. McCloskey, T. Foley, and S. H. Rosecrans. This proposal was seconded by his brother, Most Rev. Peter R. Kenrick, Archbishop of St. Louis. Dr. Philip Tancioni, rector of the College of the Propaganda, insisted that Rosecrans be the rector.[30] The ultimate, unanimous choice of the U.S. bishops for the position was Father William G. McCloskey, a professor at Mt. St. Mary's Seminary, Emmitsburg.

In 1861 Archbishop Purcell went to Rome for his decennial visit and while there petitioned the Holy See for a coadjutor; first on the list of nominees for the position was Father Rosecrans. The other bishops of the province objected, if the title would imply a right of succession[31], and so on December 8 the Holy Father sanctioned his appointment not as coadjutor but as auxiliary bishop, without any right of succession. The appointment was made official on Dec. 16. By Apostolic Letters dated January 7, 1862, Rosecrans was named Titular Bishop of Pompeiopolis and was appointed auxiliary bishop to Archbishop Purcell. The Apostolic Letters arrived in Cincinnati on February 15, 1862.[32] On February 19 Rosecrans wrote letters of thanks to the Propaganda and to the Holy Father.[33] He made a retreat at St. Martin's in Brown County[34] and was consecrated on March 25, the Feast of the Annunciation, in St. Peter's Cathedral. The event was described in the *Telegraph*:

This solemn event took place...in St. Peter's Cathedral, which was crowded to its utmost capacity. A large number of our separated brethren, ladies as well as gentlemen, could be distinguished among the dense congregation....

About 10 o'clock the bishops, priests, members of religious orders, and ecclesiastical students entered the sanctuary in procession, two and two, headed by the grand-cross bearer. The prelates present were the Most Rev. Archbishop..., the Right Rev. Bishop [Martin J.] Spalding of Louisville, the Right Rev. Bishop Luers of Fort Wayne, the Right Rev. Bishop Carrell of Covington, the Right Rev. Bishop De St. Palais of Vincennes, and the Bishop elect, the Right Rev. Dr. Rosecrans. Among the ecclesiastics present, we noticed the Very Rev. Edward Purcell, V.G., who delivered the sermon of the day on the text of the Annunciation, the Very Rev. H. Ferneding, V.G., the Rev. A. M. To[e]bbe, assistant priest, the Rev. C. Driscoll, deacon of honor, Rev. R. Tilmore [Gilmour], sub-deacon of honor, Rev. J. Dwinger [Dwenger], deacon of office, Rev. J. Alberink [Albrinck], sub-deacon of office, Rev. C. H. Borgess, master of ceremonies, Rev. W. J. Halley, assistant ditto, Rev. Father Soprania, Visitor of the Jesuits in the United States, Rev. W. P. Morrogh, New York, and the Rev. Fathers Walshe, Macleod, Stoehle, Banchet, Henge, Guilfoyle, Garvey, Bouche, Vogt, Hengehold, Corcoran, T[h]isse, P. B. Donahue, N. Donahue, Wachten, Kelly, Whytler, &c.

Pontifical High Mass was celebrated by the Most Rev. Archbishop, at whose hands with those of the Right Rev. Prelates of Louisville and Fort Wayne the Bishop elect was consecrated. The blending of the two essentially different but equally significant, beautiful, and edifying ceremonials of High Mass and the Consecration was new to many and impressively solemn to all. The chaunting of the Kyrie and the Litany by the choir of ecclesiastics, and the glorious outbursts from the orchestra were not only a religious, but an intellectual treat of the highest order, in the enjoyment of which three full hours flew away like so many minutes. After consecration the new Bishop, accompanied by the two assistant prelates and preceded by the grand cross, took the circuit of the church and bestowed his benediction on the congregation.

At 3 o'clock another large assemblage was in attendance at the Cathedral where Grand Vespers were conducted by the new prelate in full canonicals, assisted by the Rev. Messrs. Gilmore, Hally and Macleod in deaconical robes. On this occasion the Right Rev. Bishop Luers delivered a very emphatic and telling discourse on the festival of the day.[35]

On the day of his consecration, some of the priests who were graduates of Mount St. Mary's of the West presented a massive pectoral cross and chain to the new bishop, with the following address:

Rt. Rev. and Dear Professor:

It is a pleasing duty for the undersigned, your former pupils, to offer to you our heartfelt congratulations on your elevation to the Episcopacy by the Holy See. We avail ourselves willingly of this auspicious occasion to express our feelings of lively gratitude to you, and to assure you of our undiminished affection and esteem. Our good wishes, with our humble but fervent prayers, will follow you in the wider sphere of influence and apostolic labors for which your eminent talents and virtues so well fit you.

Please accept, dear Professor, this cross and chain, as a token of the well-deserved esteem and gratitude of your old pupils. We pray God to grant you many years of usefulness, for the salvation of souls and the advancement of our holy religion. We beg your prayers and blessing for ourselves and hope you may ever have reason to remember with pleasure

This was signed by Fathers D. Kelly of Dayton, J. B. O'Donohue of Milford, J. N. Thisse of Piqua, B. F. Hemsteger of Columbus, P. Garvey of Johnstown, Pa., Jos. Whittler of Cumminsville, T. O'Shea of Washington, Pa., A. M. Toebbe of Cincinnati, T. J. J. Coppinger of Columbus, J. J. Menge of Alton, Ill., James O'Donohue of Portsmouth, John D. Duffy of Circleville, Ed. Fitzgerald of Columbus, B. Gels of Pomeroy, E. P. Corcoran of Hamilton, B. Menge of Cincinnati, Jos. Dwenger of Auglaize County, P. Sheehan of Pittsburgh, J. Shiff of Dayton, W. Fernending of Cincinnati, Mich. O'Donohue of Hillsboro, F. J. Goetz of Dayton, W. Boeker of Lockland, and A. Gerts of Cincinnati.

The new bishop replied:

Reverend and Beloved Friends:

The rich present and kind address with which you favor me at this time of my assuming a new and awful responsibility to carry before God, until His judgment day, are inexpressibly pleasant to me.

It is pleasant to be assured that you reciprocate the affection with which your docility, cheerful obedience and earnest piety inspired me while you were in the Seminary; and still more so to be the object of your esteem, now that years of priestly fidelity have shown in you that the faithful Seminarist always becomes the good priest, and have won for you the veneration and confidence of your flocks. While thanking you most cordially, I beg you not to forget your promised prayers in my behalf; and as I wear the cross you gave, outwardly on my breast, I may wear the Redeemer's deeply in my heart, and never at any moment forget that, whether God requires it all at once, or piecemeal only, "bonus Pastor animam suam dat pro ovibus suis."

Invoking on you all the blessing of Almighty God, Father, Son and Holy Ghost, I remain your friend and brother in Christ,

S. H. Rosecrans, D.D.,

Bishop of Pompeiopolis and Aux. Cin.[36]

It seems rather strange but, after having agitated long for a coadjutor and receiving an auxiliary bishop, Archbishop Purcell in the summer of 1864 proposed Bishop Rosecrans for the vacant see of Albany.[37] But he said then that he and his auxiliary were on the best of terms.

Chapter III
Auxiliary Bishop, 1862-1868

The Civil War

The War Between the States was a difficult time for Bishop Rosecrans, for, despite any personal leanings, and despite accusations of supporting the military cause of the Union or immediate abolition of slavery, he sought in public to steer clear of policy issues. In this he was carrying out the directions of the Third Plenary Council of Cincinnati. This council of the eight prelates of the province (in Ohio, Kentucky, Indiana, and Michigan) was held in Cincinnati in May 1861, when the war had just begun. Father Rosecrans was one of the two secretaries, along with V. Rev. Peter Hennaert, Vicar General of the Diocese of Detroit.[1] Under section III, "Our Country—Invocation for Peace," the resulting Pastoral Letter said:

> The spirit of the Catholic Church is eminently conservative, and while her ministers rightfully feel a deep and abiding interest in all that concerns the welfare of this country, they do not think it their province to enter into the political arena. ...Wherever Christ is to be preached and sinners to be saved, there she is found with her ministrations of truth and of mercy. She leaves the exciting question referred to precisely where the inspired Apostle of the Gentiles left it, contenting herself, like him, with inculcating on all classes and grades of society the faithful discharge of the duties belonging to their respective states of life... Beyond this point her ministers do not consider it their province to go, knowing well that they are the ministers of God, who is not a God of dissension but of peace and love.[2]

Two years later, in May 1863, Bishop Spalding of Louisville sent to Rome a "Dissertation on the American Civil War" in which he wrote of the country's bishops:

> ...our prelates have not been bothered any more, at least directly, on this matter; and excepting two or three—among whom is found my Metropolitan—our archbishops and bishops limit themselves now to the spiritual and to prayers, according to their repeated and published declarations, and their uniform manner of acting in the past. And this is—I am definitely convinced—the most prudent and wise rule to be followed in our present circumstances.[3]

Despite the fact that his brother and many of his friends were in the armies of the Federal government, Bishop Rosecrans followed this "prudent and wise rule."

Archbishop Purcell, the Metropolitan of whom Bishop Spalding wrote, became an advocate for Union victory and immediate emancipation of the slaves. And while one might consider this postion the morally correct one, Archbishop Purcell was one of only a handful of American bishops to advocate it publicly. Bishop Spalding thought that Purcell had been influenced by Bishop Rosecrans in this position, and that the bishop had been influenced by his brother the General.[4] Many have taken up this accusation since that time, but there is no evidence to support it.

During the days leading up to and in the early part of the war, Father Rosecrans was still editor of the *Catholic Telegraph*. His thoughts no doubt were expressed in the editorials summarized here (though not necessarily written directly by him):

- May 29, 1858: Abolitionists' sole idea of sin is conveyed by the word "slavery." To disobedience they add spiritual pride, self-will, and private judgment. They attack human authority and the country, rulers, states, courts, judges, and legislatures. In the end they ridicule the Bible and every form of religion.
- May 6, 1860: Claiming rights for the people as an unorganized body, in opposition to the organized body or government, leads to anarchy and licentiousness. "We deny the right of any State to secede from the Union," which a

state could do only on the basis of conditions laid down in the Constitution. But that instrument recognizes no such contingencies.
- December 1, 1860: The Catholic Church has said both to North and South, be just, be moderate, patient, and charitable.
- December 22, 1860: A revolution is inevitable. The experiment in self-government seems to have failed. We fear we shall be left without a nation. The imagination shrinks from the consequences.
- January 16, 1861: There can be no forcing people to remain in the Union, unless by actual abandonment of the principles for which you pretend to fight. We have nothing to say as to the policy to be pursued.
- January 23, 1861: The duty of Catholic citizens is to adhere most devotedly to the Union. In Union there is strength not only for the Nation, but for Catholics.
- February 23, 1861: A government of the people has a right to protect itself from a rebellion of a few factious and criminal men. But where whole communities repudiate its authority, that authority is by the very fact of their opposition at an end. You may regret the catastrophe of secession, but you cannot prevent it by force nor attempt to prevent it without revolutionizing the government.
- March 16, 1861: The Southern people have had grounds of complaint, and have a right to be heard. It would be impolitic and unjust to attempt to force them into submission to wrong whether real or imaginary.
- April 20, 1861: Individual opinions must yield to our obligations to the Union. It is our solemn duty to support the laws and the national honor.
- August 31, 1861: The war is upon us; all talk of peace is now useless. The results of war are tragic but may turn our people to God.
- Jan. 15, 1862: On the slavery issue, the Southerners refuse to listen to reason; the Northerners are in favor of extreme measures. God grant the government have the power to crush the one and the firmness to resist the other. Emancipation as a war measure seems incendiary

and stupid, involving the horrors of servile war, ending in the desolation of the South and the ruin of the North. The *Telegraph* was strictly following events and calling for peace and order, while pointing out truth along the way. Until March of 1862, when Rosecrans left the *Telegraph* just before his consecration, the selection of war news and articles did concentrate on the Union forces, which was natural for a paper published in a Northern state. But the vast majority of editorials, usually one or two per issue, but sometimes more, especially when Rosecrans's school duties would have been fewer, were on religious and philosophical subjects.

The 1863 election for Governor of Ohio pitted Peace Democrat Clement Valandingham against John Brough. Brough was a strong supporter of the Union's war effort and the anti-slavery direction it was taking. The Wheeling *Daily Intelligencer*[5] noted that during this campaign the *Telegraph* did strong and powerful service to the Union cause. While other Catholic papers followed after the "Democratic gods," the *Telegraph* exhorted its readers to do their duty to their country by upholding its rulers and overthrowing its enemies. By this time, the paper's sole editor was V. Rev. Edward Purcell, the Archbishop's brother.

The *Cincinnati Commercial* stirred up trouble by reporting that "the venerable Catholic Archbishop Purcell, accompanied by Bishop Rosecrans, appeared at the polls in that city at the late election, for the first time in twenty-five years, and voted the Union ticket."[6] Other papers reported that the Archbishop and Bishop attended the polls and labored for the whole Union ticket.[7]

Bishop Rosecrans seems to have never uttered or written a word about these reports. Archbishop Purcell, however, on the evening of November 1 gave a lecture in Mozart Hall in which he defended his actions in voting for the Republican ticket. He and Bishop Rosecrans "had been charged with standing at the polls all day, with hands full of Union tickets, exerting their influence among Catholic Democrats" against Mr. Valandingham and his companions. "This, he said, is utterly false. He did not go to the polls with Bishop Rosecrans; he had gone quietly there alone, and deposited his unconcealed suffrage—a suffrage which his conscience approved, and for which he was answerable to God. He voted as he did out of fear 'that if Valandingham were elected the attempted withdrawal of Ohio soldiers in the field—with [General] Rosecrans—would ensue, and that the State of Ohio would be tossed with revolutionary opposition to the war policy. He feared that raids would be invited, the parallel of which might be found in Quantrell's barbarous and inhuman invasion of Kansas.'" Further reasons were threats that the Southerners would never extend the hand of friendship and trade if they succeeded in separating from the U.S. and his wish to see every man free. "The Catholic Church has ever been the friend of human freedom. It was Christ's mission to set men free, and Christian people disregard his precepts and example when they seek to uphold and perpetuate involuntary human servitude."[8] This may have represented Bishop Rosecrans' thinking as well, but he never articulated a position in public or, as far as we know, in private.

Bishop Rosecrans wrote to Rome[9] that he was counted among abolitionists by the newspapers, mainly because of a speech or lecture, delivered in Columbus in 1863 (on January 6 in Naughton's Hall). He also delivered it in Cincinnati in 1860, and in the Cathedral in Fort Wayne on St. Patrick's Day, 1863. This lecture praised the work of the congregation of Trinitarians, who were founded in the twelfth century to free Christians who had been enslaved by Muslims, the "First Emancipation and Anti-Slavery Society."[10] The closest this lecture came to a general position on action to be taken with regard to slavery was the following, which certainly does not show support for warfare or rabid abolitionism:

> 2. The means which they employed to accomplish the liberation of slaves were such as grew naturally out of the spirit of divine charity which animated them. That charity which is the true golden bond that binds the moral world together, unlike the tinsel counterfeit philanthropy, is never harsh, vindictive, impatient, selfish or unjust to any one.
>
> It prepares no knives, or pikes, or hatchets for the hands of slaves; it counsels no treachery, no murder, no violence, no incendiarism. It never seeks to influence

wounded pride into wrath, or sullen discontent into midnight insurrection. But it gently and sweetly seeks to remedy evils without inflicting wrong, and where the evils are irremediable, to soothe affliction with the hope of recompense at the hand of God. Though it could strike the fetters from every slave beneath the canopy of heaven by a single blow, yet it would not strike unless the blow were just. Though it could soothe a single pang of a bondman by a lifetime of labor, it would cheerfully undergo the labor and look to God for reward.[11]

In this same letter to Rome, Bishop Rosecrans noted that he had never spoken publicly about political affairs, a statement that is supported, in a negative way, by the lack of any such words in the public record. In addition, his reticence was expressed in a letter to Father Sorin at Notre Dame University, October 25, 1865, wherein he expressed himself reluctant to endorse the new *Ave Maria* magazine because he did not want to intrude himself on the notice of the public.[12]

On Saturday, August 15, Feast of the Assumption, 1863, Bishop Rosecrans administered Confirmation in St. Raphael's Church in Springfield, Ohio, and in the evening he lectured in the public hall at the court house on "Law and Liberty." The story was picked up by a news service and, in some papers, the Bishop was made into a hawk, "Law" having become "War": "Bishop Rosecrans, of Cincinnati, brother of the General, was announced to speak for the war and liberty; at a grand Union picnic in Clark county, Ohio, August 15th. His patriotism has never faltered, and he adds another name to the list of true-hearted Catholic prelates."[13]

A different news service provided a better account, according to which the Bishop gave a metaphysical lecture. He declared liberty and law inseparable, defined liberty to be the free exercise of that which is right; declared the observance of just law the fulfillment of liberty, and insisted upon the obligation of the people to observe law because it was ordained of God. He concluded "that he had been advertised to make a speech on the so-called topics of the day; but his vocation would not permit him to interfere in things that are the subjects of merely momentary interest."[14] The intention of the speech or lecture was to promote peace and order, in light of the feelings of many related to the New York draft riots that had taken place the previous month.

Bishop Josue Young of Erie, Pennsylvania, formerly pastor at Lancaster, Ohio, not only did not think Rosecrans was too strong a supporter of the Union forces and abolition, he was said to have accused Rosecrans of disloyalty to the cause. In letters written on August 10 and 16, 1862, from Piqua to the Archbishop, Rosecrans mentioned that he had complained of a report circulated in Lancaster by Young according to which Rosecrans was disloyal. This complaint provoked Bishop Young to call Rosecrans a lunatic.[15] But the fact that the rumor spread attests to Rosecrans's silence on the public matters.

Rosecrans did mention talk among the Catholics of resisting the state military draft and thought action might be necessary to prevent evil consequences of this spirit. This stance, however, was consistent with that of many other bishops who spoke for peace and order, not necessarily for a Union military victory or immediate abolition of slavery. Bishop Rappe in Cleveland in a sermon in his cathedral on July 19, 1863, denounced the draft rioters in New York and advised his hearers to submit to the laws of their adopted country and, if drafted, to go to fight its battles. He told them to avoid any crowd or tumultuous assembly and to preserve the domestic peace.[16] Bishop Rosecrans himself was nearly caught up by the U.S. draft law. Clergymen who were in charge of congregations were exempt, but others were not. Three Jesuit priests and two students at St. Xavier College in Cincinnati were actually drafted. One of them was too ill to serve and the $300 each to purchase substitutes was found for the others. Rosecrans was among the clergymen conscripted, but the authorities let his case slide.[17]

Bishop Rosecrans visited his brother and the Union troops in his command, but nothing indicates that these were anything other than pastoral visits. Such visits were a great necessity, for Catholic chaplains in the army were a rarity. The first such visit took place after General Rosecrans' victory over Confederate General Price at Iuka, Mississippi, on September 19, 1862, and before the battle of Corinth on October 3 & 4.

CLERICAL BON MOT.

When at dinner, the other day, at the residence of a mutual friend, Bishop Rosecrans being at the table, the conversation naturally turned upon the recent fight at Iuka, under command of his brother, General Rosecrans.

"It would seem to me, Bishop, that you and your brother, the General, are engaged in very different callings," remarked a gentleman to his worship.

"Yes, it appears so," returned the Bishop. "And yet," he continued, " we are both fighting men. While the General is wielding 'the sword of the flesh,' I trust that I am using 'the sword of the Spirit.' He is fighting the rebels, and I am fighting the spirits of darkness. There is this difference in the terms of our service: he is fighting with Price, while I am fighting without price."[18]

He was not in Mississippi long, for he carried out episcopal duties in the Cincinnati archdiocese on each Sunday that September and October.

In the spring of 1863 Bishop Rosecrans again visited his brother and the Catholic soldiers, this time at Murfreesboro, Tennessee. He left Cincinnati on Monday, April 6 and had returned to Cincinnati by April 19, visiting Bishop Spalding in Louisville on the return trip.[19] A newspaper report from Murfreesboro, dated Sunday, April 12, stated:

Under the auspices of the Christian Commission regular religious worship has been established here, and to-day old church-goers were reminded of home and its blessed privileges by the sacred sound of church bells. There were Protestant services at the old Methodist Church, and at the Christian Church Bishop Rosecrans (brother of the General) held forth to those of the Catholic faith. They were both well attended... To-night the Bishop lectured at the same place to a crowded house of soldiers. Another odd occurrence, especially so to one raised under the strictest Protestant discipline, was that immediately upon the close of the services a grand serenade was given to the General and his brother at headquarters.[20]

This occasion was still remembered in 1890 as a Thanksgiving Day, but was confused with Thursday, April 30, which President

Lincoln had proclaimed a day of humiliation, fasting, and prayer, on which "we attended church, and heard a sermon by Bishop Rosecrans, the general's brother."[21] The tenor of these two trips, implied in these short notices, is of a spiritual, not a political, nature.

Despite the tightrope he walked, avoiding political advocacy on the one side while advocating law and order and supporting the soldiers on the other, it is clear that Bishop Rosecrans was a patriot. In editorials against the Know-Nothings in 1853 and 1854, among other thoughts, he wrote against those who said that true liberty and freedom of religion was an impossible dream of the founders; wrote of the devotion of Catholics to the Constitution, as opposed to the Red Republican "reformers;" encouraged respect for the law, against Know-Nothing incitements to riot, in order to preserve the country's republican form of government; wrote of our fathers bleeding for true liberty, freedom of conscience, and true republicanism. In a letter written in 1863 in support of the Sanitary Fair for the wounded soldiers, he told of the unexpected visions of his beloved homeland that came over him in 1848 when he saw the Stars and Stripes run up on an American gunship in the port of Genoa.[22]

Local Activities in the War Era

Meanwhile, the work of the Church continued. In June 1863, Bishop Rosecrans and two priests and two laymen were appointed by Archbishop Purcell as a Board of Examiners of applicants as school teachers in the diocese.[23] As Bishop, Rosecrans continued teaching Theology and living at the seminary until a fire in October 1863. At that time he moved once again to the archepiscopal residence but he continued teaching until 1864. In 1865, though no longer teaching there, he moved back to reside again at the seminary.

On the night of Saturday, December 23, 1865, Rosecrans stayed late at the Cathedral hearing confessions. Though urged to remain there because of the late hour, he ordered a carriage to meet him and began walking toward the seminary. At the bend of the road near Mr. Wilder's, less than a quarter of a mile from the Seminary, he was set upon by two robbers who demanded his money. The Bishop refused to comply with the "modest request," and sought to escape by running from the pair. They fired a navy revolver at him and the shot passed through one leg and lodged in the other. He continued on foot to the seminary and, hurrying to his quarters so as not to disturb anybody, tried to extract the ball from his thigh with a pocket knife. He was discovered in this operation by one of the household and a surgeon was called. The ball had lodged so close to the femoral artery that it could not be removed without great danger and ever afterwards it was a source of pain and discomfort. He was able to offer Mass on Sunday and on Christmas Day, Monday, but the seminarians were obliged to support him on either side before Mass was finished. When remonstrated with and told that he would kill himself by over exertion, "he smiled in his own genial way" and said, "Well then I should only die." Early in the new year he visited the Ursulines at Brown County and at the Sisters' request left with them the bullet that had been taken from his leg.[24]

A different and probably less trustworthy, yet interesting, version of this incident is given by one who said he heard it from the Bishop's own lips. According to this version, after hearing confessions on Saturday nights his practice was to walk to the foot of the hill, about half way to the seminary, and there would meet a man with a horse and buggy to carry him the remainder of the distance. On this night the connection was not made and the Bishop continued up the hill on foot, "until he came to a 'cut' with a high bank of solid clay on his left, and a steep precipice on his right, where stunted oaks grew thick enough to partially conceal a couple of men who sat on the edge, apparently resting. As the Bishop passed these two he heard the murmur of their voices, but paid no attention to them. When a step further on, another man passed him, evidently going cityward. This man halted, and said, 'Say, Mister, I see you've got a watch—tell us the time.' The Bishop replied, without stopping, something to the effect, 'It's time for honest folks to be a-bed, and rogues a-thieving.'" A few seconds later he was shot. A man at the seminary gate, a few rods away, hurried to meet the Bishop and asked, "Did you hear that shot?" "Yes, and I think I felt it, too," was the Bishop's reply. "The words were barely uttered when

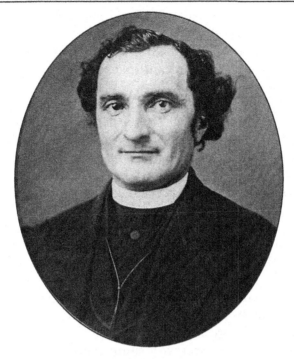

*Rev. Sylvester Rosecrans, c. 1860
(Ohio Province Archives, Sisters of Notre Dame de Namur)*

he succumbed from loss of blood. The students and neighbors hurried to the rescue, he was carried into the house, and his physicians, the Drs. Bonner, father and son, were speedily called.

"On examining the wound, it was found that the ball had passed so near the femoral artery that probing at that time would endanger the Bishop's life. The wound was dressed and the ball left for further investigation. It dropped by its own weight to another position, and when Gen. E. P. Scammon called to inquire for the Bishop's health, he found him industriously engaged trying to dig the bullet out of his own leg with a penknife." According to this account, the perpetrator was never known, and it was thought that perhaps the deed had been an attempt to assassinate General Rosecrans in revenge for men he had executed in St. Louis during the war.[25] The attack on the bishop was announced in a wide range of newspapers and even became known in Rome, where many in the Propaganda offices were concerned about him.[26]

Almost a year passed before a man was arrested for the crime. The city detectives had investigated the shooting and strongly suspected Charles Ross, a farmer aged about twenty-one, but before they had gathered sufficient evidence to justify his arrest he went out West. He returned to Cincinnati early in November 1866, and on the 11th was arrested and jailed. He was arraigned in Police Court in December, but Bishop Rosecrans did not appear so he was discharged.[27] The Bishop perhaps did not want to make more difficult the life of a young man who was the same age as the college students he loved so well.

In all his acts we see lived out the personal humility Rosecrans maintained as a bishop, as described in 1878: "Vested with one of the highest offices of the Church, he aspired to no distinction as a prelate, but delighted in the simplicity of a humble priest; content with a change of clothing for his private use, he gave little heed to the fashion of hat or coat, so long as his garments were clean and entire; yet he could think of the white dress for a protege's commencement, remind her of the need of a Communion veil, and himself supply the money to produce them, so that she should appear as well clad as her companions. Once during these years as auxiliary bishop he casually remarked, 'I don't believe I ever had fifty dollars ahead in my life, and I don't suppose I ever shall.' Scarcely had he finished speaking when he began planning to complete the education of a poor waif (who was destined to cause him no little disappointment by failing to reach the high standard the Bishop had anticipated). His thoughtfulness for others often induced him to send his physician, at his own expense to attend in cases of mildest character"...[28] And yet, as a bishop Rosecrans was a formidable and beloved leader among the Catholics of the Archdiocese and beyond.

Episcopal Activities

Immediately upon his consecration, Bishop Rosecrans embarked on a flurry of episcopal activity—confirmations, ordinations, and church cornerstone layings and blessings. The year 1862 was an especially busy one because Archbishop Purcell

Known Episcopal Activities of Bishop Rosecrans Within the Archdiocese of Cincinnati						
	1862	1863	1864	1865	1866	1867
Confirmation Ceremonies	43	21	14	9	17	7
Ordination Ceremonies	12	7	3	1	3	1
Church or Cornerstone Blessings	6	2	1	6	7	4
Religious Profession Ceremonies	2					
Graveyard Blessings	1				1	
Altar Consecrations	1					
Banner Blessings	1			1		1
Bell Blessing	1					
Cemetery Cross Blessing			1			
Missions Preached			2			

went to Rome, at the invitation of the Holy Father, to attend the canonization of the Japanese Martyrs. We know of some 43 Confirmation ceremonies, twelve ordination ceremonies, six cornerstones or churches blessed, two ceremonies for the reception of Sisters, and a few other miscellaneous blessings—a huge number even for a man as young as Rosecrans then was. As the Civil War dragged on there were fewer churches built and the Archbishop shared the Confirmation schedule, but the new Auxiliary kept very busy. In 1866 many and in 1867 the majority of the Confirmation ceremonies he administered were in parishes that were destined to be part of his new Diocese of Columbus. According to a later account, the bishop was impressively fitted for these ceremonies. "The Bishop... possesses, in an eminent degree, the happy faculty of imparting additional solemnity to the very impressive character of the imposing ceremonies reserved for the Episcopal Order of the Priesthood, by the exquisite cadences of a fine musical voice, a remarkably prepossessing countenance, and the easy, because natural, grace of a dignified deportment."[29]

Popular Lecturer

As a preacher Bishop Rosecrans was inclined to be reserved, but his great simplicity, depth, and originality of thought was wonderful, while he always displayed a love of God and charity to man that at once marked him a true apostle. Though his language was not emotional, he preached from the head and the heart, feeling what he said, and making his hearers feel the same, without regard to what people might think or say. This was his success as a preacher. No person, clerical or lay, ever listened to a sermon of Bishop Rosecrans's without learning something.[30]

Besides preaching at religious ceremonies, the bishop gave lectures before many groups, including students, alumni, and the general public. Although he was not a great orator in the style of the Nineteenth Century, he was a thought-provoking and captivating speaker. He did not reach the orator's flights of wordy eloquence and his figures of speech were few and simple, but he engaged the attention of his audience, and the learned and unlearned alike understood him. It was said that as a speaker he was "rather pleasing in manner." His fine logical powers and ability as a lecturer soon became well known around the diocese and beyond.[31] His lectures were "ever-pleasing, never tedious."

The earliest lecture we know of, aside from addresses given as a student, was given to the students of St. Joseph's College near Somerset on Independence Day 1855, mentioned above. The earliest known series of lectures was delivered on the afternoons of Sundays from May 30 through June 1859, in St. Peter's Cathedral in Cincinnati. The subject was the Divinity of Christ.[32] The lectures were not published at the time but probably formed the basis for his book, *The Divinity of Christ: together with Thoughts on the Passion of Jesus Christ*, first published in Cincinnati by J. P. Walsh in 1866. It was republished in 1878 in New York by Benziger and in 1924 the Paulist Press excerpted and printed the *Thoughts on the Passion of Jesus Christ*.

In July of 1859 with Rev. Dr. Keogh of Pittsburgh Bishop Rosecrans visited the East, stopping to see Rosecrans's former co-worker at the Cincinnati Cathedral, Bishop James Wood, in Philadelphia. For two or three days they were the guests of their good friend and former associate in the Propaganda at Rome, Rev. Dr. Morrough, at St. Joseph's Seminary, Fordham, and on July 12 Rosecrans addressed the graduating class at his alma mater, St. John's College, Fordham.[33]

Auxiliary Bishop

Other known lectures and lecture series he delivered within the diocese were:
- 1860, March 25, Sunday; address at the first anniversary of the Catholic Institute at Metropolitan Hall, corner of Ninth and Walnut streets. It was "a very graphic and beautifully written sketch of the Order of Mercy, and its efforts during the Middle Ages to relieve the Christians enslaved by the Musselmen."[34]
- 1863, January and February, several lectures in St. Peter's Cathedral on "the importance of religious instruction."[35]
- 1863, June 24, Wednesday, a lecture in the Union Hall in Urbana for the benefit of the local Catholic school. The topic was "the importance of inquiring for the true Religion."[36]
- 1863, August 15, lecture in the public hall at the Court House in Springfield on "Law and Liberty."[37]
- 1864 Nov. 13, lecture in St. Mary's Church, Marion on "The Rule of Faith"[38]
- 1864, November 21 (or 14?), lecture in the public hall in Newark for the benefit of St. Francis de Sales Church on "Catholicism and Civil Liberty."[39]
- a series beginning after Vespers on Sunday, Feb. 12, 1865 and continuing through Lent, in the Cathedral.[40]
- 1866, Feb. 18, lecture at Mozart Hall on "Our Country from a Catholic Point of View," with the proceeds to replace the organ in the seminary chapel.[41]
- 1866, Feb. 25 and the following Sundays after Vespers, a series of lectures in the Cathedral.[42]
- 1866, April 16, lecture in Piqua in the City Hall.[43]
- 1867, Nov. 7, lecture at St. Gabriel's Church, Glendale, with a concert by St. Peter's Cathedral choir.[44]
- 1868, Jan. 30, lecture in Crowley's Hall in Kenton. "He discoursed of the Church as in contact with persecution. He defined from St. Thomas the Catholic teaching in reference to the propagation of the Faith and stated that the several kinds of allegations which are made use of to controvert her teaching were devoid of fact. He disposed of the inquisition in a persuasive manner. Eminent jurists of the county who were present made favorable remarks on the lecture."[45]

- 1868, Lenten Sundays, a series of lectures after Vespers at St. Patrick's in Columbus.[46]

Journeys Outside Ohio as Auxiliary Bishop

As Auxiliary Bishop, Rosecrans took one or two major trips each year beyond the confines of the archdiocese. Most of these were of a pastoral nature and on most of them he made good impressions.

In June 1862 the bishop, accompanied by Rev. R. Gilmour, pastor of St. Patrick Parish in Cincinnati, made a somewhat leisurely journey to Boston for the dedication of St. Francis de Sales Church on Bunker Hill. They left Cincinnati on Wednesday, June 11, and went as far as Cresson Station, where they left the railroad to visit the Catholic localities on the summit of the Alleghenies, the establishment of which is originally due to the zeal and generosity of the illustrious and princely Father Demetrius Gallitzin. They were hospitably entertained by the Pastor of Loretto. On Thursday morning, they visited the Convent of the Sisters of Mercy, St. Mary's Church, and the monument erected by his devoted parishioners to the memory of Father Gallitzin. In the afternoon, they paid a visit to the pastor of the Summit, and proceeding to the highest point of the mountains enjoyed the magnificent panoramic view of the surrounding country. On Friday morning they visited St. Francis' Monastery and Academy at Loretto, under the charge of the Franciscan Brothers. Before leaving Loretto, the Bishop was serenaded by the excellent string band formed by the pupils of St. Francis', who executed very creditably and skillfully several appropriate pieces of music. In the evening the travelers took the Eastern train on the Pennsylvania R. R., on their way to Boston.[47]

The dedication took place on Tuesday, June 17, anniversary of the famous victory of the American forces over the British at Bunker Hill in 1775. Archbishop Purcell had blessed the cornerstone of the new church in 1859 and Rosecrans was substituting for him on the current occasion. In the presence of nearly fifty priests and some five thousand of the laity, Bishop Rosecrans dedicated the church and Bishop Goesbriand of Burlington offered the Pontifical Mass. Bishop Rosecrans delivered the sermon, of which *The Boston Pilot* had this to say:

> Bishop Rosecrans evidently felt the solemn importance of the occasion. His sermon was such as we like to hear from our Pastors. It was from the heart, and it was delivered in the full conviction of a Catholic soul. Bishop Rosecrans, himself a convert, addressed a mixed congregation with the consciousness of his conviction and of his authority, an authority which only a Catholic Bishop possesses. The more we were pleased with his sermon, the more we felt the truth of what he said, as his words were extemporaneous, and he had been suddenly called to address the people.

A synopsis of the sermon, dealing with private judgment, faith, and obedience, was published in the *Pilot*.[48]

As mentioned above, Bishop Rosecrans made at least two visits to his brother and the Union troops, in 1862 and 1863.

In 1864 the Bishop returned again to his alma mater, St. John's College, Fordham, and addressed the annual commencement on July 7 with a speech on "Faithful Leadership." He had been invited by the newly formed alumni association of the college. He also attended the alumni association's first annual dinner that evening, at Delmonico's. That December 8 he preached at the profession of 38 novices at St. Mary's Convent, Notre Dame, Indiana.[49]

In 1865 he took a trip east that seems to have been purely a much-needed vacation. It may have been taken in part to spend time with his brother, who was planning to move to California in the immediate future. He arrived at the Astor House in New York to meet William on June 20. On the 23rd he went by streetcar to Coney Island and took a plunge into the breakers. On the 24th he went with William to Orange and stayed over into Sunday. Later he was to go to Roslyn on Long Island and dine with Rev. Dr. Ely, a retired Presbyterian preacher, William Cullen Bryant, Parke Godwin, General Dix, and others.[50]

In 1866, the year after he had been shot, Bishop Rosecrans did not leave the Archdiocese until July, when on the 22nd he laid the cornerstone of Sts. Peter and Paul Church in Sandusky, Ohio, at the invitation of the Bishop of Cleveland.[51]

Later that year, from October 7 until October 21, Bishop Rosecrans attended the Second Plenary Council of Baltimore, a meeting of all the bishops of the United States. This was the only such council he attended, the next earlier one having been held in 1852 and the next later not occurring until 1884. It was presided over by Archbishop Martin J. Spalding of Baltimore as Delegate Apostolic. The press remarked that the discussions were all private, and in Latin. But the cathedral was crowded on the evening of Monday, October 8, to hear Bishop Rosecrans deliver a sermon titled "Faith Cometh from Hearing." He took time to write a description of the procession and opening Mass to his niece Mary (Mamie).[52]

The council's decrees were signed by seven archbishops, thirty-nine bishops or their procurators, and two abbots. The decrees were under fourteen titles such as: Concerning the Orthodox Faith and Present Errors; Concerning the Hierarchy and the Government of the Church; Of Ecclesiastical Property; Of Promoting Uniformity of Discipline; and Of the Education of Youth. Of particular concern to Rosecrans was Title xiii, Concerning the Creation of New Bishoprics.

Chapter IV
New Diocesan Ordinary, 1866-1873

Movement Towards the New Diocese

The Fathers of the Second Plenary Council of Baltimore requested that the Holy Father divide the Archdiocese of Cincinnati by the erection of the Diocese of Columbus and they suggested appointment of Bishop Rosecrans to the new see.[1] In December Archbishop Purcell wrote a letter to Propaganda in which, among other subjects, he commented on the choice of Bishop Rosecrans for the new see and named the counties that would compose its territory. At the request of the Prefect of Propaganda, Purcell indicated again the proposed boundaries of the two dioceses in a letter of April 26.[2]

The origin of the boundary is given in a story, according to which Archbishop Purcell at one point called Rosecrans to his rooms and said that he was thinking about making such a request to Rome and asked Rosecrans what boundaries he would suggest to divide the new diocese from Cincinnati. Not suspecting that he would be named ordinary of the new see, Rosecrans had walked over to a map of Ohio hanging on the wall and had drawn his finger along the lines that seemed favorable to him, saying, "I think that would be about right." When issued, the papal brief drew the boundary line as Rosecrans had suggested, dividing the two dioceses along the Scioto River south of Franklin County, and along the western boundaries of Franklin, Delaware, and Morrow counties. Rosecrans came to rue this suggestion. The exclusion of prosperous Marion and Chillicothe by this boundary hampered the new diocese, leaving it poorer and less populous than necessary. In addition it was an awkward arrangement that made it necessary for the Bishop of Columbus to pass through Chillicothe, in the Archdiocese, to get to Portsmouth, in his own diocese. Bishop Rosecrans realized this as early as April 23, 1870, when he suggested, in a letter to Purcell, that the boundaries be altered to include all of those portions of the counties through which the Scioto flows, south of Franklin County.[3] This, however, did not happen until 1944.

For a time, the city of Lancaster was considered a candidate to be the see of the new diocese. It was attractive because of its more well-to-do, though smaller, Catholic congregation, its long history, and its new St. Mary Church that would have made a fine cathedral. It also was more centrally located than Columbus within the proposed diocesan boundaries. But Columbus was chosen, probably because the seat of state government was there and because of its growing prominence as a commercial center and its ease of access by railroad.

On Sunday, February 3, 1867 Right Rev. Edward Fitzgerald, D.D., who had been Pastor of St. Patrick Parish in Columbus for the preceding ten years and was to become Bishop of Little Rock, was consecrated in that Columbus church by Archbishop Purcell. Bishops John J. Lynch of Toronto and Rosecrans were co-consecrators.[4]

Bishop Rosecrans was assigned to St. Patrick Parish, Columbus, as pastor, replacing Bishop Fitzgerald. This appointment was a preliminary step in the erection of the new diocese. On his arrival in Columbus he walked down Naghten Street from the railroad station with a tattered old carpetbag in his hand, and, arrived at the rectory, announced to the housekeeper that he had come to take charge of the parish.[5] He was in Columbus on Sunday and Monday, March 3 and 4, when he wrote a letter to the Archbishop.[6] He scheduled a meeting of the Cathedral Building Committee for Tuesday.

About March 26th[7] he was in Cincinnati for a short time and the ecclesiastical students of Mount St. Mary's of the West, as a token of their esteem, gratitude and love, gave him, on the occasion of his departure for Columbus, some beautiful and valuable presents. The Theologians presented him with two rich sets of dalmatics and stoles—red and purple. The Philosophers gave him a black cloak lined with purple. The first division of the Preparatorians presented him with a costly cassock. The second division of the Preparatorians gave him a white stole, and a traveling toilette box. Among those present on this occasion were his future clergymen in the Diocese of Columbus, Fathers Gallagher, Campbell, Dues, Fladung, Specht, Cull, Meara, and Fitzgerald.[8]

This spring he began to familiarize himself with the institutions and parishes in his proposed diocese, visiting the Good Shepherd Convent on the West Side of Columbus and the convent of the Sisters of Notre Dame de Namur, where he acted as extraordinary confessor. In April he confirmed in Delaware and preached in the throngled church.[9] On May 14 he was present for the close of a ten-day mission at Holy Cross Church in Columbus and delivered a few well-timed remarks on the fruits of the mission. These acts were in addition to his ordinary duties as Pastor of St. Patrick Parish and Confirmation at Holy Cross on May 19. He called another meeting "to take measures for further progress towards the erection of the new cathedral" on May 12.[10]

On Monday, May 20, 1867 Archbishop Purcell, Bishop Rosecrans, Bishop John Quinlan of Mobile, and Bishop Henry D. Juncker of Alton, Ill. left Cincinnati, bound for New York City. Together with Bishop Michael Domenec of Pittsburgh and Rev. John C. Albrinck of the Cincinnati Archdiocese and Rev. John B. Hemsteger of Columbus, along with several students for the American College, they were going to Rome, scheduled to embark on the steamer *New York* on May 22.[11] They were going to Rome to help celebrate the Centenary of St. Peter's Martyrdom. They were in Rome by June 2, when the Archbishop suggested to Propaganda that instead of appointing Bishop Rosecrans to Columbus he be assigned to succeed the late Bishop Timon in Buffalo. He proposed a terna of Fathers Augustus M. Toebbe, Patrick J. Ryan, and Caspar H. Borgess for Columbus. This must have been discussed in the U.S., for on the next day Archbishop John McCloskey of New York wrote to Propaganda from New York making the same suggestion for Buffalo. On July 28 it was reported in Buffalo that Rosecrans definitely would become Bishop there. Later in the month, Archbishop Martin Spalding of Baltimore, in Rome, gave his support to Rosecrans for Columbus.[12]

Cincinnati's archbishop and auxiliary bishop spent quite a while in Rome. Rosecrans filled out a statement of his expenses there on July 3 and later in the month the New York newspapers reported them still there.[13] It was in 1867, while in Rome, that Rosecrans was honored by being named Assistant to the Pontifical Throne. By July 10 the two Cincinnati prelates had left Rome and arrived in Ancona, accompanied now by Bishops James Wood of Philadelphia and James Bayley of Newark as well as Rev. Mr. Lancaster and Peyton Boyle. Purcell wrote, "Since leaving Rome, the spiteful Victor Emanuel, as if there were cholera in Rome, which there is not, has had us fumigated in every little or large town in his usurped dominions. A horrible ordeal of villainous odors, compounds, and chemicals..."[14]

Bishop Rosecrans, at least, examined various churches while in Europe to obtain ideas for St. Joseph Cathedral. He probably also visited Ireland, for he later gave a lecture called "Glimpses of Ireland in 1867." He reached Columbus by September 18, in excellent health, much improved by the trip.[15]

Rome in time acted on the requests of the Plenary Council of Baltimore. On Feb. 26, 1868 Propaganda issued decree no. 26 regarding that Council. By decision of the general congregation of Sept. 16, 23, and 27, 1867, and sanctioned by the Pope on Oct. 6, 1867, the Diocese of Columbus was created out of the Archdiocese of Cincinnati. On the same day, in decree no. 25, Bishop Sylvester H. Rosecrans was appointed to the new see. Word of these decrees reached Cincinnati by February 19. Propaganda wrote a letter to Rosecrans informing him of his appointment, which he received on March 2. On the same day, the newly appointed ordinary wrote from Columbus to Propaganda, acknowledging the appointment and describing the ecclesiastical and general conditions of the new diocese. Apostolic Briefs were issued on March 3, 1868, creating the new diocese and appointing the new bishop.[16]

Rosecrans as an Ordinary

Bishop Rosecrans seems at first to have disliked his appointment to Columbus. He remarked that Archbishop Purcell had compelled him to take the position, which he called a melancholy promotion.[17] He thought Columbus a "corner," of the archdiocese, apparently, which one can understand. Columbus had only three parishes, compared to a dozen or so in Cincinnati, not counting those in its suburbs, and Cincinnati had many Catholic institutions and convents, compared with just one hospital and two convents in Columbus. Rosecrans once told Purcell that Columbus was the only place he had ever been to which he had a rooted aversion.[18] This may have been because of both its strongly Protestant citizenry and the level of politics constantly stirring the state capital. But in addition to the small proportions of the Columbus Catholic body, the attitude of many was a source of vexation. He once noted in an editorial, "Many of them do not seek for Catholic news, do not interest themselves in the Church at home or throughout the world, do not know what Catholic enterprises are afoot in their midst, and think they do enough for religion by subscribing something because solicited. ...They never think of being prominent in any project of charity or piety. They seldom inquire of their pastor whether he needs help for the poor and the orphans he must relieve." But he came to love his diocese so greatly that it was known among the episcopate that he seldom was absent from it. "He was so intently bent upon the work to which he had been assigned, that he felt that it would be wronging his people if, for any reason whatsoever, he went away or separated himself from them."[19]

His view of the episcopacy, at least as a diocesan ordinary, and specifically that of a new diocese, he expressed in his sermon at the consecration of his former pupil, Rev. John Lancaster Spalding, as first Bishop of Peoria in 1877. "In conclusion," he said, "let me say to the young chosen one who today has received the episcopal consecration, who goes forth on the same mission and with about the same resources as that undertaken by the apostles, that henceforth he must be alone in the world. His duties, his position, will necessarily make him without any one to lean upon; but all will expect to lean upon him. ...Our Lord invites him by this consecration to a closer relationship in His holy family; for truly, when the gold cross is hung around his neck, then the heavy cross of sorrow, disappointment and responsibility will also be hung on his heart. He is to wear the crown of thorns, and it will press more sharply around his brows than if he had never been promoted to this high dignity."[20]

Despite discouragement at his new position, in a short time Rosecrans became a noble type of a true Bishop.

He believed it was better to wear out than to rust out. His life was one of hard labor, ceaseless devotion to his spiritual subjects, and humble charity to all. Regular and exact in the performance of the least duty, he always found time for all that was required of him. From 4 o'clock in the morning till 9:30 in the evening he did all his work. Only serious indisposition or inconvenience would prevent his daily celebration of Mass or delay until unseasonable time the reading of his Office. In these things he was almost scrupulously exact.[21] He was a man of prayer, and in this he was an example to his brother priests, and a moral to his people. To this he owed his greatness as a prelate.

His poverty was well known. In Cincinnati he remarked that he had never had fifty dollars ahead. In Columbus he probably could have lowered that figure to fifteen. At his death his personal property consisted of a watch that had belonged successively to his nieces Mamie and Annie (at Brown County), a few pictures on the walls of his room, and a few other trifles.[22]

He strove always for mastery of self but he was generous and lenient to the faults and mistakes of others. On the other hand, when obliged to censure an errant one, duty could move him to severity. But he never failed to smooth away the harshness, and temper with kindness, the pain of such a just censure. The exercise of the power of absolving the repentant sinner was one of his greatest works of love. Besides being confessor for the inmates of the convents of the Good Shepherd and of the Sacred Heart, he was regularly and promptly with his clergy in the Cathedral confessionals on Saturdays and vigils of holy days, happy to bear a share in listening to the tales of sin and woe. While he fasted, observing scrupulously every precept of the Church in this regard, he exercised his rightful authority to dispense those of his penitents who suffered from ailments that prevented their keeping the fast. Some who knew him intimately remarked that he took it upon himself to do penance and fast for those who were too weak morally and physically to bear the burdens.[23]

Perhaps his best-known characteristics were earnestness and love for children; he found his greatest enjoyment in the company of little ones. "While his nature was essentially a loving one and he found great happiness in the society of a few chosen families, the moment he felt that the object of his friendly attachment loved God the less and him the more, that moment he began to direct the soul to God, and by the angelic zeal which characterized his whole life, made manifest his ardent desire to win affection for the Creator instead of the creature."[24]

On the other hand, he was "a man's man" who could enjoy a cigar and had a dog (named Jack).[25] It was well known that, on episcopal visitations, after the religious duties and ceremonies were accomplished, he would enjoy an evening game of cards with his priests and sometimes with local society.[26]

He was "the most talented man of Ohio...a model Bishop, a faithful and generous priest, a father to the orphan, a protector to the feeble and homeless, a man made after God's heart..."[27]

Organizing the New Diocese
Statistics

The new Diocese of Columbus comprised all of 27 counties and parts of four more, containing in all 13,900 square miles. There were 29 county seats. The total population was about 787,000. Estimated Catholic population of the new diocese was 40,000, or about 5% of the total. They were, in order of decreasing numbers, Irish, Germans, Americans, a few French, and a scattering of Italians. The diocese included all of the hilly southeastern part of the state, with some of Ohio's worst agricultural land. In those days, however, some of those areas were booming with coal and iron production and railroad operating centers.

The new diocese was poor in Catholic population and wealth in comparison with the archdiocese Bishop Rosecrans had left. One handy statistic demonstrating this is the annual reports of seminary collections published in the *Catholic Telegraph*. These show collections in the territory of the new diocese to have been about 27% of the archdiocesan total in the war years of 1862 and 1863, but only 18% in the perhaps more typical post-war year of 1866. The collection in St. Peter in Chains Cathedral alone typically was larger than the total collected within the boundaries of the new diocese.[28]

When the diocese was erected, as best we can determine there were available to serve it 42 priests (see Table 2), counting the Bishop and including nine Dominican Fathers. These clergymen tended 32 parishes, 42 missions with churches but no resident pastor, 10 stations with no church, a hospital, and four convents (three of them with schools attached).[29] (See Table 4.) These figures include two mission churches that were inactive at the time and never were opened again. Twenty-three parish schools had total attendance of about 3,100 pupils.

First Acts

Although the news of Rome's erection of the new diocese reached Ohio in February 1868, the official letters did not reach Bishop Rosecrans until July. On July 16 he signed his first pastoral letter as Bishop of Columbus, addressed to the clergy and laity. He expressed his regret at severing his close ties with Archbishop Purcell and his "profound dread of the new responsibility" he was undertaking. He named V. Rev. John B. Hemsteger Vicar General and Rev. Gerhard H. Ahrens Chancellor. In addressing the clergy he laid out his development program of cathedral, seminary, orphan asylums, and colleges and asked for their cooperation. The priorities of the clergy, few in numbers for a vast harvest, were to be providing the sacraments, providing religious education, and then approaching the mass of unbelievers among whom the Catholics were scattered. For the laity he begged an increase in faith and charity, that their lives might preach to the unbelievers.

The letter, together with translations of the documents erecting the diocese and appointing him bishop, was printed in the *Catholic Telegraph* in Cincinnati and the *Daily Ohio Statesman* in Columbus.

It was necessary for Bishop Rosecrans to employ an official seal, and in a discussion with Father Ahrens on the subject the latter suggested a rosary as the most appropriate, it signifying in itself the name of the Bishop—Rose-crown, or Rosenkranz. This the Bishop, in his modesty, considered too personal. Father Ahrens then suggested the rosary entwined with a crown of roses but the Bishop rejected the idea of the crown of roses while he seemed to think well of the rosary if used with some other device. He himself suggested a dove as signifying Columbus, and the motto "Mors Christi Vita Mea." "When the seal finally reached the pastoral residence it was completed as we all now know it—the rosary entwined with the crown of thorns, the dove in the center, the Episcopal hat above, the motto beneath and the scroll above all with the words 'Diocese of Columbus.'"[30]

On Holy Thursday, March 25, 1869, the consecration of the sacred oils took place for the first time in Columbus. All the clergy of the city, and Rev. Wm. F. O'Brien, of Zaleski, assisted on that day. V. Rev. J. B. Hemsteger presented a massive crozier to Bishop Rosecrans in the name of the clergy of the diocese, hoping he might bear it through many years of health and prosperity.

In 1873 a solemn consecration of the diocese to the Sacred Heart of Jesus was carried out, at the invitation of Pope Pius IX. Beginning about the end of November, a novena of prayers, instructions, and benedictions of the Blessed Sacrament was begun. After Pontifical Vespers on the evening of December 8, Feast of the Immaculate Conception, after a sermon was preached on the devotion, during the singing of the *O Cor Amoris* the Blessed Sacrament was exposed and then the Act of Consecration of the diocese to the Sacred Heart of Jesus was made; Benediction followed.[31]

Diocesan Officials

The bishop appointed the following officials:
· Vicar General was V. Rev. J. B. Hemsteger from 1868 until his death in 1878.

· Others with this title were Rev. Louis Cartuyvels of Newark in 1871 and Rev. John A. Rochford, O.P., 1870-1871.[32]
· Chancellor for all of Bishop Rosecrans's time was Rev. Gerhard H. Ahrens.
· The Bishop's Secretary was Rev. John B. Eis, at least from 1877 to 1878 and perhaps as early as 1875.

Synods

The first Synod of the Diocese of Columbus opened on Aug. 20, 1869, preceded by a three-day retreat preached by the Bishop. Secretary was Rev. M. J. D. Ryan and notary was Rev. Michael Ahern. It seems that the retreat was the important matter and the Synod was held only as a formality. "The Rt. Rev. Bishop declared as received and binding in the diocese the decrees of the Provincial and Plenary Councils of Baltimore, and the decrees and statutes of the Archdiocese of Cincinnati." He also charged the clergy to keep careful and exact accounts of the financial affairs of their churches.

Bishop Rosecrans held two additional synods. The second opened on Aug. 22, 1873, in St. Joseph Cathedral. A three-day retreat had been conducted by Rev. J. V. Bokel, O.P., Prior at St. Joseph's near Somerset. Officials were V. Rev. J. B. Hemsteger, promotor; Rev. N. A. Gallagher, secretary; and Rev. D. B. Cull, notary. Five committee reports were made. First, it was reported that it would be better to continue the existing system of voluntary contributions to support the seminary and construction of the cathedral rather than imposing a tax on the congregations. Second, it was thought not a good time to found a diocesan newspaper. Third, it was deemed impractical to establish clerical conferences. Fourth, after considerable discussion, it was determined, and approved by the Bishop, that Catholic parents must send their children to Catholic schools when such were available. Fifth, those who contracted marriage before a non-Catholic minister were to be considered excommunicated by the general law of the Church. Confessors could absolve them after referral to the Ordinary; confessors could absolve those who contracted marriage before a civil magistrate, again after referral to the Ordinary. The acts were published by Bishop Rosecrans, with his approval and further explanation. The third Synod was held on August 26, 1876, and dealt only with the diocesan debt. (See the brief discussion in Chapter IX.)

Troubles with Archbishop Purcell

In his initial pastoral letter July 16, 1868, Bishop Rosecrans wrote that Archbishop Purcell "has been as a father to us since entering the ecclesiastical state." Rosecrans had dedicated his book in 1866, "To my father and friend the Most Rev. John Baptist Purcell, D.D., Archbishop of Cincinnati, the inspirer of this and countless worthier undertakings, for the honor of Jesus Christ..." And in his sermon at the Requiem Mass for Bishop Rosecrans, Bishop Foley of Chicago noted that "He [Rosecrans] was always one of his [Purcell's] beloved sons, and he was always obedient." But their relationship became very strained during the early years of the new diocese, to such an extent that in contrast with the first four years, there was almost no news from the Diocese of Columbus in Cincinnati's *Catholic Telegraph* for 1872. It would seem that either the Bishop would not submit news or the Archbishop would not allow it to be published. The contention concerned the division of seminarians and clergy and, later but of greater impact, ownership of a convent in Newark.

Divvying up Seminarians and Clergy

In principle, Archbishop Purcell took care to be sure not to remove clergy from the parishes of the new diocese as it was being formed. But as to seminarians, he did not see that any should belong to the new diocese even though their homes were within its boundaries.

Bishop Rosecrans thus saw several seminarians lost to him, whose ordinations should have greatly helped him in his early struggles in the new diocese. Rosecrans mentions a Kennedy, an O'Dea, and two Fitzgeralds. And Bishop Rosecrans never dreamed that Anthony Ullrich or Nicholas A. Gallagher (the latter from Noble County) did not belong to the new diocese, but Purcell claimed them. Purcell did offer Ullrich to Rosecrans, but Rosecrans preferred that, if anyone be given him he should be Irish, for the greatest need was at

St. Patrick Parish in Columbus. Gallagher was agreed to and Rosecrans ordained him in 1868. Rosecrans had to ask if there were any seminarians in Cincinnati that were considered to belong to Columbus. He mentioned a student named Skinner who belonged to him as well as a young Stambaugh who would begin in the fall of 1868. (Oddly, none of the seminarians mentioned by Bishop Rosecrans ever were ordained for either diocese, except John J. Kennedy, who was ordained for Cincinnati in 1873.) Archbishop Purcell eventually softened and four of the ordinands of the new diocese in 1870 and three in 1871 are known to have studied at Mt. St. Mary's. (These were Fathers J. J. Slevin, J. A. Murray, E. L. Fladung, C. L. Grimmer, and J. C. Goldschmidt; and Fathers Jessing and D. B. Cull, each of whom was adopted by Bishop Rosecrans just before ordination.) Several of the early students at St. Aloysius Seminary in Columbus were on the rolls of Mt. St. Mary's in 1870.

Even with regard to current clergy the Archbishop's principle did not quite hold up; he did "remove" some clergymen from "this side of the boundary." Purcell removed Father Nicholas Pilger from Woodsfield without Rosecrans's consent, though he soon allowed him to return. Father Joseph Fitzgerald had been serving at St. Patrick Parish in Columbus when he had obtained an *exeat* to depart from the Archdiocese before the new diocese was erected; yet Purcell refused to replace him. About the time the dioceses were separated, Father Conway of London and Father Mallon of St. Patrick's in Columbus were to exchange assignments. But then the Archbishop decided to send Father Mallon to Sedamsville while not sending Father Conway to Columbus to replace him. Purcell thought that sending someone to replace Mallon should be in the nature of a temporary loan.[33]

Despite such problems, Bishop Rosecrans made peace with the Archbishop, whom he refused to consider anything other than his spiritual father.

In 1870, just after Purcell's return from the Vatican Council, controversy over seminarians arose again and was compounded by misunderstanding. Bishop Rosecrans on July 16, 1870 ordained to the priesthood Rev. John Joseph Jessing, who in time became the founder of the Pontifical College Josephinum. Jessing, and another German seminarian named Heisser, had been students of the Cincinnati Archdiocese. The Archbishop wrote to Rosecrans in late July or early August, apparently berating him for ordaining Jessing. Rosecrans replied in August that he did not know that Jessing's ordination was not satisfactory to all who knew him. He had not even looked at Jessing's *exeat* when he came to Columbus, but had understood that Father Edward Purcell had given him one; and that Heisser's situation was similar. Archbishop Purcell seems to have advised or asked whether Rosecrans could refrain from sending students to Mt. St. Mary's Seminary, but Rosecrans replied that he could not avoid the practice at that time.

Purcell apparently then asked Rosecrans that the two new priests (Jessing and, apparently, Murray) pay their debts to the seminary. He also made some remarks about the debt that Rosecrans was accumulating for construction of the cathedral and was unable to pay. In a letter of August 20 Rosecrans admitted that the two would have to pay their seminary bills. But he was crushed by what he took as the Archbishop's sarcasm about the cathedral debt. On the letter at this point, after reading it, the Archbishop wrote "Bad mistake," meaning that he had intended no sarcasm. The Archbishop wrote back to Rosecrans immediately, explaining his earlier remarks. In reply to this, Rosecrans on August 25 wrote to Purcell, saying how sorry he was that he had misunderstood Purcell's remarks, and in the same letter addressing matters that were more routine. In another letter dated September 5 he returned to the subject, describing the situation preliminary to the ordination of Father Jessing and verbal promises received from Father Purcell, and saying that he had not knowingly done any wrong to Purcell. This seems to have closed the subject.[34]

Sisters of Charity of Cincinnati

More serious than concerns over seminarians was the controversy that developed between Bishop Rosecrans and Archbishop Purcell over ownership of the convent of the Sisters of

Charity in Newark. Shortly after being named Bishop of Columbus, Rosecrans found the little town of Newark to be embroiled in a storm of controversy, whose outer ripples reached even to Rome.[35]

Archbishop Purcell

The pastor, Father Louis Cartuyvels, had obtained the services of the Sisters of Charity, headquartered at Cedar Grove in Cincinnati, to staff the parish school. Early in 1865 Sisters Cecelia Griffin, Francis Xavier Clements, Agatha McGuire, and Genevieve Spitznagel (who soon were joined by Sister Sylvester Williams) took up residence in a house on Granville Street. In addition to their residence there was the former church, used as a parochial school, and a cottage for a select school, which they called the St. Francis de Sales Academy. (This cottage much earlier had been the residence of the two celebrated missionaries Rev. J. B. Lamy and Rev. Projectus Macheboeuf. It stood to the west of the church then in use.) In all, the property included three acres. Attendance at the Academy required advance payment for board and tuition, with the number of boarders limited to twenty.

Things seemed to be progressing nicely until 1870 when, the "views of Superiors and Pastor did not agree." According to a much later history, the difficulty seems to have arisen over the support of the Sisters. The sisters were expected to support themselves by payments received from the parents, "but Father Cartuyvels seems to have been given some of this money which he applied to the costs of operating the parish." This must have been payments for students in the parish school, since the Academy was self-sustaining. The parish was also expected to pay $1,000 a year to the Sisters, but did not do so.

The Sisters had purchased their house and lot from Edward Brennan but mortgaged it to him and could not pay for it. The misunderstanding could not be resolved and the sisters withdrew from Newark and returned to their Cincinnati motherhouse in the summer of 1870. They took their furniture and carpets and rented out the house.

The dispute over the house continued to simmer. Bishop Rosecrans supported Father Cartuyvels, stating to Archbishop Purcell that the house was purchased for the use of the Sisters but not as a donation to them. He appealed to Purcell as superior of the Sisters to end the scandal. But Purcell would not. Both sides wrote to the Congregation de Propaganda Fide and some of the Newark parishioners supported the position of the Sisters. Cardinal Barnabo replied in August 1871, that, based on all the statements he had received, it did not seem reasonable that the house be acknowledged the property of the parish. In November he wrote again that Rosecrans should come to some agreement with Purcell to resolve the issue.

On January 3, 1872, Rosecrans wrote to Purcell, quoting Cardinal Barnabo's letter. He stated again that the Sisters had not used their own funds to purchase the house. He also noted that the deed stated that the house could not be alienated from the congregation, and that his statements were true, despite what the Cardinal thought. He offered three ways of settling the issue, the last of which was for him to give up the See of Columbus. But Archbishop Purcell cooperated by sending to Rosecrans the affidavits and other documents he had received from Newark and Rosecrans made notes of and on them and returned them to Cincinnati. He noted "wicked falsehoods" in a letter that had been sent to Cincinnati and he hired a detective to investigate the secretary of the "gift scheme," who had opposed Father Cartuyvels, and who falsified the "protest" sent in by parishioners. He noted, in a letter to Purcell, that what was going on in Newark was also going on in Coshocton against Fr. Jacquet and that he could not yield to the subversion of order and justice.

In reality the views of the Bishop and the Archbishop were not too divergent. Bishop Rosecrans and Father Cartuyvels argued that the Sisters' house in Newark had been purchased "with money from the offering of the faithful" and so the house should belong to the parish. The Sisters said they had purchased the house with their own funds, but it is clear that some of these funds were indeed donations from the faithful of the parish, but which the donors had intended to belong to the Sisters and had not intended to be tied back to the parish. Propaganda, based on conflicting documents received from Columbus and Cincinnati, in May 1872 at last threw up their hands and told Bishop Rosecrans that he and Archbishop Purcell would have to try again to resolve the issue. The Sacred Congregation's only other alternative would have been to deputize a neighbor bishop to investigate the matter and this does not appear ever to have been done.[36]

How the two old friends, Rosecrans and Purcell, resolved the issue is not known, but it seems that the younger man at last deferred to the elder. At meetings held in Newark in June 1872, to investigate the financial matters of the congregation, under Father Louis DeCailly as representative of Bishop Rosecrans, one conclusion reached was that the parish owed $2,000 to "Father Purcell."[37] This no doubt was Father Edward Purcell, treasurer of the Archdiocese. It may be that this amount was admitted to settle accounts with the Archdiocese on behalf of the Sisters of Charity.

After the withdrawal of the Sisters of Charity, Bishop Rosecrans obtained the services of the Sisters of St. Dominic from St. Mary's of the Springs to educate the children of St. Francis de Sales Parish.

The Sisters of Charity had also taken charge of parish schools at St. Peter in Steubenville, Sacred Heart in Pomeroy, and Holy Redeemer in Portsmouth in the late 1860s, but they also withdrew from Pomeroy and Portsmouth in the early 1870s and Steubenville in 1880[38] and they never returned to the Diocese of Columbus, as such. Beyond any fallout from the Newark controversy, the Sisters were impelled by the fact that their primary mission was to the Archdiocese of Cincinnati and they were short-handed for that task. However, they served in several parishes that became part of the Diocese of Columbus when the western boundary was extended in 1944.

Chapter V
Clergy, Journeys, and Family Vocations, 1868-1878

Diocesan Clergy

In directing his clergy, from the least to the greatest, Bishop Rosecrans acted more the part of a brother than of a superior. In their adversity he was a friend, an adviser, and a helper, whose heart was ever open to the appeals of distress.[1] The mutual respect of the clergy and the Bishop is exemplified by the visit of the clergy of Columbus to the Bishop on St. Sylvester's day, 1877. "On that day the clergy of the city were accustomed to annually visit the reverend prelate and extend their felicitations. Little entertainments in the different educational and charitable institutions, too, commemorated the day. ...Many there were who recalled the happy little address of Vicar-General Hemsteger to Bishop Rosecrans on last St. Sylvester's day, when he spoke in behalf of the clergy and referred to the labors of the good Bishop. As well were remembered the response of the prelate, in which, with characteristic humility, he referred all that had been accomplished to the exertions and zeal of the priest working under Divine Providence."[2]

He knew most of the priests well. Among those whom he had taught in the seminary in Cincinnati were Fathers Thomas Tuomey, J. Murray, J. J. Slevin, Caspar Goldschmidt, Daniel Cull, Francis Campbell, M. M. Meara, Henry Dues, M. M. A. Hartnedy, Joseph Tuohy, B. M. O'Boylan, and John Meara.[3] Most of those ordained after 1871 he taught, at least for a time, at St. Aloysius Seminary in Columbus. (See Table 3.)

He inherited 33 priests from the Archdiocese; of these twelve left or were expelled by him during his eleven years as

Bishop of Columbus. He had much better success with the 24 he ordained for the diocese; of these only one left and one was expelled. In addition to these 56, at least another 54 secular priests served in the diocese for periods of various length. Some of these proved suitable to the task while others did not. Twenty-four of these left for their own reasons or were expelled by Bishop Rosecrans time while he still lived, but at least sixteen stayed the rest of their working lives.

Of the fourteen priests either inherited from Cincinnati or ordained for Columbus who left during Rosecrans's time, only one who publicly renounced the faith was treated harshly, as was necessary.

Four priests inherited from Cincinnati were lost within two years. Archbishop Purcell had suspected that Father Henry Fehlings of Delaware would be a problem and he proved to be so. Bishop Rosecrans removed him in 1869 but allowed him to return to his monastery in Europe without making the problem public. (But he died in Utica, N.Y., in 1888.) Father Christopher Pindar of Circleville renounced the priesthood and abjured the faith in public, at Mass, in 1869. Bishop Rosecrans went to Circleville at once and pronounced him excommunicated.[4] Father John E. McSweeney was "a failure" at Zaleski, with legal and health problems, and could not work. Bishop Rosecrans sent him to South Bend in 1869.[5] Father John Nordmeyer, who had caused concern, transferred to St. Louis in 1869.

Father Philip J. O'Donoghue was suspended by Rosecrans and removed from Ironton in 1871. Bishop Rosecrans later rescinded the suspension so that he could find work elsewhere. Archbishop Purcell received him back into the Archdiocese and assigned him to Marion, from which place he pestered Rosecrans and the Congregation de Propaganda Fide for years, seeking compensation for the supposed mistreatment he had received.[6]

Father William O'Reilly was suspended from his post in Ironton by Bishop Rosecrans in 1875. Twenty years earlier, in Cincinnati, as a young priest Bishop Rosecrans had seen the problems that could result from accusations of inappropriate conduct against a priest, whether true or not. They had to be

Table 2
Priests Inherited from the Archdiocese of Cincinnati

Name	Nativity	Ordination	Death
Ahern, Michael M.	1840, Cincinnati	1863	1910, Frontenac, Mich.
Ahrens, Gerhard H.	1841, Cincinnati	1866	1884, Columbus
Bigelow, William T.	1842, Lancaster, O.	1864	1872, Steubenville
Brent, Julius	1827, Engand	1851	1880, Mt, Vernon
Brogard, Joseph	c 1810, France		unknown
Brummer, John W.	1824, Germany	1851	1872, Columbus
Cartuyvels, Louis	1811, St. Trond, Belg.	1839	1874, Chicago
Daly, Patrick J.	1840, Ireland	1866	1870, Bellaire
(O')Donoghue, Philip	1831, Ireland	1855	1914, Ft. Worth
Eppink, Magnus	1842, Germany	1865	1884, Zanesville
Fehlings, Henry	1823, Germany	1854	1888, Utica, N.Y.
Fischer, Herman	1819, Baden		1878, Columbus
Heimo, Joseph A.	1816, Switzerland	1843	1869, Calmoutier
Hemsteger, John B.	1827, Alt Scherenbach	1854	1878, Columbus
Hillebrand, Bernard	1834, Westphalia	1866	1917, Crescent Spgs, Ky.
Jacquet, John Mary	1817, France	1844	1896, Galveston, Tx.
Kalenberg, John F.	1839, Germany	1863	1893, Miamisburg, O.
Karge, Francis	1810, Gratz, Austria	1834	1875, Delhi, O.
Klueber, Damian J.	1817, Fulda, Ger.	1860	1883, Fulda, O.
Mallon, Francis C.	c 1835, Ireland	1866	1883, Cincinnati
Mayrose, Herman H.	1834, Münster, Ger.	1866	1898, Shelbyville, Ind.
McSweeney, John E.	Ireland	1866	unknown
Nordmeyer, Johann	1838, Germany	1864	1894, Rengel, Mo.
Pilger, Nicholas E.	1842, Treves, Prussia	1865	1905, Lancaster, O.
Pindar, Christopher	1842 (place uncertain)	1865	1906, St. Matthews, Ky.
Rauck, John Joseph	1817, Germany	1841	1894, Pine Grove
Rosecrans, Sylvester	1827, Homer, O.	1852	1878, Columbus
Rudolph, Francis R.	1842, France	1867	1906, Indiana
Ryan, Michael J. D.	1838, Providence, R.I.	1862	1870, Marietta
Specht, Francis X.	1840, Osnabrück, Ger.	1864	1913, Columbus
Thienpont, Emmanuel	1802, Belgium	1833	1873, Logan
Walker, Augustine O.	1822, Somerset, O.	1850	1900, Somerset
Wismann, J. Bernard	1842, Cincinnati	1865	1891, Mt. Vernon

Table 3
Priests Ordained for the Diocese of Columbus

Name	Nativity	Ordination	Death
Gallagher, Nicholas A.[1]	1846, Temperanceville	1868/12/25	1918
O'Reilly, William	1843, Ireland	1869	1890
Tuomey, Thomas M.	1840	1870/3/24	1873
Slevin, James J.	1839, Moxahala	1870/7/2	1909
Murray, Jeremiah A.	1844, Cumberland, Md.	1870/7/16	1924
Jessing, Joseph J.[2]	1836, Münster	1870/7/16	1899
Fladung, Edward L.	1847, Fulda, Ger.	1870/12/17	1922
Grimmer, Charles Louis	1844, Baden, Germany	1871 March	1902
Goldschmidt, John C.	1840, Kaltensundheim	1871/6/10	1923
Steyle, Philip	1846, Meurtke, France	1871/6/25	1915
Cull, Daniel B.	1848, Chillicothe	1871/10/5	1883
Heery, Patrick M.	c 1847, Co. Cavan	1872/12/20	1924
Campbell, Francis J.	1850, Columbus	1873/12/20	1896
Meara, Michael M.	1850, Cincinnati	1874/5/30	1925
Dues, Henry B.	1850, Cincinnati	1874/5/30	1886
O'Boylan, Bernard M.	1851, Co. Cavan	1875/1/23	1928
Hartnedy, M. M. A.	1846, Co. Galway	1875/4/17	1912
Tuohy, Joseph	1843, Ireland	1876/6/10	1915
Fitzgerald, Richard J.	1849, Limerick, Ireland	1877/3/3	1897
Montag, John G.	1853, Canal Dover	1877/5/29	1902
Meara, John J.	1853, Columbus	1877/5/29	1878
Weisinger, Simon P.	1846, Pittsburgh	1877/5/29	1932
Lane, Thomas J.	1847, Walpole, Mass.	1877/12/21	1891
Woesman, Francis M.	1854, Cincinnati	1878/4/13	1922

1 Bishop of Galveston
2 Founder of the Pontifical College Josephinum

handled quickly to avoid scandal. Priests who had problems with intoxication or immorality sometimes were sent to other dioceses where the bishop knew nothing of the problem and as a result caused scandal there.[7] Rosecrans wrote a letter of dismissal for Father O'Reilly that, if used, would have made the accusations against him known. When O'Reilly complained, and by this time he had vehemently denied the accusations, Bishop Rosecrans charitably wrote a second letter that simply dismissed the priest from the diocese and allowed him to visit Ireland and Rome. This earned for Rosecrans a figurative rap on the knuckles from the Congregation de Propaganda Fide.[8]

Father Michael Ahern, "tired of life," left the diocese for the South in September 1878 but remained a faithful priest.

Father Francis Mallon, as mentioned above, was moved back to the Archdiocese by Archbishop Purcell. Father Hillebrand, who was not very robust at that period of his life, transferred to Covington in 1874. Fathers John F. Kalenberg, Francis Karge, and Francis Rudolph all returned to the Archdiocese of Cincinnati. Father Jeremiah A. Murray, in poor health, was allowed by Rosecrans to live with his brother, Father John B. Murray, in Chillicothe, and then to transfer to the Archdiocese.[9]

Relations with the Dominican Fathers

The Dominican Fathers were the pioneer Catholic clergy of Ohio, having first visited in 1808 and having established the first parish in the state, St. Joseph's near Somerset, in 1818. They were the only religious order of priests represented in the Diocese of Columbus in Bishop Rosecrans's days, comprising about one-fifth of the priests in the diocese when it was erected. The Bishop seems always to have had good relations with them. Likewise, the relations between the Dominican Fathers and the diocesan clergy in Perry and the adjoining counties were always those of the closest comradeship. The doors of the one were always open to welcome the men of the other.[10] While their service was limited because the majority of the Dominicans were at the priory at St. Joseph's near Somerset, even these were made available to Bishop Rosecrans to send temporarily to other parishes if he was in great need.

The Dominicans staffed several churches in the new diocese in 1868:
- St. Joseph's near Somerset, with its priory (Fathers Joseph Dunn[11], Patrick Keogh, James Edelin, Dominic Noon, and Leo Adams)

- St. Dominic at McLuney (west of Crooksville); St. Patrick in Jackson Township (Clarksville or Junction City); St. Pius at South Fork (west of Moxahala); and St. Rose at New Lexington, all served from St. Joseph's
- Holy Trinity in Somerset (Fathers John Rochford and John Collins)
- St. Thomas Aquinas in Zanesville (Fathers Bernard Brady and Thomas Cady)

At the end of 1869 the Dominican Fathers broached with Bishop Rosecrans the subject of relinquishing to him the smaller Perry County churches and missions. Naturally he objected strenuously, for this would force him to find pastors for them, but his objection was made in his usual affable manner. The Dominicans let the subject drop for a time until an opportunity arose when Father Nicholas (Thomas) Burke came from Europe to the American province as a visitator in the fall of 1871. Knowing the Bishop's high regard for authority, they had Father Burke use his influence with the Bishop. The result was that at the end of November 1872 the Dominicans relinquished to Bishop Rosecrans all control of the Perry County congregations of McLuney, South Fork, St. Patrick's, and New Lexington.[12] The Dominicans apparently continued to attend them until early the next year as a favor to him.[13] The Bishop seems to have been unconcerned that legal title to these properties remained with the Dominicans.

Bishop Rosecrans knew most of the Dominicans who were provincials during his years. Father Joseph F. Dunn was elected to that post in 1869. He had been reared near Junction City, made all his studies at St. Joseph's, and had served his years as priest until that time at Zanesville and Somerset. He had a splendid mind but great humility; his brother priests and the people where he served all spoke most highly of him.

Father Dunn was succeeded as provincial in 1873 by Father John Rochford or Rotchford (1834-1896), who had a very close working relationship with the Bishop. In May 1869, Bishop Rosecrans had asked the Dominican provincial and the Vatican to allow this "talented and exemplary Friar Preacher" to assist him in the ministry in Columbus.

Father Rochford had been ordained in 1859; he had been president of St. Joseph's College near Somerset in 1860-1861 and in 1869 was Pastor of Holy Trinity Parish in Somerset. He was described as a brilliant man whose Latin flowed easily, a leader and "smart operator," a forceful preacher and missionary, and one of the most respected priests in the Midwest, who besides was a man of handsome and commanding appearance. He loved the Dominican Order and had worn its habit from the age of 13. But at this time he and some of his brother Dominicans were punished, unjustly he thought, by their provincial, Irishman V. Rev. William O'Carroll. The priests had wanted a provincial who was known to their French master general, Most Rev. Alexander Jandel, and so could mollify Jandel's low opinion of the American province and his opposition to the two Dominican secular colleges in this country. But the man they elected turned down the office and Jandel appointed O'Carroll to the position in 1864. He turned out to be high-handed and as lacking in understanding of the province as Jandel was.

Bishop Rosecrans asked for Father Rochford's temporary service and, given his situation at the time, Rochford was glad for the opportunity. Permission was granted in June of 1869 and Rochford moved to St. Patrick Church in Columbus to live with the Bishop and the other clergy. He was the first priest assigned to lead the Cathedral congregation when it was organized in 1870 and began to worship in Naughten Hall. He taught at St. Aloysius Seminary after its opening in 1871. He is said to have been a vicar general for Bishop Rosecrans and we know the Bishop had him try to calm the parishioners in Newark during the contention over the former house of the Sisters of Charity. Late in 1872 the Dominicans recalled him, to work at St. Vincent Ferrer's in New York City.[14] As provincial from 1873 until 1877 he continued to live in New York but this would not have hindered any working relationship between the province and the diocese.

Father Stephen Byrne was elected to replace Father Rochford as provincial in 1877. He had been educated at Mt. St. Mary's in Cincinnati and at St. Joseph's near Somerset and had worked for a time in Ohio.

In practice, the cooperation of the priors at St. Joseph's near Somerset probably was more critical to Bishop Rosecrans than that of the provincials. During Rosecrans's years in Columbus these priors were:

- V. Rev. Joseph F. Dunn, 1868 and 1869.
- V. Rev. J. D. Sheehy, 1869 to 1871.
- V. Rev. John Albert Bokel (the elder), 1871 to 1874.
- V. Rev. Peter Clement Coll, 1874 to 1877
- V. Rev. Hugh F. Lilly, 1877 to 1883.

As Bishop of Columbus, Rosecrans happily cooperated with the Dominicans by ordaining several of their members to the priesthood (as he had done in Cincinnati as auxiliary bishop in 1863):

- 1871, October 18, in St. Joseph's Church near Somerset, Rev. Arthur Higgins (a native of Perry County)
- 1872, October, at St. Mary's of the Springs, Rev. George Raymond Dailey, O.P.
- 1873, May or June, in St. Joseph Cathedral, Revs. Edward P. De Cantillon, John R. McGarvey, and Patrick J. Scannell
- 1874, August 6, at St. Joseph's near Somerset, Revs. John A. Bokel (the younger), James D. Hoban, Charles V. Metzger, Jeremiah C. O'Mahoney, William Quinn, and Thomas A. Scallon (Fathers Metzger and Scallon were from this diocese.)
- 1875, Aug. 4, at Somerset, Rev. John Ambrose Durkin
- 1877, January 11, at St. Joseph Cathedral, Rev. William Francis Linahan
- 1878, April 26 or 27, at St. Joseph's, Somerset, Rev. John H. Garvey

As will be mentioned below, Bishop Rosecrans seems to have been especially close to Dominican Father Ambrose Durkin in 1878.

Bishop Rosecrans in 1871 happily gave his approbation and approved publication of *Catena Aurea or A Golden Chain of Evidences Demonstrating from "Analytical Treatment of History" that Papal Infallibility is no Novelty*. This was written by Bishop James Whalen, O.P., who was living at St. Joseph's near Somerset and at St. Thomas Parish in Zanesville in his retirement. Because he lived as a simple friar, no accounts, other than those focusing on Bishop Whelan, mention that this second and older bishop was resident in the Diocese of Columbus during almost all of Bishop Rosecrans's tenure, until his death on February 18, 1878.

Vatican Council Avoided

When Pope Pius IX. called for the Vatican Council, it was considered the highest privilege and honor for a Bishop to be invited into that august assembly by the head of the Church, to take part in the important transactions which transpired there. Bishop Rosecrans, on the contrary, was so wrapped up in the labor of his office and so interested in building the Cathedral that he asked the Holy See to permit him to remain at home, considering himself too humble and too unimportant to be found necessary to go to Rome. He wrote to Propaganda on Feb. 13, 1869, of the poor state of temporal affairs in his diocese, saying he did not know how he could afford to go to the Council and asking to be dispensed from attending. In a reply of May 1, Cardinal Barnabo wrote, "I did not fail to communicate to the Holy Father what you say to me in regard to the Ecumenical Council, and I am now glad to let you know that in view of the circumstances laid before him, his Holiness has vouchsaved to dispense you from the obligation of attending it."[15]

Several American bishops asked to be excused from the Council, but in the end Rosecrans was one of only five active bishops and two vicars apostolic who did not attend. Forty-eight American bishops and one abbot were there. Bishop Thomas Foley of Chicago later put it this way: "The Holy See granted his prayer, and allowed him, amongst a few other Bishops, to remain at home to take charge of his own Diocese, and to look after the interests of other Dioceses in the country, whose Bishops were then in the council." On January 9, 1870, Bishop Rosecrans was the principal consecrator of Bishop August Toebbe for the Diocese of Covington, in St. Philomena's Church, Cincinnati. Bishop James Duggan of Chicago became mentally incompetent in the spring of 1869 and was confined to an asylum. Bishop Rosecrans was co-consecrator of Thomas Foley, to be coadjutor of Bishop Duggan, in Baltimore on Feb. 27, 1870. On April 24 he was the principal consecrator of Caspar H. Borgess, who would be administrator of the Diocese of Detroit, in the Cathedral in Cincinnati. That same day he left for New Orleans to consecrate its Bishop Napoléon Perche on May 1.[16] He also confirmed and blessed churches in the dioceses of Cincinnati and Cleveland while the Council was in progress and ordained four priests for the Diocese of Pittsburgh and one for Cincinnati at St. Patrick Church in Columbus on March 24, 1870.[17]

Father Isaac Hecker, founder of the Paulists, was anxious to attend the Council (though his reason is unclear) as a member of a religious community, as one active in the apostolate of the press, and as an American. He was told by Cardinal Barnabo that he was not entitled to a seat at the Council as Superior-General of the Paulists. Cardinal Barnabo later told him that bishops would not be accompanied by theologians, so that route to the general sessions also was closed to him. Finally he applied to Bishop Rosecrans for an appointment as his procurator, to which the bishop agreed in mid-June 1869.[18] This perhaps was through the agency of the Bishop's nephew Louis Rosecrans, who had joined the Paulists in 1867. When the large attendance at the Council made it impossible for procurators to be admitted to the general sessions, Hecker obtained the position of theologian to either Archbishop Martin J. Spalding or Bishop Gibbons (secondary sources at hand disagree as to which). This gave him access to the Council documents, the meetings of the American bishops, etc. But he did not keep Bishop Rosecrans posted on events, never writing a line to him after reaching Rome. Because of this, and because Hecker did not know him well enough to present his views without instructions, Rosecrans did not mind that Hecker had no vote at the Council. Hecker left the Council prematurely in April 1870, seemingly discouraged that the vote for Papal Infallibility had disproved his one-sided, progressive view of on-going Church history.[19]

Bishop Rosecrans's more important role came after the American bishops had returned from the Council and tried to explain to their people their positions relative to, and the meaning of, Papal Infallibility. He was worried about Archbishop Purcell's reaction to the definition. The Archbishop had opposed the Council's action, believing at least that it should await a more opportune time, and left Rome before the vote was taken. On August 16, 1870, Rosecrans wrote to the Archbishop, implying that the latter should accept the definition. He said that on the previous Sunday he had had the Council's chapters on the Church read in church and had remarked to the congregation his own welcoming of the end of the long discussion by a proclamation of the Ancient Faith; and that the Council had been legitimate and had received papal approval. He added that he had been sorry to read Archbishop Kenrick's *Concio*, which had contended that the Church could not declare the pope infallible.[20] Purcell tried to clarify his position in newspaper articles and in a speech in Mozart Hall in Cincinnati. Rosecrans, perhaps alone, thought this an effective effort and read the speech aloud to three priests after dinner on August 21.[21]

Episcopal Visitations

As Ordinary of the Diocese of Columbus, Bishop Rosecrans continued the rounds of episcopal visitations that had become his practice as auxiliary bishop of Cincinnati. Although our records are far from complete, his first year in Columbus shows the energy he expended to reach out to his people, visiting, confirming, and sometimes delivering lectures to benefit local needs.

In March he delivered a series of lectures at St. Mary's, Lancaster. In May he visited Circleville to clear up confusion regarding the new church being built; and he administered Confirmation at both churches in Zanesville and at Holy Cross and St. Patrick's in Columbus. June saw him farther afield, in Delaware, Marysville, Somerset (St. Mary's Academy and St. Joseph's), Junction City, and Logan. In July he was at the distribution of premiums at St. Patrick's parish school and confirmed in Newark, Steubenville, and in Columbus at Holy Cross Parish. August took him east to Bellaire, Batesville, Harrietsville (where he blessed the new church), Fox Settlement (another new church to bless), Archer's Settlement, and Fulda. In September he went south to visit both parishes in Portsmouth, St. Peter's at Lick Run (Wheelersburg), St. John's Church at Lilly, St. Mary's at Pine Grove, and both St. Lawrence and St. Joseph in Ironton. October called for a trip northeast to St. Joseph's at Canal Dover, Marges and Malvern

(Lodi) in Carroll Co., and in Holmes County Ste. Genevieve's at Calmoutier, Millersburg, and Napoleon (Glenmont). In November he dedicated the Church of St. Mary, Mother of God, in Columbus.

Although the more convenient places could be reached by railroad, some of the remote areas could be reached only by spending many hours on rough roads. On his journeys in October 1868, in two days he traveled 73 miles in a wagon and then by carriage some 75 miles to Millersburg. It is said that once an old farm wagon being used as his episcopal carriage broke down and he and his attendants alighted while temporary repairs were made. "There happened to be a peach orchard by the road and the Bishop suggested a little feast, provided the owner of the orchard didn't object. The house was sought and the farmer gladly agreed to sell the party some peaches, but when he learned of the Bishop's presence he ejaculated with a good round oath, 'not a cent from the brother of 'Old Rosy',' meaning General Rosecrans of Iuka, Corinth and Civil War fame. The Bishop then suggested that the farmer accept a cigar, of which he availed himself and down on a log by the road sat the genial Bishop and the farmer and chatted about crops, etc., until the wagon was ready to resume the journey."[22]

Travels Outside the Diocese

Bishop Rosecrans was not quite the stay-at-home prelate that his friend Bishop Foley of Chicago later portrayed him to be. He attended occasional meetings of the bishops of the province at Cincinnati. He frequently visited St. Martin's, Brown County, sometimes for rest or retreat, sometimes for ceremonies for the Sisters, sometimes to visit with his nieces and other friends among the congregation. He also occasionally carried out episcopal functions in Archdiocese of Cincinnati, for example the blessing of a new bell at St. Patrick church in London on St. Patrick's Day, 1870.

Longer journeys or those that threw him before larger crowds of people usually happened only once per year and most of these were of a personal nature involving his family, former students, or others whom he knew well.

Clergy, Journeys, and Family Vocations

On August 16, 1868, he preached at the consecration of Bishop Machebeuf in Cincinnati.[23]

On July 9 and 10, 1870, he went to Canton, in the Diocese of Cleveland, to lecture in Harter's Hall and to lay the cornerstone of the new St. John's Church.[24]

On May 23 to 25, 1872, he was in New York City, where in the Paulist church on West 59th Street he conferred minor orders for the Paulists, including James Kent Stone, and ordained some to the priesthood, including his own nephew, Rev. Adrian Louis Rosecrans.[25]

On Sunday, Sept. 6, 1874, he was scheduled to preach at the cornerstone laying of Sacred Heart Church in Lake George, New York.[26] In 1875, on May 23, he was present at the consecration of Bishop John Kain in Wheeling.[27]

The next year, in May, he made the sad journey to New York to officiate at the funeral of his nephew, Paulist Father Louis Rosecrans. Later that same month he attended the golden jubilee of Archbishop Purcell in Cincinnati.[28]

On May 1, 1877 Bishop Rosecrans had the joy of seeing one of his former students, Rev. John Lancaster Spalding, consecrated to be the first Bishop of Peoria. The ceremony took place in St. Patrick's Cathedral in New York City and Rosecrans delivered the sermon.

In June of 1878, he seems to have attended the graduation ceremonies at St. John's College, Fordham, and that evening he was elected president of the alumni association.[29]

Family Religious Vocations

Bishop Rosecrans had three nieces and a nephew who followed him into the priesthood or religious life. As children no doubt they were following the good example of William and Ann in taking their religion seriously, as Sylvester himself had done, but the Bishop had his own impact on their lives. While he was president of the college at Mt. St. Mary's and through the Civil War, the home of William and his family was practically next door, in a former convent they called "Roccabella," a quarter of a mile down a quiet lane from the seminary (said to be the house at 2935 Lehman Road, Price Hill, Cincinnati). As remembered by his niece Lily,

Lily Rosecrans Toole

William S. Rosecrans

Rev. Adrian Rosecrans, C.S.P.

Annie, Sr. M. Kostka, O.S.U.

(Lily, Adrian, and Sr. M. Kostka, courtesy of the Ursulines of Brown County; William Courtesy of Tom Wolke.)

Clergy, Journeys, and Family Vocations

Never was there a more devoted uncle. Outside of his college and church duties he seemed to live for his little nieces and nephews. Every evening brought him to the house, and once there, he surrendered himself entirely to the children, romping with them like a boy, telling stories and teaching them to sing. Then when the evenings grew long and cold, he brought over books from the college library and read aloud works that could be enjoyed by all the family. In this way, when Anita was only eight years old [c. 1865], she had become familiar with nearly all of Dickens', several of Bulwer's, Washington Irving's and numerous short stories, poems, etc. of leading authors, to say nothing of books of travel.[30]

During the summers of the Civil War, he would visit Annie and the children in Yellow Springs, Ohio, where they lived with General Scammon's family (at 136 South Walnut Street, a house still standing).[31] As a bishop he saw their religious lives flourish.

Rev. Adrian L. Rosecrans, C.S.P.

Adrian, oldest son of the General to survive childhood, was born in 1849 and was educated at Notre Dame University, followed by private studies at home in Cincinnati, with the goal of assisting his father in the mining business. He worked for his father in California for a few months and then worked for the revenue department before discerning a call to the priesthood. In order to make complete "the sacrifice of ties of blood" he did not join the ranks under his uncle but instead joined the Paulists in 1867. Bishop Rosecrans ordained him in 1872 when just short of 23 years of age. He was an impressive preacher of singularly amiable character and modesty. He worked on a Paulist mission in California but his health soon forced him to retire to the headquarters in New York City, where he died suddenly on May 10, 1876.[32]

Bishop Rosecrans made the sorrowful journey to New York to offer the Requiem Mass on May 13 in St. Paul the Apostle Church on West 59th Street. He rode in a carriage to the place of interment, at St. Patrick's (Old) Cathedral on Mulberry Street.

The Bishop always was a most honored and welcome guest in the home and family of General Francis Darr in New York. (The General had been a staff officer of General Rosecrans during the early part of the war.) The Bishop visited them after the funeral and while there wrote an account, ostensibly for *The Catholic Columbian*, of his nephew's death. He read it to the General, who expressed a wish to have a number of copies of the paper in which it would appear. The Bishop considered for a little time and then remarked, "I shall lay this away until I am convinced that family pride had nothing to do with my writing it."[33] This no doubt is the article that appeared on the editorial page of the *Columbian* on May 20, 1876.

Sister Mary of St. Charles Rosecrans, O.S.U.

Mary Louise or Mame was the oldest daughter of William and Anne, born in 1851. Bishop Rosecrans received her vows as an Ursuline Sister at her profession on Dec. 8, 1875 at St. Martin's in Brown County. She died there only three years later, on March 2, 1878. She had had a hemorrhage of the lungs in August of 1877 and others from time to time after that. She also suffered from tuberculosis.[34]

The following poem dedicated to her appeared on page 237 of the Ave Maria magazine dated April 13, 1878. It is signed "S.A.R." and one has to wonder whether that middle initial should have been "H."

> She placed it on the altar,
> As she knelt in silent prayer—
> "Take this little gift, St. Joseph,
> Which I've culled with loving care,
>
> "'Tis a fragrant little blossom,
> In thy name, dear heavenly friend,
> Let its sweetness be the emblem
> Of the message which I send.
>
> "It blooms in consecration
> Of the sun's first brilliant ray,

On the sacred month we honor,
And to greet thy festive day.

"Now I ask of you a favor
Which I pray you'll not refuse,
That you guide me to my Saviour,
Ere your chosen month shall close."

Sister Mary Kostka Rosecrans, O.S.U.

Annie Rosecrans, youngest daughter of the General and Anne, was born in 1857. On Friday, March 29, 1878, just after her sister's death, the Bishop conducted her from Columbus to Brown County and he was present on Sunday for her admission as a postulant. She received the habit as Sister Mary Kostka on September 5. The Bishop was to have been present, but arrived too late for the ceremony.[35] Some years later she became ill and was released from her vows. She went home to assist her father and later her brother-in-law, Governor Toole of Montana. She died in Montana in 1903.

Sister M. Imelda Rosecrans, O.P.

Mary or Mayme was the only child of the Bishop's brother Charles Wesley or Wes Rosecrans. She was born in Iowa about 1863 and was orphaned by her father's death in 1865. She was raised by her uncle and aunt, Henry C. and Elizabeth Rosecrans, also of Keokuk County, until the age of thirteen. Late in 1876 she came to Columbus and enrolled in the Dominican Sisters' Sacred Heart Academy, where the Bishop then was making his home. She had never been baptized, for her father had never joined the Church, and that step was taken on May 19, 1877. She was the only family member present at the Bishop's death and entombment.

She moved with the academy to Somerset in 1879 and received the Dominican habit and white veil there on August 15. She moved with the little congregation to Texas in 1882, where she taught at Sacred Heart Academy in Galveston and at Holy Rosary School for Colored Children. She died on September 6, 1902.[36]

In addition to the above, William's daughter Lily, born in 1854, attended St. Martin's Academy in Brown County, where she was the only graduate in 1872.[37] She married Joseph K. Toole, who became Governor of Montana, and had three children.

Chapter VI
Academies for Young Women, 1862-1878

Most of the institutions founded in the new diocese by Bishop Rosecrans were run by religious Sisters and several of them served women and girls only. In this regard it was remarked, "his reverence for womanhood was not the least of his admirable traits; in innocent girlhood he beheld the future Spouse of the Immaculate Lamb or the devoted wife and mother, whose virtues crown a husband's life with the brightest jewels of home and whose children 'rise up to call her blessed.' In all his intercourse with girls his conduct tended to inspire them with the true idea of a woman's worth as a pure maiden, a faithful wife or a devoted religious."

Many of the existing and new institutions were schools. Speaking of Rosecrans's devotion to educating the children of his diocese, Bishop Foley said, "His great solicitude for the establishment of schools, his great care for the young; his deep interest in them; so deep that, I venture to say, he has done that which scarcely any other Bishop in the United States has done. He made himself a teacher of the young. It was his pleasure, his enjoyment, to enter the schools and teach a class, like any other teacher employed in them, and what illustrated more strikingly than this the interest that your beloved Bishop took in the young, and the desire that he had to keep them in the faith, and the hope he had that his humility, and his kindness, and his teachings would forever attach these young to himself, and through him, to his divine Master, in whose service he was a faithful laborer. And, beloved people of this grand city, you should never forget these acts of charity and noble condescension and great humility which your Bishop has exhibited for your children. He felt, as every Bishop must feel, that if we save the children we save the family, and saving the family, we save the whole flock. It was the highest wisdom that prompted him to do this work which he has done so humbly and so faithfully, in your midst. He might, perhaps, have mounted the chair of eloquence, and, by his learning, which was profound and extensive, he might have attracted the admiration of vast audiences; but he was more pleased to go among the children and teach them the way of life, in the hope that he might communicate, through them, to the families to which they belong."[1]

Dominican Sisters' Academies

At the request of Bishop Fenwick of Cincinnati, a small group of Dominican Sisters had come from Springfield, Kentucky, to Somerset in 1830 to found St. Mary's Academy. The school and convent, and in time its free-standing chapel, stood across South Columbus Street from Holy Trinity Church, on the site of the later parish school, the open space in front of the present school. The community struggled and prospered there, attracting new members and drawing boarding students from a wide area along with many day students and support from the heavily Catholic local population.

Recently consecrated Bishop Rosecrans visited Holy Trinity Parish on the weekend of August 9 and 10, 1862. He arrived at New Lexington by railroad and was conveyed to Holy Trinity Church by Hon. William E. Finck, member of the Ohio Senate. The children were assembled in the church to welcome their Bishop; and when he had entered the sanctuary two little girls, one representing the children who were to make their first Communion and the other those who were to be confirmed the day following, pronounced the following addresses:

Right Rev'd Father in God!

With hearts full of gratitude to God, do we hail you, thrice welcome, amongst us! Well are we aware of the inestimable gifts, the heavenly benediction, this, your first visit brings to us. Long and anxiously have we expected you, and earnestly have we prepared ourselves to become in some small measure, worthy of your benedictions. With your name, Esteemed Father, has been heralded to us the bright hope now to receive for the first time into their souls the most adorable Body and Blood of the Redeemer of the world. This, then, is to us a day of joy; and while we live, we shall cherish the remembrance of this your first visit. Welcome, then, Dear Father, thrice welcome are you, and may the best gifts of Heaven ever be yours.

SECOND ADDRESS.

Yes, we welcome you, Father with hearts full of joy,
A heavenly joy, free from earth's base alloy,
For the fruits and the gifts of the spirit of Love,
Do we hope to receive through your hands from above.
May your pathway sublime, be free from earth's care—
May angels around you, their bliss with you share,
May the blessings of Heaven replenish your heart,
A share of which, now, we implore you'll impart.

To these addresses the Bishop replied in a few appropriate words of kind encouragement. If these girls were not students at St. Mary's, certainly the students were present!

On Sunday the 10 o'clock High Mass was offered by the Rev. J. V. Edelen, O.P., the Rev. Fathers Raymond Young, O.P., of Zanesville, and O'Brian, O.P., of Somerset, assisting with the Bishop, who delivered a clear, logical and solid discourse after the Gospel. After Mass Confirmation was administered.

That afternoon the Bishop visited St. Joseph's, near Somerset and after Vespers preached a beautiful discourse on the reasonableness of the faith of Catholics in the sacraments and mysteries of the Church. He then administered Confirmation, followed by solemn benediction of the Blessed Sacrament, in which he was assisted by several members of the Dominican Convent. He spent the evening of Sunday there.[2]

A fire broke out in the chapel at St. Mary's on June 6, 1866, which spread quickly and destroyed the whole property. The Dominican Fathers moved their novitiate from the former St. Joseph's College building to Kentucky and allowed the Sisters to use the college building as convent and school for the next two years.

Bishop Rosecrans visited the Sisters in October 1867, offered Mass for the community, and gave the pupils a recreation day.[3] As of 1868 Bishop Rosecrans was the superior of these Sisters, to whom they owed obedience. This was the result of a Vatican decision of 1863, fully in place by 1866, that jurisdiction over the Sisters did not rest in the Dominican Order but in the local bishop.[4]

At the end of this academic year, on Sunday, June 21, 1868, he visited once again. Three young ladies of the academy were baptized and received first Communion; they then, along with others, were confirmed by him. Rose Taggart made her profession as a Sister of St. Dominic and two young ladies received the white veil at six o'clock Mass in the Academy Chapel. Ten o'clock High Mass was offered by the Dominican Fathers at St. Joseph's Church, with the girls of the Academy as the choir. After Mass the bishop preached and administered Confirmation. This may be the occasion, placed in 1867 in *Make the Way Known*[5], when the students put on Cardinal Wiseman's *The Hidden Gem* in a big shack, once a sheepfold and by then a laundry, on a temporary stage. "The bishop loved it and showed his appreciation by giving the school a holiday." He visited St. Patrick's Church, Jackson Township, that afternoon.[6]

Accepting a generous offer from Theodore Leonard, the Sisters moved from their temporary home to Shepard, northeast of Columbus, in the summer of 1868. They arrived at the Union Depot on July 8 and were met there by Bishop Rosecrans, Mr. Leonard, Mr. Miller, and others, who conducted them to the new site in their carriages.

The next morning the Bishop went to the new convent with altar breads and an altar stone to offer Mass for them. Dominican Father Clarkson "had found and unpacked their little harmonium and he played while the Sisters sang hymns." Bishop Rosecrans promised them full cooperation in their new work. No one had considered a name for the new convent. "Saint Mary's was so much a part of them that it was taken for granted they would use that name in the new home as they had in the old. But when they said that, he had a suggestion. 'There are so many springs on your grounds,' he said, 'why not add of the Springs to distinguish it from the old Saint Mary's?'" So the new institution became St. Mary's *of the Springs*.[7] At the Springs, the academy's student body was composed entirely of boarders. Though "near" Columbus, the site was over four miles from the population center, a long distance for any day students to travel in those days. This made the continued existence of the institution more of a struggle than it had been in Somerset.

Bishop Rosecrans's visits to St. Mary's of the Springs were quite frequent. Aside from general visits, he received the Sisters' vows, administered Confirmation, handed out diplomas, and gave retreats. He knew the students well enough to write poems and letters to them after their graduations, mentioning their friends and giving them news of the school and the diocese.[8]

Although the Sisters often were short-handed for all the work they were doing, they acceded to the Bishop's requests to staff St. Francis de Sales Parish school in Newark, replacing the Sisters of Charity, in the fall of 1870 and the Holy Redeemer parish school in Portsmouth (where they stayed only a few years), St. Lawrence parish school in Ironton, and St. Mary parish school in Lancaster in the fall of 1872.[9]

The two leading Dominican Sisters in this era were Sister Rose Lynch and Sister Mary Agnes Magevney. Sister Rose was born in Ireland, lived in Zanesville, and joined the community in 1832. A cornerstone of the community, she was elected prioress in 1849. She served several additional terms and was in that position when the disastrous fire struck St. Mary's in 1866. Sister Mary Agnes was a daughter of Eugene Magevney, the leading Catholic of Memphis, Tennessee, a businessman and schoolmaster. She had been educated by Dominican Sisters there and joined the congregation at Somerset in 1863. Something of an extremist, she always insisted on the most patched habit in the house and took her meals in the kitchen from an old tin pan. She was named novice mistress in 1868 and secretary of the community in 1869.

Dominican Sisters from Somerset had opened a school at St. Thomas Aquinas Parish in Zanesville in 1854. In 1856 the Sisters, including Sister Rose, had opened St. Columba's Academy in an adjoining building. This was the beginning of a new Dominican foundation with a novitiate separate from Somerset, but the two houses often supported each other with personnel exchanges. St. Columba's seems to have had academic problems. The students at the "free or poor school," as the people called the parish school, frequently surpassed the pupils of the prestigious Academy in the annual public exhibitions.

This separate house made sense early on, but with improving travel and communications, Bishop Rosecrans did not see its necessity and probably saw problems having two similar communities in his diocese. He called the Sisters from Zanesville to St. Mary's of the Springs to effect a reconciliation and to explain that the house in Zanesville would be entirely under the control of the motherhouse. On his orders, St. Columba's Academy was suppressed. The last superior of the Zanesville house was Sister Catherine Brown, who upon its closing was sent to teach in Lancaster.

The leaders of the Springs' congregation, rather than circumstances, were blamed by some of its members for the problems it had at this time. They thought the congregation's recent history lamentable, having gone deeply and unnecessarily into debt through the expense of building St. Mary's of the Springs. (The new convent and school had cost almost eight times the money received from insurance and the sale of the bricks of St. Mary's in Somerset.)

Sister Rose Lynch, many-times superior of the Dominican Sisters, having heard of dissatisfaction among some of the Sisters, in the summer of 1873 tendered her resignation as prioress to Bishop Rosecrans and informed him that under no circumstances would she be a candidate for re-election. On July 17 the Sisters' Council elected Sister Catherine Brown, formerly superior of St. Columba's, as prioress and Bishop Rosecrans approved the election.

Sister Rose was sent to Lancaster and Sister Mary Agnes was removed as novice mistress and was to go to Ironton. Both were disappointed with the outcome of the election (which they said was illegal because Sister Mary Agnes had been sent away for training just before it was held) and declared that they would not recognize Sister Catherine as prioress.[10] At some point, just when is not clear, Bishop Rosecrans came to the support of these two, so that they were not disobedient to him, but Sister Rose, at least, was given a public penance by the chaplain.

Academies for Young Women

Bishop Rosecrans saw clearly the need for a "select" day school in the Cathedral parish, to take away all excuse from parents who were sending their little girls to the public schools, which in those days were virulently anti-Catholic. His requests to the Sisters of Notre Dame de Namur to start a select school had not yet produced results by 1873. So, when Sisters Rose and Mary Agnes would not recognize the election of Sister Catherine, despite his earlier suppression of the independent house in Zanesville, he encouraged them to start such a school near the Cathedral. In January 1874, they opened a school in a house on the southwest corner of Gay and Fifth Streets, north of the Cathedral, and Bishop Rosecrans appointed Sister Mary Agnes "Superioress of the House called the Cathedral School of the Sacred Heart." This was the beginning of the Dominican Sisters of Texas.

The new school, soon called Sacred Heart Academy, at once attracted a large number of students and for at least its first three years it did not have enough teachers. Bishop Rosecrans, in its earliest days, would walk over from the Cathedral and help with the classes. For several years he insisted that St. Mary's of the Springs supply three or four sisters to help and, reluctantly but obediently, they did so. This was a major irritant to them.

When the Bishop would visit the Springs, he would talk with the children and sometimes take part in their games. He would allow the student who had the highest grades for the week to wear his amethyst ring during his visit. He always took along his big collie, who, it was said, was so loyal to his master that no one could get him to eat meat on Friday. The visits would be genial and pleasant, but the Sisters' smiles "vanished if Sacred Heart Academy was even remotely mentioned."

In August 1874, Sister Mary Agnes purchased a large house on the southeast corner of Broad and Seventh Streets (Grant Ave.) in her own name and moved Sacred Heart convent and school there. A year later she purchased the next house east, which became the academy while the house on the corner became exclusively the convent.

Shortly after the purchase of the second house, Bishop Rosecrans took up residence in the two front rooms of its second story. The quiet provided by this residence, and the silence and regularity of the convent next door, lessened the Bishop's stress and prolonged his life. The Sisters later told of his strict observance of lent, keeping "black lent" as they termed it, and only taking a piece of dry bread with a cup of tea for his breakfast. While they spread his table with such fare as their hearts inspired, it was only to see him rise from it and leave every dainty untouched. Occasionally he would fill his hands with fruits or cake and distribute the "goodies" among the children of the academy, and then he would laughingly tell some friend of what a good joke he had played upon the Sisters by "hooking out" the goodies for the children. If he expected to eat out he would take a simple meal at home first, and then while other guests enjoyed the viands spread before them, he engaged in conversation, eating little or nothing, but making his host believe he was enjoying the repast to the full.[11]

Sister Mary Agnes and Bishop Rosecrans worked together closely on their finances. Her account books indicate that

Sacred Heart Academy, left, and Convent. Bishop Rosecrans made his home and died in the upstairs front rooms of the Academy. (Catholic Record Society-Diocese of Columbus)

she made loans totaling about ten to fifteen thousand dollars to the Bishop, funds that apparently were never repaid, and she jointly signed notes with him for other loans. This money was used for the growth of the institutions of the new diocese, though not necessarily for construction of the Cathedral. The only major work done on that edifice after 1872 was the plastering of the ceiling in 1878. Existing records indicate that Mother Mary Agnes and Bishop Rosecrans co-signed notes totaling $3,150 in 1878, which may have been for that purpose.

The Dominican Sisters in Texas, on the basis on memories of Sister Rose Lynch, have held Bishop Rosecrans responsible to some extent for the failure of their Sacred Heart Academy in Columbus. The property had been burdened with several mortgages and was lost to creditors in 1879. An analysis of the surviving records[12] has indicated that Sister Mary Agnes was in debt far beyond what the Bishop owed her, to a total of about sixty thousand dollars.

Having lost their Columbus foundation, the Dominican Sisters of the Sacred Heart moved to Somerset and began anew in rented facilities. They began a new structure on the old site across from Holy Trinity Church, but were unable to complete it. Bishop Watterson at length decided, as Bishop Rosecrans had regarding the two Dominican communities at St. Mary's and St. Columba's, that he did not want two Dominican motherhouses in the diocese. In 1882 the Dominican Sisters of the Sacred Heart moved to Galveston to assist Bishop Nicholas A. Gallagher, who had been the first priest ordained for the Diocese of Columbus. One can only speculate whether Bishop Rosecrans would have allowed the Sacred Heart effort in Columbus to fail and whether he would have allowed the two separate motherhouses to continue.

Meanwhile, relations between the Bishop and St. Mary's of the Springs deteriorated. He initially had told Mother Catherine that Sacred Heart would be a completely independent institution and he would provide for its needs, so the continuing call on the older community for teaching sisters for Sacred Heart caused great consternation. In 1875 one of these Sisters, not able to get along with Mother Mary Agnes, returned to the Springs without permission from either her or the Bishop. Mother Catherine explained to him that her action was "justified by the customs of the community," but he rejected this. In a letter of March 6 he reviewed Mother Catherine's various complaints and declared that her vow of obedience had been slighted. He continued,

> If I have contented myself to visit the house [the Springs] and promote its interests in every way without making my office felt, I do not wish to do so any longer. For my own peace I would much rather stay away from your house altogether—would rather you would migrate as long as I cannot—but I cannot do it without losing my soul. . . . This is the last effort I am going to make to have a square understanding with you. If it fails I will have to confine myself to a strictly official course as the one best calculated to promote peace, or best fitted to prepare the way for disorders that may follow.[13]

Mother Frances Lilly, who was elected to replace Mother Catherine in 1876, thought the Bishop had wronged the community. The story is told that once when the Bishop came unexpectedly for a visit, and was asked to wait for Mother Francis Lilly in the parlor, he refused and waited for her in the corridor. Mother Frances was so upset at a recent order to supply Sisters to Sacred Heart that she did not want to see the Bishop at once, so she had a ladder brought, climbed out the window, and walked around to re-enter by the front door, in order to be more composed when she met him.[14] Bishop Rosecrans and the Sisters at the Springs were not reconciled by the time of his death.[15]

The Sisters and the successors of Bishop Rosecrans did repair the relationship and St. Mary's of the Springs continued to operate its academy until 1966. A college was started in 1924 which today is Ohio Dominican University.

St. Joseph's Academy

The Sisters of Notre Dame de Namur had come to Cincinnati in 1840 at the request of Bishop Purcell. In 1855 the two Columbus pastors, Father Borgess of Holy Cross Parish and Father Meagher of St. Patrick's Parish, asked the Sisters to take over teaching the girls in the existing schools in their parishes. The Sisters accepted and they arrived that fall. Their first convent was a frame house on Gay Street east of Washington Avenue and west of the Insane Asylum; in 1856 they moved to a larger frame house on the west side of Cleveland Avenue, north of Long Street, with ample ground for a garden.

On the Feast of St. Joseph in 1858 the Sisters purchased a long, narrow, brick building large enough for school and convent, on the northwest corner of Oak and Young streets. They moved their convent into this building and opened a "select school" there. Attendance at the school was too small for it to continue and they were forced to close it after two years.

The Sisters persevered through many early trials and were still at their two parish schools when Bishop Rosecrans arrived as Pastor of St. Patrick's Parish in 1867. One of his first acts as pastor was to visit their convent, on March 26, 1867. He acted as their extraordinary confessor for many years. He would walk from St. Patrick's to their convent, no matter what the weather. When the Sister Superior wanted to send a conveyance for him he would not allow it. Often the portress had to hang his coat and hat near the fire to dry during the time of confessions.

As early as May 1873 Bishop Rosecrans asked the Sisters to establish a day school. He assured them that many prominent men of the city promised their assistance. Waiting for an improved economy and for pledges of security from prominent citizens, the Sisters did not accede to the Bishop's request at once. They finally purchased a site for the school in May and October 1874. Meanwhile, Dominican Sisters Rose and Mary Agnes had withdrawn from St. Mary's of the Springs and in January had opened Sacred Heart Academy. When Sister Mary Ligouri Hemsteger of the Sisters of Notre Dame learned of this, her reaction was that one academy was as much as the city was ready for and furthermore she did not want to complete with another community. She went to the bishop and told him how far her plans had progressed but that she was willing to abandon her whole scheme. He replied that if he had not wanted an academy he would not have asked her to establish it. So both schools went ahead but, as seen above, the Dominican foundation failed within a few years, though not for a lack of students.

On April 15, 1875 the cornerstone of St. Joseph's Academy was laid by Fathers Hemsteger, Goldschmidt, and Eis. Classes opened on September 6 and shortly thereafter Bishop Rosecrans visited the school in the unfinished building. He returned on October 4 to offer Mass and on November 4 he presided at the distribution of awards and blessed the building. His friendship with the school continued; he was present for the midterm exams in February 1876 and for the distribution of awards on July 8. At the graduation ceremony for the school's first graduate on June 24, 1878, he and four priests were in attendance.[16]

The Sisters of Notre Dame de Namur created a long history of teaching in various parish schools in Columbus, as well as at the Academy. The latter closed in June 1977.[17]

St. Aloysius Academy

In 1875 Bishop Rosecrans asked the Sisters of St. Francis of Penance and Christian Charity, the order who were running St. Vincent's Orphan Asylum in Columbus, to take over the shell of a new school that had been started near New Lexington.[18]

Owen Donnelly, an aging bachelor farmer, a native of Ireland, in 1870 donated a large farm lying southwest of New Lexington to Bishop Rosecrans, in hopes that it could be used for a school. Bishop Rosecrans asked Father Francis Moitrier to take charge and the institution-to-be was named St. Eugene's, in honor of Mr. Donnelly. Father Moitrier, who in January of 1873 became the first diocesan priest appointed to the pastorate of St. Rose Parish in New Lexington, was enthusiastic and even made his home at the academy when a room could be made ready, but the project languished. By 1875 the eight-room school was far from complete when Bishop Rosecrans asked the Franciscan Sisters to take over the project.

Mother Gonzaga Brexel, newly arrived from Germany, accompanied by Father Goldschmidt and another Sister, set out to inspect the new school. They found an ugly brick structure without doors or windows or roof, surrounded by weeds and brush several feet tall. There also was a small frame house, in bad condition. They found that Father Moitrier was being sued by several contractors for payment for the work completed to date. They visited Father Schmitt in Lancaster, whose opinion coincided with theirs, that there was no use in opening a school on such a spot and that no students would ever go there. It was voted to give up the project.

Father John Eis, however, who was Pastor of Sacred Heart Parish in Columbus and was Bishop Rosecrans's secretary, thought the undertaking could be successful and offered to travel to New Lexington from time to time to supervise matters. Bishop Rosecrans agreed with him. The Sisters who had intended to settle at the school spent the winter of 1875/76 at St. Vincent's in Columbus. Meanwhile they engaged a German farmer named Wieser to take charge of the farm at the school in December. The Sisters went to New Lexington in March 1876 and found that a storm had torn off the new roof of the school and damaged the plaster and that not a room was ready to be occupied. They stayed in a room of Mr. Wieser's frame house until the new building could be prepared for them. The first room completed was the chapel, where Father Philip Meschenmoser, who replaced Father Moitrier as Pastor at St. Rose in New Lexington, offered Mass and reserved the Blessed Sacrament. The Sisters moved into the building in June and in August dismissed the workmen.

The school was opened and soon had a small band of pupils. On October 4, 1876, the Feast of St. Francis of Assisi, Bishop Rosecrans blessed the house. The chapel was placed under the patronage of the Immaculate Conception and the school under that of St. Aloysius.

The Sisters were asked to repay the loans taken out for construction of the building, but the funds they had brought were far from sufficient for this and all the other costs of furnishing and opening a school. Father Eis came to St. Rose Church and there announced that he would be responsible for all these debts and he asked for and received all the claims.[19]

St. Aloysius Academy flourished through the decades as a girls' school, a military academy, and a coeducational high school. It survived until 1969.

Father Eis had the Franciscan Sisters of Penance and Christian Charity operate the new school at Sacred Heart

Parish in Columbus when it opened in 1876. In time they came to staff several other schools in the diocese, as well as St. Ann's Infant Asylum, St. Rita's Home for Working Girls, St. Therese's Shrine, St. Charles Seminary (housekeeping), the St. Francis Evangelization Center in McArthur, and the St. Philip Neri Center for outreach in Murray City. Sister Christina Pecoraro, Provincial Minister, noted as late as 1984, "The Diocese of Columbus, which welcomed our first sisters, pioneers from Germany, in 1874, has continued to be a source of life, in Spirit and Truth for all of us."

Chapter VII
Institutions and New Parishes, 1868-1878

The struggles of Bishop Rosecrans to establish the institutions required in his new diocese, in the face of very limited resources, were phenomenal. The only two Catholic institutions in the City of Columbus when it became the see were St. Francis Hospital and the Good Shepherd Convent. In addition to these and the academies for young women mentioned above, he founded a diocesan seminary, an orphan asylum (and encouraged a diocesan priest to found another), a boys' school, a Catholic cemetery for the city of Columbus, and a diocesan newspaper.

St. Francis Hospital

The Sisters of the Poor of St. Francis operated St. Francis Hospital, which they had opened in a converted house on East Rich Street in 1862. In 1865 they obtained a lease and moved into a large portion of the Starling Medical College at State and Sixth, where they ran the hospital until 1955.

The Sisters' congregation had begun in Aachen in 1845. In 1858 Sarah Worthington Peter, originally of Chillicothe, brought some of them to Cincinnati where they founded St. Mary's Hospital. Doctors William McMillen, John W. Hamilton, and Starling Loving brought them to Columbus.

The Sisters of course were on good terms with Bishop Rosecrans, but we have no record of any formal meetings or interaction with him. Early during his time the hospital had eighty-five beds. The second story was devoted to sick and infirm women and the third to sick and infirm men. About five hundred patients were received each year. The hospital expanded into additional rooms in the building in 1875. The patients were of every class, race, religion, and worldly condition. Preference was always given to the poor, with the intention being that the hospital be a public, charitable institution.[1]

Good Shepherd Convent

The Good Shepherd Convent and its school were operated by the Order of Our Lady of Charity of the Good Shepherd of Angers, which had been founded in France. The object of the order was to establish and sustain houses of refuge for fallen but penitent women and girls of all ages, to rescue female children from dangerous occasions of crime, and to train and instruct them in useful employment.

The Sisters had been encouraged to come to Columbus near the end of the Civil War by Father Edward Fitzgerald, pastor of St. Patrick's Parish. He was concerned for the lives and souls of the young women who followed the soldiers to their camp near the city. Four Sisters came from Cincinnati in the spring of 1865 to temporary quarters on Spring Street. Nine months later they moved to the former Sullivant mansion at the southwest corner of West Broad and Sandusky Streets. (Sandusky Street is now the right of way of Route 315).[2]

There were three classes of "inmates" in the convent. Penitents were women who wished to do penance for the actions of their prior lives and to lead a Christian life. Any Penitents who desired to remain for life were admitted to vows and formed the class of Magdalens. They formed an austere, contemplative community within the convent and followed a rule of prayer, penance, and manual labor. The third class was made up of girls who had been secured from danger before they had fallen or had become stained by serious crime. This Preservation Class, opened in the Columbus convent in 1867, in time became the largest of the three classes here and required the most effort on the part of the Sisters. Most of the girls had one or both parents living and many were returned to their homes within a short time but others remained until adulthood. Girls as young as four were often admitted. The students came not only

Institutions and New Parishes

from throughout the Diocese of Columbus but from other parts of Ohio and even from surrounding states, especially western Pennsylvania and West Virginia.

We know of several visits that Bishop Rosecrans made to the Good Shepherd Convent, beginning before he took up residence in Columbus. Through the years from 1866 until his death he administered Baptism, First Communion, and Confirmation, offered Mass, was part of a committee of school visitors made up of local clergy and laymen, and received women into the class of Penitents.

This institution continues today as a school only, but has not been considered a Catholic institution since 2001.

St. Aloysius Seminary

Bishop Rosecrans's first concern being for the priesthood of the diocese, in 1871 he established St. Aloysius Seminary on the West Side of Columbus, in part due to the pressure of disagreements with Archbishop Purcell, but also, and perhaps more, due to his own desire to devote his personal attention to the education of the clergy of his new diocese. "No trouble, no inconvenience, no suffering, no illness that could be overcome, was ever allowed to interfere with this labor of love..."[3]

In May 1871 Bishop Rosecrans purchased for $7,000 a block of land west of the Scioto River in Franklinton in an area that was then in the process of being annexed to the City of Columbus. It was bound by what later were named Sandusky, Shepherd, Grubb, and Culbertson streets and measured 198 by 231 feet, about an acre. On the property were two houses and a barn. The smaller house was at the corner of Grubb and Shepherd. The larger house, on the middle of the Shepherd Street side, consisted of a two-story brick portion about thirty feet square with a frame addition stretching about 65 feet to the rear. Immediately to the west across Sandusky Street was the convent of the Sisters of the Good Shepherd. The seminary opened on September 1, 1871 with 34 students, four more than its nominal capacity of 30.

Rev. Nicholas A. Gallagher from Belmont County, the first priest ordained for the diocese and assistant pastor of St. Patrick

Parish, was principal of the school and Rev. Gerhard Ahrens, chancellor and assistant at Holy Cross Parish, was procurator. The professors were priests of the diocese and, for the younger students, some of the seminarians. The Bishop is said to have devoted many hours to instruction there himself. The courses covered eight years and included typical Classical and Scientific courses of the day as well as the theology program.

Bishop Rosecrans closed the little seminary in 1876 during one of the great economic depressions of the nineteenth century. Despite appeals to the people for its support, it was a financial failure and the diocese had no resources to subsidize it.[4] After St. Aloysius closed, Bishop Rosecrans again sent his seminarians to Mt. St. Mary's in Cincinnati. (That institution closed in 1879 and remained shuttered for several years, during the financial crisis of the Archdiocese caused by the failure of Father Edward Purcell's "bank." The Columbus students then went to other seminaries, such as Our Lady of Angels in Niagara, N.Y.)

The names of fifty students of St. Aloysius Seminary are known, of whom thirteen were ordained for the Diocese of Columbus and one for the Diocese of Milwaukee.

St. Vincent Orphan Asylum

The need for a Catholic home for Catholic children from poor or broken families was apparent early on in Bishop Rosecrans' days in Columbus. Early in 1869 he responded to the plea of a Catholic man whose children were being kept from him by the Hannah Neil Mission. In 1868 two girls aged about twelve and fourteen years named Ellen and Jane Curran, whose mother had been in the poorhouse, had been entered into the hands of the matron at the Mission. By early 1869 their father had become established in the West and was in a position to support them, but he could not get them from the Mission or find out where they had been placed. He enlisted the help of Bishop Rosecrans, but the Bishop, on visiting the Mission, was met with insult and told that he had no business among the guardians of other people's children with inquiries as to their whereabouts. The platform of the institution seemed to be this: on the one hand, gull the public by giving out that you help the poor; on the other, drive away all the poor but those you can proselytize. In this view, the woman called the matron hunted up families of children that were helpless and secured the little ones, in order to give them an "education" in her anti-Catholic ideas. There was at the time another child in this same "den" whose helplessly poor father had found a place for him but could not get him out of it.[5]

The 1870s were a very difficult time for many, a time of economic depression when jobs were hard to find. Some parents were unable to buy food or pay rent or otherwise care for their children. Other parents had lost a spouse and could not care for little children alone. Such little ones were found abandoned at the doors of the Sacred Heart Academy on Broad Street. The Dominican Sisters took them in and clothed and fed them. Some remained in their care for a number of months, but in time the parents usually returned to claim them. Some very small children also were cared for by the Sisters of the Good Shepherd on the west side. But this was not the main apostolate of either the Dominican or the Good Shepherd sisters. The question of how to provide for such Catholic children weighed heavily on the mind of Bishop Rosecrans.

It was on a June day in 1874 that a knock on the door of the Bishop's residence brought an answer. A messenger had come from St. Francis Hospital, requesting an audience for a Sister from Germany who was visiting there. Rather than set up an appointment for her, the Bishop at once set out for the hospital to see her. There Mother Aloysia Lenders, a Sister of St. Francis of Penance and Christian Charity, told him their story. She and some companions had been driven from Germany by the *Kulturkampf* of Chancellor Bismarck and were in America seeking a home and work. They had been invited to Buffalo by the Jesuit pastors of two German-speaking parishes, but on their arrival there earlier that month they had been told that the bishop would not welcome them into his diocese. A novena of Masses, prayers to the Sacred Heart, and a second visit to Buffalo's bishop seemed to secure no help. When one of the Sisters had become ill, the Jesuits had suggested that she be taken to the hospital of the Sisters of the Poor of St. Francis in Cincinnati.

While in Cincinnati pondering their situation, one of the young Cincinnati Franciscans remarked, in a suggestion that seemed to come from Heaven, "Mother, there is no orphanage in Columbus, Ohio; could not the sisters open one there?" Mother Aloysia had set out for Columbus the next day. Bishop Rosecrans was very pleased at the idea of these Sisters locating in Columbus and at once engaged them to take charge of the orphanage he intended to build. "His fatherly kindness fell like a balm on the heart of the anxious Superior, and seeing in these events, the Hand of God, she at once promised the Bishop that her nuns would take charge of the orphans." It took a little longer than expected, however, for the Sisters to settle in Columbus, for in the meantime the bishop of Buffalo had changed his mind and decided to accept them! For various reasons, the Sisters accepted his offer, and founded the Stella Niagara Motherhouse, but they never for a moment forgot the kindness of Bishop Rosecrans and their commitment to him.

Three Sisters arrived to settle in Columbus on the evening of December 22, 1874 and were received again by the Sisters at St. Francis Hospital. Bishop Rosecrans was notified and at once, accompanied by V. Rev. John B. Hemsteger, his Vicar General, called upon them to bid them welcome.

Bishop Rosecrans obtained from Louis Zettler his house and seven acres (mostly covered by orchards) at Rose (now Kelton) and East Main Street, at a cost of $25,000. Mr. Zettler donated $10,000 of this and took a note for the remainder. The two-story brick house, converted to accommodate the Sisters and orphans, contained nine rooms and a chapel. On February 2, 1875 some 500 Catholics of the city, led by the St. Patrick's Total Abstinence Society, the St. Patrick's School Society, and the Pope Pius IX Cadets, assembled at St. Francis Hospital with the three Sisters and processed in silence to the new orphanage, which was to be named St. Vincent's Orphan Asylum. The building was dedicated by the Bishop, assisted by Fathers J. B. Hemsteger, J. B. Eis, J. Cassella, M. M. Meara, and the students of St. Aloysius Seminary. The first residents were eight little girls who until then had been cared for by the Sisters of the Good Shepherd.[6]

Bishop Rosecrans assigned young Rev. John C. Goldschmidt as chaplain of the orphanage, where he remained faithfully until his death in 1923.

The Bishop began two major expansions of St. Vincent's. On Sunday, Aug. 29, 1875 he laid the cornerstone of a three-story building to house kitchen, refectory, school, and dormitories. He dedicated it on Easter Sunday, April 16, 1876. In 1878 he came to St. Vincent's on May 12 to administer Confirmation and he laid the cornerstone of the "new north main building." He hoped to dedicate it, but he did not live to see its completion.[7]

The orphanage was "the charity" of the Diocese of Columbus for many decades, to which a special Christmas collection was dedicated. It is now represented by the St. Vincent Family Center.

St. Joseph's Orphan Asylum

The second orphanage in the diocese was the work of Father Joseph Jessing. After ordaining him, Bishop Rosecrans assigned Father Jessing to the pastorate of Sacred Heart Church in Pomeroy. Soon Father Jessing became deeply concerned about the orphan boys in his parish. With the assistance of the Brothers of Saint Francis, he established St. Joseph's Orphan Asylum for them. Bishop Rosecrans dedicated the building, which stood next to the parish church, on May 2, 1875.

Father Jessing began a German-language newspaper called simply *Ohio* (soon changed to *Ohio Waisenfreund*, the Ohio Orphan's Friend), to support the German Catholic immigrants against the corrupting American Protestant society in which they lived. He wrote and personally published this newspaper and soon his time was all given to the orphans and the paper, income from which supported the institution. Bishop Rosecrans sent another priest to take over as pastor in 1876 so that Jessing could continue this ministry.

Looking for larger quarters, Jessing moved the orphanage and newspaper to 821 East Main Street in Columbus in 1877. To the orphanage and printing press Father Jessing added a trade school.

From this beginning came the Collegium Josephinum, a seminary, in 1888, intended to produce clergy for the German immigrants throughout the country. It became a pontifical institution in 1892 and its first graduates were ordained in 1899. It moved to its present site on High Street north of Worthington in 1931. Care for orphans was phased out some years later.

St. Joseph's Seminary

After the closing of St. Aloysius Seminary, Bishop Rosecrans invited the Sisters of St. Joseph of Ebensburg, Pa., to use that property for a day and boarding school for young boys. The school was opened in the spring of 1877 by Mother Hortense Tello and Sisters Agnes Downing, Teresa Sweeney, and Zita Wolfe.[8]

In April, Bishop Rosecrans appointed Father Richard C. Christy chaplain of both these Sisters of St. Joseph and the sisters at the Good Shepherd Convent. It had been this Father Christy who in 1869 as pastor of St. Patrick Parish in Ebensburg, Pa., had introduced the Sisters there from Flushing, Long Island. Father Christy had been chaplain of the 78th Pennsylvania Volunteers in General Rosecrans's Army of the Cumberland; that service caused his health to begin to deteriorate so that he had to retire from his pastorate in 1874. It is thought that it was through the agency of General Rosecrans that Father Christy was introduced to Bishop Rosecrans and came to Columbus in semi-retirement.[9] Bishop Rosecrans was anxious for these Sisters to establish a novitiate in Columbus and Louis Zettler offered property for the purpose, but the Sisters had to turn the offer down because their numbers were too few for the project.[10] St. Joseph's was a boarding school for boys aged eight to fourteen and also was attended by day scholars.[11] It is not clear when the boys' school was closed, but the 1879 city directory still listed "St. Joseph's Seminary" and the Sisters announced the opening of the upcoming term on August 7, 1879. The Sisters staffed the Holy Family parish school when it opened (apparently after 1879) and stayed until 1912. They also provided housekeeping staff for St. Joseph Orphanage beginning with its move to Columbus in 1877 and to St. John parish school in Bellaire in the 1878-1879 academic year.

Mt. Calvary Cemetery

The small, old Columbus Catholic Cemetery on what later was Mt. Vernon Avenue, dating from 1846, had become overcrowded by the 1860s. The site for a new cemetery, to be named Mt. Calvary, was purchased in 1865 in the name of trustees. The cost and ownership were to be split between the two Columbus parishes. The property was encumbered by debt and, in 1867, Bishop Rosecrans had to suspend construction of the cathedral because the cemetery note was coming due and St. Patrick Parish did not have the money for both church and cemetery. Burials in the new cemetery began as early as the spring of 1867. The 27 3/8-acre tract was transferred to Bishop Rosecrans in August 1868.

Bishop Rosecrans consecrated the ground on All Souls' Day, 1874. A procession formed in front of the Cathedral and proceeded to High Street, south to Mound Street, and west to the cemetery. Two bands made the procession merry and eleven Catholic societies of the city in full regalia made it colorful. Patrick Egan and Patrick Bresnahan were mounted marshals while the bishop and clergy rode in carriages.

"Many carriages followed the procession to the Cemetery, and the sides of the road were lined with pedestrians bound for the same destination. A large crowd was already at the Cemetery to witness the approach of the imposing pageant. The procession moved through the main gate of the Cemetery... and toward the cross in the center of the grounds. Near the cross the bands took position while the societies formed two lines, between which the Bishop and clergy walked to the cross, where half a dozen Seminarians were already stationed. A number of altar boys, appropriately dressed, preceded the Bishop and clergy, who appeared in robes peculiar to their offices. A dense mass of people surrounded the clerical group.

"Bishop Rosecrans then addressed the multitude, stating that the ceremony would be a long one; that he had not a good place from which to speak, and might not be able to make all understand the proceedings; but he reminded the people that the ceremony was a religious one, and asked all to pray for the souls of the dead." Some 1,400 already had been interred there.

"There were five crosses planted on the ground so as to define the shape of a cross. Each of these crosses had four candles burning before it on a stand a little above the ground.

"The cross in the center was visited first. A short prayer and the Litany of the Saints were chanted before it. After this the procession of ecclesiastics made a circuit of the whole ground, chanting psalms, and the Bishop sprinkling it with blessed water. On the return to the central cross, it was blessed by a particular prayer and by incensing. ...Each cross was incensed, and three lighted candles placed on the top and arms. At the close the Pontifical blessing was given, and the crowd dispersed."[12]

Mt. Calvary now contains some 40,000 graves, including that of Bishop Watterson, and is lovingly maintained by the staff of the Catholic Cemeteries of Columbus.

The Catholic Columbian

Late in 1874 Bishop Rosecrans asked seminarian Dennis A. Clarke to produce a newssheet to promote the Cathedral Fair. This was such a success that the Bishop asked him to begin a weekly diocesan newspaper, *The Catholic Columbian*, to begin in January 1875. The Columbian Printing Company was incorporated on December 15 by Father M. M. Meara, Dennis A. Clarke, Luke G. Byrne (attorney), and O. T. Turney, but the company never was organized.[13] Bishop Rosecrans himself was the editor at least as far as editorial content was concerned. (Aside from statements to that effect, it is quite obvious from the decrease in content of the editorial page when he was away from home.)

During the Bishop's life the *Columbian* was "a journal... vigorous and world-famed through the ability the Bishop brought to it in his editorial contributions." The *Catholic Universe* of Cleveland said, "It was a pleasure to read his organ, the *Columbian*. He brought to that sphere as to all others his characteristic frankness and genial good humor." Said *Ave Maria* magazine, "The short, pithy paragraphs which adorned the editorial page of the *Columbian* week after week were the productions of his pen, and as a proof of their worth we might say that they were copied far and wide by the Catholic press. There was in the few lines that he penned more truth (and it was better expressed) than in a half column from the pen of an ordinary writer."[14]

The editorial columns of the *Columbian* allowed Bishop Rosecrans to bring the teachings of the Church to a broader audience than his sermons or lectures would reach, beyond the local and even national Catholic community. Editors of general and anti-Catholic newspapers of the day would read them, searching for items on which to hang their diatribes, but some Catholic truth must have come through to them. The *Ohio State Journal* on many occasions had running editorial battles with the *Columbian*, but the editor usually gave the Bishop fair play. The Bishop's editorials were on every topic related to the Church but the majority were intended to expose anti-Catholicism, both that which was overt and that which was disguised in politics, church-state relations, and government schools. Many column-inches were devoted to explanations of the nature of the Church and the papacy, the virtues, sin and the loss of faith, and relations between the Church and the world.

New Parishes

Bishop Rosecrans organized two new parishes in Columbus, counting the Cathedral Parish; he started two parishes and four missions outside of Columbus. Four other churches whose early beginnings had been fostered by the Archdiocese were brought to parochial (three) and mission (one) status by Bishop Rosecrans and he dedicated the church for one parish already officially established (St. Mary in Columbus).

Begun by Archdiocese

St. Rose Parish, New Lexington—The mission of the Dominican Fathers at New Lexington was begun as a station in 1867, with Father Leo Adams in charge. A brick building was purchased in 1868 to be used as a church. Bishop Rosecrans assigned Father Francis Moitrier as pastor, who lived at the new St. Aloysius Academy, and sent Father Meschenmoser as first resident pastor in the town in 1876.

St. Sylvester Parish, Zaleski—Catholics at Zaleski were attended for many years before having a church building. St. Sylvester Church was begun when the cornerstone was blessed by Bishop Rosecrans on October 8, 1863. It originally was to have been named St. Patrick, but by that year had been re-named in honor of the Bishop and his patron saint. The Bishop was scheduled to dedicate it on Christmas Day, 1869.[15]

St. Henry Parish, Harrietsville—Land was donated for a church near Harrietsville in Noble County and the cornerstone was laid in 1867. On Aug. 27, 1868, Bishop Rosecrans blessed the new church. After the dedication, High Mass was offered by the pastor, Rev. Damian Klüber of Fulda, and a sermon was preached by the Bishop.[16] Bishop Rosecrans sent Father Edward Fladung as resident pastor in 1871.

St. Mary Mother of God Parish, Columbus—This parish had been started in 1865 as an offshoot of Holy Cross Parish, with Father Specht as pastor. On Sunday, Nov. 29, 1868, Bishop Rosecrans officiated at the dedication of the church. Pontifical Mass followed, the choir having an orchestral accompaniment to one of Weber's Masses. The Bishop made a few remarks in English after the Gospel.[17]

Table 4, Part 1
Churches, Stations, and Pastors, March 3, 1868

Place and County	Church	Pastor	Status
Anthony, Athens	St. John the Baptist	at Zaleski	M
Archer's Settlmt., Noble	St. Michael	at Fulda	M
Athens, Athens	St. Paul[1]	at Zaleski	M
Batesville, Noble	St. Mary	Jacquet	P
Bellaire, Belmont	St. John the Evangelist	at Batesville	M
Bolivar, Tuscarawas	St. Martin	at Canal Dover	M
Brownsville, Knox	St. Michael	at Mt. Vernon	M
Calmoutier, Holmes	Ste. Genevieve	Heimo	P
Canal Dover, Tusc's	St. Joseph	Wismann	P
Cardington, Morrow		at Delaware	S
Chapel Hill, Perry	St. Francis of Assisi	Brogard	P
Chauncey, Athens	Seven Dolors	at Logan	M
Churchtown, Wash'n	St. John the Baptist	Eppink	P
Circleville, Pickaway	St. Joseph	Pindar	P
Clinton Furnace, Scioto		at Lick Run	S
Columbus, Franklin	Holy Cross	Hemsteger	P
Columbus, Franklin	St. Patrick	Rosecrans[2]	P
Columbus, Franklin	St. Mary	Specht	P
Columbus, Franklin	St. Francis Hospital	Hillebrand	C
Coshocton, Coshocton	St. George	Nordmeyer	P
Crane's Nest Monroe	Sts. Peter & Paul	at Fulda	M
Danville, Knox	St. Luke	Brent	P
Deavertown, Morgan	St. Michael, Archangel	at Chapel Hill	M-I
Delaware, Delaware	St. Mary	Fehlings	P
Dresden, Muskingum	St. Matthew	at Coshocton	M
Durbin Church, Vinton	St. James	at Minerton	M
Fox Settlement, Wash'n	St. Patrick	at Fulda	M
Franklin Twp., Cosh'n	St. Nicholas	at Coshocton	M
Fulda (Enoch), Noble	Immaculare Conception	Klüber	P

1 Not yet dedicated.
2 Assisted by Fathers Ahrens and Mallon.

P=Parish, M=Mission, S=Station, C= Chapel, I=Inactive

Table 4, Part 2
Churches, Stations, and Pastors, March 3, 1868

Place and County	Church	Pastor	Status
Gallipolis, Gallia	St. Louis	at Pomeroy	M
Geneva, Fairfield	Sacred Heart	Brummer	P
Glenmont, Holmes	Sts. Peter & Paul	at Calmoutier	M
Good Hope, Fairfield	O.L. of Good Hope	at Geneva	M
Hanging Rock, Lawrence		at Ironton	S
Harrietsville, Noble	St. Henry	at Fulda	M
Hessian Hills, Tusc's	St. Peter	at Canal Dover	M-I
Ironton, Lawrence	St. Lawrence O'Toole	O'Donoghue	P
Ironton, Lawrence	St. Joseph	Fischer	P
Jackson, Jackson	Holy Name	at Zaleski	M
Jersey, Licking	St. Joseph	at Col's St. Pat'k	M
Junior Furnace, Scioto		at Lick Run	S
Killbuck, Coshocton	St. Elizabeth	at Coshocton	M
Lancaster, Fairfield	St. Mary	Rudolph	P
Leatherwood, Guernsey	St. Patrick	at Batesville	M
Lewis Center, Delaware	St. Aloysius	at Delaware	M
Lick Run, Scioto	St. Peter	Mayrose	P
Little Scioto, Scioto	St. John	at Lick Run	M
Lodi (Malvern), Carroll	St. Francis X.	at Canal Dover	M
Logan, Hocking	St. John the Evangelist	Thienpont	P
Long Bottom, Meigs		at Pomeroy	S
Marges, Carroll	Immaculate Conception	at Canal Dover	M
Marietta, Washington	St. Mary	Ryan	P
Martins Ferry, Belmont		at Wheeling	M
Mattingly Sett., Musk'm	Nativity of B. V. Mary	at Newark	M
McLuney, Perry	St. Dominic	at St. Joseph	M
Meigs Creek, Morgan	St. James	at Marietta	**M**
Miltonsburg, Monroe	St. John the Baptist	Pilger	P
Minerton, Vinton	St. Mary	Ahern	P
Monday Creek, Perry	St. Peter	at St. Joseph	M
Monroe Furnace, Jackson		at Lick Run	S

P=Parish, M=Mission, S=Station, I=Inactive

Table 4, Part 3
Churches, Stations, and Pastors, March 3, 1868

Place and County	Church	Pastor	Status
Mt. Vernon, Knox	St. Vincent de Paul	at Danville	M
New Lexington, Perry	St. Rose of Lima	at St. Joseph	M
Newark, Licking	St. Francis de Sales	Cartuyvels[1]	P
Phillips Church, Fairfield	St. Joseph	at Geneva	M
Pine Grove, Lawrence	St. Mary at the Furnaces	at Ironton St. J.	M
Pomeroy, Meigs	Sacred Heart	Kalenburg	P
Pond Creek, Scioto[2]	Holy Trinity	at Portsmouth	M
Portsmouth, Scioto	Nativity	Karge	P
Portsmouth, Scioto	Holy Redeemer	Walker	P
Rainbow Ck., Wash'n	Ave Maria	at Churchtown	M
St. Joseph, Perry	St. Joseph	Sheehy, O.P.[3]	P
Somerset, Perry	Holy Trinity	Rochford, O.P.[4]	P
South Fork, Perry	St. Pius	at St. Joseph	M
Steubenville, Jefferson	St. Peter	Bigelow	P
Stockport, Morgan	St. James	at Marietta	M
Syrcuse, Meigs		at Pomeroy	S
Taylorstown, Franklin		at Columbus	S
Washington Furnace, Lawrence		at Lick Run	S
Wills Creek, Coshocton	St. Ann	at Coshocton	M
Wills Creek, Monroe	St. Joseph	at Miltonsburg	M
Woodsfield, Monroe	St. Sylvester	at Miltonsburg	M
Worthington, Franklin		at Columbus	S
Zaleski, Vinton	St. Sylvester	McSweeney	P
Zanesville, Muskingum	St. Thomas	Brady, O.P.[5]	P
Zanesvlle, Muskingum	St. Nicholas	Rauck	P

1 Assisted by Father Daly
2 Even though within the Archdiocese of Cincinnati
3 Assisted by Fathers Keogh, Edelin, Noon, and Adams, O.P.
4 Assisted by Father Collins, O.P.
5 Assisted by Father Cady, O.P.

P=Parish, M=Mission, S=Station

St. Joseph Mission, Cardington—Father Henry Fehlings of Delaware purchased land at Cardington in 1864, but whether this was sanctioned by the Archbishop for the start of a new parish is not known. A church was built by October of 1868 and the property was transferred to Bishop Rosecrans in 1870. On June 26, 1870 the Bishop blessed the church and administered Confirmation.[18]

Begun by Bishop Rosecrans

St. Mary Mission, Groveport—In 1870 the Catholics of Groveport in southern Franklin County petitioned Bishop Rosecrans to establish a mission there. The Bishop appointed Rev. Nicholas Gallagher, of St. Patrick Parish, to organize the mission and in 1871 they purchased a small brick church from a defunct protestant congregation. Bishop Rosecrans dedicated it on Sunday, June 25, 1871, "after which he delivered an interesting and instructive sermon."[19]

St. Augustine Parish, New Straitsville—In 1871 Bishop Rosecrans appointed Rev. Emmanuel Thienpont of Logan to organize a mission in New Straitsville and to visit it once a month. Lots were donated for a church, construction was begun in 1871, and, it is reported, it was dedicated in 1872. Bishop Rosecrans sent Father Joseph Laffan as resident pastor in 1873.

St. James the Apostle Mission, Hammondsville—It is not clear who took the lead in establishing this Jefferson County mission of the Steubenville parish. Father Bigelow of Steubenville purchased a schoolhouse from the township board of education in 1871. It stood on the state route on the hillside on the west side of town, above where the Methodist church now stands. The property came to be placed in Bishop Rosecrans's name in 1873. The name St. James does not appear in the annual Catholic Directory until 1885.

Sacred Heart Parish, Columbus—On May 27, 1875 Bishop Rosecrans assigned Father John B. Eis to erect a building for a new parish in the north side of the city on property that had been donated in 1852. It was decided to erect a school building with a large hall that could be used as a church and that could accommodate a convent for the Sisters who would teach in the parish school. Bishop Rosecrans laid the cornerstone on Sept. 5, 1875 and Mass was offered there on Easter Sunday, April 16, 1876. The school opened on April 19 in the charge of the Sisters of St. Francis of Penance and Christian Charity. V. Rev. John B. Hemsteger dedicated the building, in the absence of the Bishop (who was at his nephew's funeral) on May 7. In 1877 a pastoral residence was added on the south end of the building and in 1886 a convent on the north end.

Immaculate Conception Parish, Dennison—Property for a church to serve the railroaders at Dennison was purchased in 1870, about a year after they had moved there with the Pennsylvania Railroad shops. The cornerstone was laid on Sunday, October 1, 1871, but an appointment elsewhere prevented the Bishop from being there for the occasion. Father William T. Hawe, assigned as pastor by Bishop Rosecrans, completed the church, which the Bishop dedicated on October 8, 1876.[20] Father Hawe also started a short-lived mission of St. Joseph at Glasgow.

Holy Family Parish, Columbus—Bishop Rosecrans appointed Rev. Richard C. Christy chaplain of the Sisters of the Good Shepherd, on the West Side or Franklinton area, in April of 1877. At the same time he was to be chaplain to the Sisters of St. Joseph who had opened a boys' school in the old seminary. He fitted up a former barn on the southeast corner of the seminary property as a temporary chapel for a new congregation. The little community used this for two months and then obtained the use of a nearby former United Brethren church, which he dedicated under the patronage of the Holy Family on June 8, 1877. The present church was dedicated in 1889.

St. Peter Mission, Millersburg—Bishop Rosecrans had visited this seat of Holmes County to give a lecture in 1868. An attempt was made to start a church about 1873 but failed when the pastor disappeared. Finally in 1877 a new lot was donated and a substantial brick church was built, which was dedicated that December 8.

St. Mary's of the River Mission, Little Hocking, Washington Co.—It was decided in the winter of 1878 that a church should be built at Little Hocking. Ground was broken in February on the bluff overlooking the mouth of the Little Hocking and the mission church was opened on June 9, 1878, under the care of Rev. M. M. A. Hartnedy, pastor at Athens. (Bishop Rosecrans was not present.)[21]

In addition to establishing the above churches, during his tenure Bishop Rosecrans sent resident pastors to Bellaire, Mt. Vernon, Athens, and Jackson and restored one to Marges.

Chapter VIII
St. Joseph Cathedral, 1866-1878

Construction

It was almost five years from the erection of the new diocese in March of 1868 until the new cathedral was ready for occupancy on Christmas Day, 1872. During that time St. Patrick Church served as Bishop Rosecrans's cathedral.

The construction of a church to serve as the place of worship of a second English-speaking congregation in Columbus was begun in 1866. That year Father Edward Fitzgerald, as pastor of St. Patrick's, formed a committee of sixteen leading Catholics who would belong to the new congregation and who would continue to interact with the bishop. These were John Conahan, Theodore Leonard, John Joyce, John D. Clarke, Thomas Bergin, William Naghten, John Caren, Michael Harding, William Wall, James Naughton, William Riches, John McCabe, Michael Hartman, John Duffy, Martin Whalen, Bernard McNally, and Michael Galvin.[1] In 1870, under Bishop Rosecrans's direction, the new congregation was organized. He leased Naughten Hall (owned by James Naughton or Naghten, a member of the building committee), on the west side of South High Street, for the congregation to use as a temporary church. The congregation was under the care of Father John Rochford, O.P., during almost all its time in Naughten Hall.

The land on which the Cathedral was erected had a frontage of 132 feet on East Broad Street and a depth of 187 1/2 feet along North Fifth Street and was purchased in Archbishop Purcell's name by Father Fitzgerald in April 1866. The price was $13,500 less $500 donated by the seller. This money apparently was collected from a pool of funds already subscribed by the community. Some $37,000 had been subscribed to the project.[2] Some time before construction commenced, the men of the proposed parish met and chose St. Joseph as its patron.

Michael Harding of 59 Spring Street in Columbus, a member of the building committee, was chosen as architect and superintendent. He was a 36-year-old native of County Tipperary who had come to Columbus via Massachusetts in 1851. By 1866 Harding had already worked on construction of the first Union Depot (1851), with John D. Clarke built St. Patrick Church (1852-1853), built the Town Street M.E. Church (commenced 1853), built Central High School at Broad and Sixth (1862), and handled the carpentry work for St. Patrick Church in London (1866).[3]

Harding brought with him the style of Irish castles and churches, which were largely influenced by their relationship to England. The building he originally designed for the new parish was in Gothic style, which for some time had been displacing the Greek revival architecture that had predominated in America, especially in the 1820s. But Harding's design was not in harmony with current styles. The American Gothic revival was developing from an experimental and noncommittal phase into a style of its own, with specific standards and characteristics. It was in transition from an earlier phase of applied decoration (frills unrelated to the structure), symmetrical forms, and traditional building materials such as brick, to the later Victorian Gothic phase.[4] Harding's plan was described as follows in the *Daily Ohio Statesman* of Nov. 12, 1866:

> The Church is to be a magnificent structure of decorated Gothic architecture, known as the "Victoria Restoration" of the fourteenth and fifteenth centuries. It is to be 183 feet in length by 75 in width. It is to have a clear-story with chancel, nave and aisles; a tower, side porch and a basement chapel, 30 by 70 feet. The aisle walls are to be 29 feet in heighth, pierced with three light windows. The clear-story walls are to be 14 feet in heighth, and also pierced with three light windows. The tops of the clear-story walls are to be 52 feet in heighth, and the whole length [height] to the apex of the roof will be 75 feet.

The aisle walls are to have deep buttresses of three stages. The front elevation is to have flared buttresses, terminated with pinnacles. There are to be three entrances in front. The tower and spire, when finished, are to be 225 feet in heighth. The tower is to have a cinque-foil window of three lights, 36 feet in heighth. There are to be three very high pointed lights on each face of the spire. The tower at the base will be 31 feet square and 23 1/2 at the height of 105 feet.

The Church is to be built of pressed brick on a sandstone base course, three feet high. The doors and windows are to have sandstone facings. The roofs and spire are to be covered with slate.

In the interior of the Church, there are to be three altars—one high altar in the chancel, and one at the termination of each aisle. The clear-story walls are to be supported by twelve cast-iron columns with responds at each end. The chancel and altars are to be divided from the nave by three lofty arches of three channeled or fluted orders, springing from clustered piers.

The roofs are to be opened, and between the tie-beams and principal rafters, are to be filed in with tracery.

At about the same time, Mr. Harding drew the plans for St. Mary Church in Chillicothe, where construction began two months after the Cathedral in 1866. At its dedication, Archbishop Purcell called this the finest church in the Archdiocese of Cincinnati.[5] The original plan for St. Joseph Cathedral, as described above, clearly was the same as that of St. Mary in everything except its grander scale.

There appears to have been no formal ground-breaking ceremony for the Cathedral. The foundation line was staked out by Mr. Harding on June 6, 1866 and excavation and masonry work commenced almost at once. Father Fitzgerald as chairman of the building committee placed an advertisement in *The Ohio Statesman* of that date, seeking proposals for excavation of the basement and foundations and for furnishing stone, sand, and lime for construction. The low level of the land is indicated by the note that the excavated dirt would be "used in filling up the lot." (The basement or "undercroft" was not completely excavated until late in the 20th century.) The excavation contract was won by Thomas J. Burke, who also had the excavation contract for the Episcopal church at Broad and Third.[6]

Auxiliary Bishop Rosecrans laid the cornerstone of the new church on November 11, 1866, amid much pomp and rejoicing on the part of Catholic societies.

> The day was beautiful but chilly. The procession of societies formed at St. Patrick's at two o'clock p.m. with Captain William Riches as chief marshal and the following gentlemen as assistants: City Marshal Patrick Murphy, Thomas Bergin, James Joyce, J. C. Nevill, Patrick Dunn, George Burke [Buerck], John Howard, William Naghten, John Caren. The procession moved in the following order: Hemmersbach's Band, St. Joseph's Mutual Benevolent Society, St. Boniface's, St. John's, St. Martin's, and St. Aloysius's societies of Holy Cross Church; subdeacon, carrying processional cross accompanied by acolytes, twenty sanctuary boys in cassock and surplice, carriages containing the bishop and clergy, Sodality of the Blessed Virgin, Holy Angels' Society, the class of boys and girls who had received First Communion and Confirmation in the forenoon that day, St. Patrick's Society from London, societies from Newark and Delaware, and finally St. Patrick's Society of Columbus. The procession, displaying brilliant regalia and beautiful banners, attracted large crowds of people as it moved to the site of the new church by way of Seventh Street, now Grant Avenue, and Broad Street. Arriving at the foundations, the societies formed a guard on the outer wall. The windows of neighboring houses, the streets and every available portion of ground for a considerable distance round about, were occupied by people anxious to witness the ceremonies.
>
> The stone was laid on the southeast corner of the building, at the intersection of Broad and Fifth streets, and in its cavity was placed the usual sealed tin box, containing the name of the church, the names of the principal officers of the National and State governments, copies of recent Columbus newspapers, the names of the reigning Pope, the Archbishop of the Province, and pastor; also the names of

the officiating Bishop and assistants and numerous other articles to serve as mementos of the occasion. The Bishop delivered an address from the temporary platform, and in eloquent and forcible language plead the divinity of the Catholic Church.

At the conclusion of the sermon the '*Te Deum*' was sung, Hemmersbach's brass band playing an accompaniment. The clergymen present were Rev. Father O'Reily of Valparaiso, Ind.; Rev. John B. Murray, of Chillicothe; Reverends Louis Cartuyvels and Daily of Newark; Rev. E. M. Fitzgerald, pastor of St. Patrick's Church; Reverends John B. Hemsteger and Francis X. Specht, of Holy Cross Church; Rev. Father Hillebrand, Chaplain of St. Francis Hospital. Special trains on different railroads brought large delegations from adjoining towns, the number in attendance being estimated at fully 6,000.[7]

At the time of this cornerstone laying ceremony it was already widely known that the church was expected to be the cathedral of a new diocese, as the *Daily Ohio Statesman* of Nov. 12, 1866, noted, saying the church "will probably, when completed take rank as a Cathedral, or resident Bishop's Church."

No work was done on the edifice in 1867 because any money available to St. Patrick Parish beyond normal operating costs was needed to pay off the debt on Mt. Calvary Cemetery. On the Bishop's arrival as pastor of St. Patrick's that spring, he found that Father Mallon had raised only $25 to meet a note of $2,000 soon due and a contract for $6,000 for stone for the cathedral foundations. At this point, he considered his promotion to Columbus to be a melancholy situation.[8]

Bishop Rosecrans saw many beautiful stone cathedrals on his trip to Europe in that summer of 1867. This experience caused him to decide that the new St. Joseph Cathedral should be built not of brick but of stone. He hired Columbus architect Robert T. Brooks to draw new plans for the church. A native of England, Brooks had come to Columbus via Detroit to serve as assistant architect for construction of the Deaf and Dumb Asylum about 1865 and he probably was in the vicinity until 1872.

As described in July 1868, the new plans called for a building "of the style known as the Early English Gothic, and built of sand stone. The building will be 190 feet long, by 105 feet front on Broad street. The tower will be three hundred feet high, the one story clear 105 feet, and the audience room 82 feet high. It will accommodate two or three thousand people."[9] A more refined version of the plans was displayed at the Cathedral Fair in December 1868 and described thusly by the *Ohio State Journal* (December 23):

> The style is the early English period of Gothic, in vertical architecture, which prevailed in the eleventh and twelfth centuries. The general plan of the Cathedral is a parallelogram, having a length of 190 feet, with a general width of 86 feet. The south front has a width of 97 feet, caused by the projection of the great Tower beyond the general line of the building.
>
> The general external facings of the walls above the ground level are of sandstone, relieved by Lithopolis stone dressings. The south or principal front shows a central gable over one hundred feet high, flanked on each side by buttresses projecting ten feet from the general line of the gable, and supported by clustered piers of Lithopolis stone resting on cut limestone bases. The central pier is surmounted by a figure of St. Joseph, double life size, in an ornamented and canopied niche. Above, in the center of the gable, are figures of the Madonna and child in a suitable niche. In the niches worked in the great buttresses, front and side, are figures of Christ, St. Peter, St. Paul and the four Evangelists.
>
> The great tower, 312 feet in height, is on the west side of and five feet back from the line of the principal gable. It contains the clock, with three dials and bell chamber arranged for a chime of ten bells. On the west side of the tower are bas-reliefs representing the birth and baptism of Christ and our Redeemer in full relief.
>
> The first is continued eastward from the central gable in the form of a Galilee [gallery?] or two storied porch; the lower part forming a continuation of the porch, which extends at the south end across the whole width of the Cathedral the upper part being occupied by the children's gallery. The porch is approached from Broad and Fifth

streets by a terrace of twelve steps. North of this Galilee is the smaller tower, 200 feet high, the lower part being occupied by the gallery stairs and part of the children's gallery. This tower is flanked on its northeast corner by a large buttress, in one angle of which is a niche containing a figure of a Bishop, the buttress terminating in a large stone cross. The five buttresses on each side are surmounted by niches filled with appropriate figures. The body of the Cathedral is divided longitudinally into nave and aisles by arcades of arches supported by cast iron clustered and foliated piers, with limestone bases. The Cathedral will accommodate about 2,500 worshippers. The altars, three in number, and of most elaborate design and finish, will be at the north end. The external roof will be of particolored slate. The building is to be thoroughly ventilated and fire proof. The sittings are to be of white walnut, open stalls, with massive covered ends. The floors of marble and freestone, in patterns.

This plan was modified considerably as time went on.

The Bishop did not hire Mr. Brooks[10] to supervise the construction of the building he had designed. Instead he hired young Joseph E. Hartman of Columbus as superintendent of construction. Hartman had been born near and was baptized at St. Francis of Assisi Church, Chapel Hill, in Perry County, in 1842, then lived in Chillicothe for a short time as a child before the family moved to Columbus. He no doubt learned masonry from his father and older brother, but he must have had additional training. His letterhead billed him as "Architect and Civil Engineer" in 1870. Receipts and other documents in the diocesan archives indicate that he was on the job by April 21, 1868, and as late as August 2, 1870.

The change from brick to stone construction required that the church's foundations be torn up and replaced with heavier ones. A most interesting report appeared in the *Daily Ohio Statesman* of September 4, 1868:

> ...We yesterday morning proceeded to the corner of Broad and Fifth streets, for the purpose of gaining some information for our readers relative to
>
> ST. JOSEPH'S ROMAN CATHOLIC CATHEDRAL
>
> now being erected at that point.

Bishop Rosecrans
(Archives, Diocese of Columbus)

...the immense structure had been commenced under the direction of Mr. M. Harding, of this city, but it was found that his plans were impracticable.—He was removed and Mr. R. T. Brooks selected as the architect, who at once proceeded to institute a number of very material and important alterations. ...It was found on tearing up portions of the walls originally laid, that there was no particle "bond" between the stones. This was the result of using "ground lime cement," which proved entirely worthless for the purpose claimed. Our informant assured us that the filling between the stones was dead, and might just as well have been composed of loose gravel from the river bed. The quality of the masonry now being laid is of the best description and reflects great credit on the superintendent, Mr. J. E. Hartman. ...there are no contracts given out for any portion of the work. Mechanics are employed and paid by the day, and each department of the entire structure is under the sole control of Mr. Hartman as chief manager and superintendent. It was the original intention to build the cathedral of brick, but on the return of Bishop Rosecrans from the tour of Europe, during which time he visited many of the most celebrated cathedrals in the world, it was determined to employ stone in its erection. Accordingly the finest quality of cut sand stone from the quarries of Mr. John L. L. Jones, of Licking county, in this State, are being used.

The tone of these comments implies that the reporter spoke with some of the workmen, but did not speak with the superintendent or any of the clergy. Mr. Harding no doubt left the Cathedral project because he had a family to support and went on to the other jobs. That any contractor as experienced as he would lay foundations with bad mortar, especially for the cathedral of his own Church, is beyond belief.

The Cathedral walls were built of Black Hand sandstone, the lower section quarried near Hanover in Licking County, and the upper near Sugar Grove in Fairfield County. The windows are cased in freestone quarried in Pickaway County and the brackets and steps are Columbus limestone. It was Joseph Hartman who, when the Bishop wanted some means of relieving the deadness of the yellow sandstone walls, suggested the chiseling of the stone faces that is seen today.[11] The horizontal chiseling, called boasting, makes shadow and light dance faintly over the church's walls, giving life to the potentially dead appearance of the sandstone. Though the effect is subtle, the horizontal lines balance well against the Cathedral's threatening height in the eye of the approaching observer.[12]

The final design of the Cathedral seems to be a fusion of styles between Harding's Irish American influences and Bishop

Rosecrans' and Brooks' English preference. English qualities are found in the shaped windows of the side aisles, south façade, and clerestory, and the interior's banded nave arcade and clustered shafts. The original architect's Irish heritage makes an appearance in the handling of the stone, keeping the interior smooth with little ornamentation, as well as the two-part elevation.

On August 16, 1870 Bishop Rosecrans wrote to Archbishop Purcell that he had dismissed the superintendent, i.e. Joseph Hartman. (We do not know the reason. Hartman lived until 1899 and was buried at Mt. Calvary Cemetery after a funeral at the Cathedral.) His replacement was George W. Saunders of Perry County. Saunders, a Pennsylvania native but long-time Perry County resident, then 61 years old, farmed immediately south of St. Joseph's near Somerset. He signed documents as superintendent in August and September 1870.

By this time Brooks' plan had been somewhat modified. The main tower remained in its offset position. The smaller, eastern tower was begun but was stopped at the roofline. The Gallilee or gallery seems to have been inaccurately described in the newspaper, for it is the vestibule and rear of the choir loft today. The many niches and statues were deleted. The buttresses and piers of the facade were reduced in depth. General Rosecrans was on hand to explain everything, to guide Saunders. While visiting in 1870 the General designed the arched windows and the supports of the clerestory. They imitate those in the side aisles, helping create continuity and order.[13] The spire that was intended to top the tower but has never been built is shown in an engraving produced by William Riches (who had been a member of the building committee) and published in Studer's history of Columbus in 1873.

One odd feature of the final design is a buttress standing directly in the center of the facade. When considering the overarching rules of architecture, chiefly the expectation of a void at the center of any façade, this choice does not align itself with professional architectural practice. The central buttress proves this unspoken rule to be true, as it overcrowds the south façade and stands tightly between two of the three entrances.[14]

George Saunders stayed on the job only a short time, to be followed by Michael Fahey of Columbus, who brought the structure to occupancy. According to Father M. M. Meara, regarding the Cathedral construction, "Not a brick nor a stone went into its erection without his care." One account reported him in charge until 1878.[15] Born in 1829, Fahey was another native of County Tipperary who came to Columbus via Massachusetts. At the age of nineteen he had taken the total abstinence pledge from Father Mathew himself and he kept it faithfully to the end of his long life. He and his wife Margaret, born O'Brien, were in Ohio by 1855 and had eight children. Michael was a carpenter, builder, and contractor in Columbus. As a carpenter he worked on the construction of St. Mary's of the Springs in 1868. The Sisters noted that for the first eight or ten days after their arrival, while construction was being completed, he continued working into the nights after his day shift, doing tasks such as putting up doors and fastening baseboards.[16] He was a member of the choir at Holy Cross Parish, then at St. Patrick's when it was formed, and then he organized the Cathedral congregation's choir at Naughten Hall. He continued a member of the choir the rest of his life and "without compensation he performed many other tasks for the Church and for God."[17]

Father Jeremiah A. Murray, pastor at St. Patrick's, was placed in the position of general supervisor of the construction and "brought to bear upon the work the business tact and shrewdness for which he was noted. He, more than anyone else, carried out the plans and ideas of General Rosecrans, making only such changes as were absolutely necessary in the course of construction."[18] The final dimensions of the structure are 185 by 92 feet, very close to the original 193 by 90 feet as designed by Michael Harding.

Financing the Cathedral Construction

The cost of the Cathedral was over $200,000, perhaps as much as $250,000, a tremendous amount for those days when a well-paid workman earned $500 per year.

The means used to proceed with construction of the Cathedral for the first years were a subscription, fairs, donations from private persons outside the diocese, collections throughout the diocese, and loans. By 1872 subscriptions totaled $24,868 (plus, apparently, the $13,000 paid for the land) and of this amount

$22,532 had been collected. No individual subscription exceeded $1,500. The annual fairs never brought in more than $6,000 and fell off as the years went by, to $3,000 and less. An economic crash in 1875 contributed to the fund-raising problem. Donations from outside the diocese were sought through promoting participation in the Perpetual Weekly Mass, which Bishop Rosecrans established for all who contributed as much as five dollars to the work. These donations exceeded all the regular subscriptions from within the city of Columbus. The annual collection throughout the diocese seldom amounted to $2,500, though the congregations of the Sacred Heart in Pomeroy, St. Mary's in Lancaster, St. Peter's in Steubenville, St. Mary's at Minerton (near Wilkesville), Zaleski, Jackson, Mt. Vernon, Danville, Coshocton, Batesville, Junction City, Delaware, Ironton, and Pine Grove made "special and praiseworthy exertion."

The Bishop was so sincere in his desire to see the Cathedral constructed that, for the Cathedral Fair in January 1868, he offered for raffle an episcopal cross and chain. The cross had been given to him at his consecration by the clergy who had been members of his theology class in Mt. St. Mary's of the West; the chain had been a present from Cincinnati gentlemen through the late S. S. Boyle Esq.[19]

When the Second Diocesan Synod met in August 1873, the first question on the agenda was, "Is it better to impose a tax on the several congregations, to furnish the Cathedraticum and to support the Seminary, or to continue the system of voluntary contributions now in use?" The committee on this question (Fathers J. B. Hemsteger of Columbus, A. O. Walker of Portsmouth, and B. Wismann of Canal Dover) reported that it was better to continue the voluntary system, because "the disposition of the people is such, that more can be hoped for by appealing to their liberality than by imposing a tax, which many will look upon as an odious burden. But that every pastor shall earnestly endeavor to make his people understand their duty in this regard, and shall give them timely notice of such collections; and that the pastor himself shall adopt such prudent means as will insure a goodly contribution; among which means, may be serviceably selected for many congregations, that whereby the pastor, in person, takes up this collection in his church; or that were the names of the contributors are written down, with the amount contributed opposite each name respectively which list is real publicly in the church, or published in some Catholic paper. Moreover, it is recommended that some determinate time be appointed for the taking up of this collection." The report was adopted and Bishop Rosecrans appointed Pentecost Sunday for the seminary and the Sunday within the Octave of All Saints for the Cathedral collection. This collection was taken up through 1884.

In the issue of the *Catholic Columbian* for Christmas Day, 1875, Bishop Rosecrans published a pastoral letter regarding the cathedral debt and the support of the seminary. He recited the previous efforts to reduce the debt and then proposed the formation of a Cathedral and Seminary Aid Society in every congregation in the diocese. "This society is to consist of persons contributing a certain monthly sum, according to their means. The names of contributors are to be forwarded to the Bishop's residence, and the amounts collected every month, and receipted for in *The Columbian*. This will require interest on the part of all members of the Diocese, and persevering attention."

The Third Diocesan Synod was held on Friday, August 26, 1876, with most of the priests of the diocese in attendance. The sole topic of discussion was the diocesan debt, which had been incurred in construction of the Cathedral. A committee composed of Fathers J. B. Hemsteger, F. X. Specht, Louis DeCailly, and John B. Eis was appointed and made a recommendation to the Synod that each congregation be taxed for support of the works of the diocese, with consideration being given to the size, debts, wealth and poverty of the people, and actual support of a school by each. This report was not implemented during Bishop Rosecrans's days but this method was used by Bishop Moeller to (almost) eradicate the debt some twenty-five years later.

In 1877 Bishop Rosecrans sent a circular letter to the clergy, noting a law binding priests to contribute $10 annually towards the Cathedral fund, which applied only to pastors. The origin of this "law" is not known.

The diocesan debt in 1878 was around $190,000, incurred almost wholly for construction of the Cathedral and to cover part of the cost of the adjacent rectory, which was built in 1875. This debt was finally apportioned to the parishes and was wiped from the diocesan books in 1905; but some parishes borrowed their allocation and needed several more years to pay those debts.[20]

Consecration of the Cathedral

Though not finished, the Cathedral was first used for services on Christmas Day, 1872, when Bishop Rosecrans celebrated a Pontifical High Mass. Father Rochford had recently returned to service in the Dominican Order and the Bishop himself was the first Rector of the Cathedral, assisted over the next few years by Fathers J. A. Murray, N. A. Gallagher, Henry Anderson, and others.

Even at that time, in its unfinished state, it was "the most substantial and imposing edifice in the capital of Ohio," after the statehouse.[21] Some complained that the solidity and cost of the cathedral seemed disproportionate to the standing and poverty of the Catholics in Columbus. Others, more harshly, complained, "What need have the Irish or Germans, the workmen in the manufactories, in the gas works, sewers, ditches, and wherever else honest sweat is earning honest bread; the apprentices, the messenger boys, the patient, toiling servant girls, seamstresses, milliners, of so grand a place of worship?" The good Bishop calmly replied, "The dwelling was for the Most Holy Sacrament. He forgot Himself for us. Should we not forget ourselves for Him? He spent more on us than we are worth. Should we fear to spend our all on Him? It is a House for God, not for men; and its proportions are for the Owner and not the visitors. To its threshold crowds will come; some in carriages, some on foot; some poorly, some richly clad. At the door all distinctions vanish, and the Master greets all alike....It is God's House, and with Him there is no distinction of persons."[22]

The Cathedral at that time was used on Sundays and holy days. It had no communion railing and the same little altar that had been used at Naughton Hall had been installed there. The sacristy windows were expected to be installed in

January.[23] Subscribers to purchase of the Cathedral windows included some of those on its building committee or involved in its construction: Mrs. Joanna, Julia, and Mary Fahey, wife and daughters of Michael, subscribed for the bull's-eye in the gallery and stair tower; John D. Clarke and James Naughton for aisle windows on the west; John McCabe, Mrs. William Wall, and Thomas Bergin for aisle windows on the east; and "Workmen at the Cathedral" for one sacristy window and General Rosecrans for another. Mrs. Mary Duffy and Miss Mary E. Joyce may have been relatives of two other committee members. Another subscriber to an aisle window on the west side was Stephen Meara, father of Rev. M. M. Meara, the later rector of the Cathedral.[24]

Bishop Rosecrans and the other Cathedral clergy lived at St. Patrick's until 1873 when Rev. Henry Anderson, by the efforts of the congregation, obtained for them the Gundersheimer house on the south side of East Broad Street, between Sixth and Seventh (Grant). In 1875 the Bishop moved into two rooms in the Sacred Heart Academy building. In 1876 he completed a residence next to the rear of the Cathedral for the clergy and sold the Gundersheimer house, but he continued to reside at the Academy building.

The plastering and groined ceiling of the Cathedral were completed in 1878 by John D. Clarke and Charles Nagel and Bishop Rosecrans began planning its consecration.

The structure was consecrated to God in impressive, solemn ceremonies on Sunday, October 20. To this grand occasion Bishop Rosecrans invited all the bishops of the Cincinnati province along with two other friends. The prelates of the province were:
- Archbishop Purcell of Cincinnati
- Bishop Richard Gilmour of Cleveland, formerly his co-worker in the Cincinnati diocese
- Bishop William G. McCloskey of Louisville (accounts differ as to his presence)
- Bishop August M. Toebbe of Covington, who had been conserated by Bishop Rosecrans
- Bishop Silas Chatard of Vincennes, consecrated just five months earlier

The final design of the Cathedral is represented by this engraving in Studer's 1873 Columbus, Ohio: Its History, Resources and Progress. *The steeple has never been completed.*

- Bishop Joseph G. Dwenger of Fort Wayne, former pupil of Bishop Rosecrans

The Bishop's other invitees were Bishop John L. Spalding of Peoria, former pupil, at whose consecration Bishop Rosecrans had preached; and Bishop John J. Kain of Wheeling.

St. Joseph Cathedral

The twentieth of October was an ideal autumn day. The coolness of the advancing season was just sufficiently moderated by the genial warmth of the bright sun to render the day all that could be desired for the occasion so anxiously anticipated by thousands who came from far and near to participate in it. The faultless arrangement of the committees having the various portions of the celebration in charge insured perfect success. The consecration ceremonies began at five o'clock in the morning and occupied nearly four hours. The consecrator was Right Rev. Joseph Dwenger, of Fort Wayne, Indiana; Assistant Priest, Rev. J. B. Schmitt, Lancaster; First Deacon, Rev. G. H. Ahrens; Second Deacon, Rev. H. B. Dues; Subdeacon Rev. M. M. A. Hartnedy; Chanters, Reverend J. B. Eis, Rev. P. Kenmert, Rev. F. Moitrier, Rev. P. Thurheimer. Other offices were filled by seminarians and sanctuary boys. The beautiful and interesting ceremony was carried out in its entirety under the direction of Very Rev. N. A. Gallagher as Master of Ceremonies, assisted by Mr. L. W. Mulhane, now [1892] Rector of St. Vincent de Paul's Church, Mount Vernon. The decorations of the auditorium [nave] and the sanctuary were in keeping with the grand and festive occasion and elicited the admiration of all.[25]

Bishop Rosecrans was happy to have a special set of vestments for Bishop Chatard to wear while offering the Pontifical High Mass. It was the finest vestment (chasuble, no doubt) worn at the ceremony. It had been made over the course of several months by Miss Mary Joyce of Columbus while a student at St. Martin's Academy in Brown County. It was pronounced by the prelates in attendance to be the finest in Ohio, perhaps in the West. "Some of the Bishops pronounced it much finer than those they had purchased in Rome."[26]

At eleven o'clock the Pontifical High Mass was begun with the following officers: Celebrant, Right Rev. Silas Chatard, Bishop of Vincennes, Indiana; Assistant Priest, Rev. J. Donahoe; First Deacon of Honor, Rev. F. X. Specht; Second Deacon of Honor, Rev. J. Jessing; Officiating Deacon, Rev. F. J. Campbell; Officiating Subdeacon, Rev. D. B. Cull. The Most Reverend Archbishop Purcell, of

Cincinnati, occupied the throne at the Gospel side, while Right Reverend Bishop Rosecrans sat on another erected at the Epistle side. Right Rev. Bishops Gilmour, of Cleveland, Toebbe of Covington, Dwenger of Fort Wayne, Kain of Wheeling, and Spalding of Peoria assisted in the sanctuary, vested in rochet and cape.[27] Seated within the sanctuary railing were about fifty priests. After the first Gospel of the Mass had been sung the Rt. Rev. Bishop of Peoria ascended the pulpit and read from manuscript a very learned discourse on Ceremonies and Symbols in which he treated of their origin, nature and meaning in rites.[28]

"We come," he said, "as sons who return to their father's house, bearing dutiful tributes of reverence and love, and the sweet fragrance of by-gone days,

> 'When all our paths were fresh with dew,
> And all the bugle breezes blew
> Reveille to the breaking morn.'"[29]

The music for the Mass was provided by a choir of over fifty very talented men and women accompanied by an orchestra of eighteen pieces plus an organ, under the direction of Professor Nothnagel. The vocal and instrumental artists were selected from different societies and bands of the city. The music was Haydn's *First Mass*, with Lambrullotte's *Cor Amoris* and his *Lauda Sion*, "the whole being so faultlessly and effectively rendered that there would be small opportunity for exceptional mention in praise or censure." "It was in the opinion of many that as a church musical performance it was never before equaled in the city."[30]

Immediately after Mass Bishop Rosecrans announced the hour for Vespers in the evening, and the funeral of the Vicar General [Father Hemsteger] on Monday morning. That good priest's body was then lying in state in Holy Cross Church. The Bishop also stated that at his earnest solicitation the Archbishop would address the people.

The venerable prelate, "The Patriarch of the West," then came forward to the sanctuary railing wearing his miter and leaning on his crosier. In a voice tremulous with emotion and from the weakness of his age, nearly fourscore years, the Archbishop referred to the rapid progress of the Catholic Church in Columbus, its beginning and growth in this city being coeval with his labors in the priesthood. He heartily congratulated the Catholics of this city upon the completion of the noble structure that had just been consecrated to the service of God. This day is surely one that the Lord hath made. The building of a Cathedral that reflected so much glory upon the Catholics of Columbus was one of the many admirable works that God had raised up Bishop Rosecrans to accomplish. Who would have thought that so much could have been done in so short a time? He referred to the fact that Bishop Rosecrans was born of Protestant parents in Licking County, and raised, almost, among the people here. The Archbishop sketched the early careers of the other prelates present, stating that he was acquainted with the father and grandfather of the celebrant of the Mass, Bishop Chatard. The speaker contrasted the ceremonies of today with those of the attending scenes of early times in Columbus, one occasion particularly being when he celebrated Mass in a place used as a saloon, down on the banks of the Scioto, and the small apartment was so crowded that he begged some of the people to go out lest he should smother. The case was entirely different today as the large and imposing building testified. The Archbishop concluded his few remarks by urging the Catholics to remain steadfast to their faith and its practices which will bring them to their highest and best place of worship---heaven.[31]

Bishop Rosecrans entertained the visiting prelates at dinner at Sacred Heart Convent. At the dinner he was the happiest of the brilliant party, rehearsing and enjoying many a hearty joke. Soon afterwards he stood on the porch of the Convent, and, with the other prelates, reviewed the grand procession of societies that came to honor the occasion. All this he saw, but referred it to the honor and glory of Him from whom all blessings flow.

In the afternoon a procession of the visiting and local Catholic societies took place. Forty-four societies, accompanied by nine brass bands, were in line. It was the greatest display that the Catholic societies ever made in Columbus, and the scene on East Broad Street as the procession moved on that beautiful thoroughfare was such as had never before been witnessed in Columbus. The handsome banners of gold, silk and satin, worked with numerous elegant patterns, their glittering mountings of gilded cross and golden cord and tassels, the many colored regalia of the different societies, the graceful plumes waving from burnished helmets, with here and there at frequent intervals our national standard floating in the gentle breeze, all conspired to present a spectacle which will be long remembered.

At the City Hall tables were provided with generous refreshment for the visiting multitudes.

The literary and musical entertainment by the young ladies of the Convent filled up the interval of the afternoon with pleasure, and after that the Bishop and Father Durkin, O.P., alone remained at the Convent.

In the evening a half past seven o'clock Right Rev. Bishop Chatard sang Pontifical Vespers and Right Rev. Bishop Kain, of Wheeling, preached the sermon, taking for his subject that most glorious of the prerogatives of the Church, the Bride of Christ, speaking to the text, "Come with me and I will show thee my spouse." It was considered a masterly oration.

At the supper table, it was observed that the Bishop was not well. He refused to take any refreshment, except a very small amount, and remarked to Father Durkin, "I am not intended for a public man. I cannot stand excitement." It was only a short time after this that he repaired to the Cathedral to assist at the vesper service.

Chapter IX
This Life's End, 1877-1878

On October 21, the day following this glorious celebration of the consecration of the cathedral, after ten years of labor, disappointment, and worry, Bishop Rosecrans died of hemorrhages, which he tended to suffer whenever excited. He had suffered slight hemorrhages at different periods of his life, but within the past two years they had become more frequent and severe.[1] He suffered one troublesome bout in the summer of 1877 while at Put-in-Bay for a rest, but recovered by the end of August.[2]

In June of 1878 the Bishop's friend Mother Julia Chatfield, leader of the Brown County Ursulines, suffered a heart attack. "Among those who visited her in her last illness, was Bishop Rosecrans. Their conversation naturally turned upon the mutual loss of old friends and acquaintances lately sustained, Notre Mère, remarking in how little time she would rejoin them in the eternal home. 'Yes, Notre Mère, that is too true, but,' said he in his usual jocular way, 'I shall be there too, to open the door for you.' There he stood apparently in the enjoyment of health, his mind occupied with perfecting the details for the consecration of his magnificent Cathedral so soon to take place, and yet, seeming to feel the constant presence of death before him. When about leaving, Notre Mère received his benediction for the last time, begging him not to forget her in his prayers after her death. 'I would pray for you,' he replied, 'but, Notre Mère, I am going before you.' With the little strength left her, she essayed to rally him out of what she considered a fit of depression, but he persistently kept to the point, and left her, saying laughingly, 'Well, I will take a morning train, you will follow in the evening!"³ He was correct. Mother Julia survived him by 12 days, until November 2.

Bishop Rosecrans seems to have been especially close to Dominican Father Ambrose Durkin this summer. Rosecrans had ordained him in 1875 and, like Rosecrans, he was a teacher. He had served at Somerset from his ordination until 1877, when he had been sent to St. Rose in Kentucky, and he had just returned to Ohio, being assigned again to Somerset, in mid-1878. Two of his sisters belonged to the St. Mary's of the Springs congregation, so he probably spent time with them, waiting for the new academic year to begin. On Monday, August 13, 1878, Bishop Rosecrans and Father Durkin left Columbus on a journey to London, Ontario, driven away from home, the Bishop said, by the extreme heat. On this journey Father Durkin would visit his birthplace while the Bishop would get a few days' rest. They sweltered all the way from Columbus to Cleveland on the Bee Line railroad. Forests and fields and villages flew by while they were wiping their faces and going to the ice water cooler. They saw a rich harvest being gathered in and the apple trees bowing under their fruit. In the towns they noted many a cross on the steeples and thanked God "that all northern Ohio is not a Know-Nothing Lodge nor a cheese Depot." At Cleveland they transferred to the train for Fort Stanley "in the land of the Kannocks'." They took the boat *Saginaw* and through the kindness of the clerk encamped separately from the throng that fiddled and danced nearly all night. The train carried them over an uninteresting twenty-nine miles to London. There they found no American newspapers and a five percent charge on their American money. They found two Catholic churches and two academies. Of interest to Rosecrans, no doubt, given the controversy over school funding in Ohio, they noted that the government kept account of school taxes paid by Catholics and handed that amount over to the Catholic Committee to be used in their schools. The local bishop, they learned, was away on Lake Huron. They found the people fondly remembered Dominican Fathers O'Brien, Rochford, Dunn, Lilly, and many others known in Ohio.⁴

The trip seems not to have improved the Bishop's health. On August 20 he was in Detroit, at St. Aloysius Pro-Cathedral.

Bishop Rosecrans in his last years

He wrote to his brother William that it was hot and he would start for home that night. He was worried about paying interest due on his loans. He was not sick but had lost thirteen pounds since the end of June.[5]

Despite feeling symptoms and receiving warnings of his disease for many weeks, Bishop Rosecrans would take no rest. The completion of a Cathedral worthy of divine worship was the central thought of his heart.[6] He had lived with an unwavering confidence in the power and protection of St. Joseph, through whom, he said, he never failed to receive what he asked, and having prayed that he might see the consecration of the Cathedral, his was sure this petition would be granted.[7]

On the night of the 7th of October 1878, he was aroused from sleep by the feeling of moisture about his neck and, examining into its cause, discovered it to be blood that had been running profusely from the temple artery. The flow of blood soon ceased, but about noon of the following day it broke out afresh, and to such an extent that his physician, Dr. Hamilton, was summoned to come in haste. The hemorrhage was stopped, and, relieved of this superfluity of blood, the Bishop expressed himself as feeling in better health than he had been for some time.

In a most joyful mood he directed the preparations for the consecration of the Cathedral. But his joy was muted by the deaths of two of his priests. Father Richard C. Christy had come to the diocese about 1876 and was chaplain of the Sisters of the Good Shepherd and founder of Holy Family Parish. His health failed and, having been relieved of his duties, he died at St. Francis Hospital on Wednesday, October 16, 1878. Then on Friday the Bishop was suddenly called to the death-bed of his saintly Vicar General, V. Rev. John Hemsteger, and, kneeling at the bedside, faltered and broke into tears and was unable to continue the litany. With characteristic courage and faith he drowned his sorrow and continued preparations to receive on Saturday the prelates who would assist in the consecration.[8] But he remarked that deaths often came in threes.

As he was entering the newly consecrated Cathedral for Vespers on Sunday evening, he was attacked by a slight hemorrhage and, almost prostrate, was taken to his room in the convent. There he suffered three more attacks. Dr. Hamilton, called to attend him, visited six times over the next 27 hours. During Sunday night the Bishop would allow no one to remain in the room with him, feeling assured that his indisposition would pass away before morning. At the usual hour in the morning he arose and prepared to go to the chapel to say Mass, but his strength failed and he returned to his bed, where he was found in an insensible condition by the Sister who sought him when he had not appeared for Mass or answered a call. He had had a hemorrhage from the stomach. Although he grew weaker it was thought he would rally—he was only 51 years old—but he was not able to attend a meeting of his clergy that he had called for eight o'clock that evening.

While the solemn Requiem Mass for Father Hemsteger was being sung at Holy Cross Church, word spread throughout the city that the Bishop was in a dying condition. Many of the prelates and priests who had remained in the city called on him on Monday morning and felt assured that his illness was not so serious.

However, at noon on Monday another hemorrhage struck him and others towards evening, the last occurring at about 7:30. It became evident that he was failing. The priests of the Cathedral and Dr. Hamilton were summoned, while the news of his dangerous condition spread with electric speed throughout the city. The city's clergy came immediately to his bedside but, not expecting his death that night and fearing the presence of so many would be harmful to him, they again departed.

When Dr. Hamilton arrived he informed the Bishop that, though he had given him encouragement earlier in the day, he now regarded his case as very serious and told him that if he had any requests to make, or last business to dispose of, he should do so. To this the Bishop replied, "My work is finished. Send me my confessor." Father John Eis, the Bishop's secretary, was present and intended to remain all night. With pious resignation the Bishop asked him to administer the last sacraments and received Penance, Holy Communion, and Extreme Unction. When asked if the blessing in articulo mortis should be given, the Bishop replied yes. When questioned about his will, he replied, "My will is made. All things, of course, will go to my successor, save my little personal articles that the family may desire for mementoes."

Conscious all the time, he lay calmly and patiently awaiting the pleasure of Almighty God to relieve him, his lips silent in prayer. At ten o'clock the death agony began, and in fifteen minutes he quietly and peacefully breathed his last, with the names of Jesus, Mary, and Joseph on his lips. Those present at the end were V. Rev. N. A. Gallagher, Rev. John Eis, Rev. T. J. Lane, Mother Mary Agnes and several sisters of the convent, D. A. Clarke (seminarian, of the *Catholic Columbian*), his brother W. J. Clarke (Prosecuting Attorney-elect), Mr. and Mrs. Joyce and their daughter Mary, Mr. and Mrs. John C. English, Miss Sallie Miller, P. J. Sullivan, and Mamie Rosecrans, the only relative of the Bishop in the city.[9]

The prelates and other clergy who had departed from Columbus were summoned to return to attend the obsequies on Friday, October 25. In the meanwhile the Bishop's remains rested at Sacred Heart Convent.

Early Friday morning Masses for the deceased were offered in the Cathedral by Bishops Dwenger, Foley, Borgess, Chatard, and Fitzgerald, the last one being attended by the children of the Catholic schools. At 9:30 the Office of the Dead was chanted with Archbishop Purcell presiding. This was followed by Solemn Pontifical Requiem Mass offered by Bishop Toebbe with the Archbishop on the throne and, in addition to the others mentioned, Bishops Gilmour and Kain in the sanctuary. Bishop Foley preached "an able and touching sermon." The remains were entombed under the sanctuary.[10]

+ + +

From the beginning of his life, Sylvester Rosecrans was given two outstanding gifts: a great intellect and a great older brother. Together, with a good education, these led him to the understanding that there is objective reality and led him to be devoted first to truth as an ideal, then to Truth itself, God the Son become man, Jesus Christ.

In his public life he was tireless in presenting the truth of the Catholic faith in sermon, pastoral letter, classroom, public lecture, and editorial. In addition, in the latter two arenas he was fearless in expounding the implications of the truth of the faith for society at large. His devotion to Truth led him to a sincerity in every aspect of life. As priest and as bishop he offered Mass daily, read of his Office, and heard confessions weekly and for holy days. As bishop he was an example and kindly father to his brother priests. His personal life was one of poverty, but, truly a man, he owned a dog, played cards, and on occasion smoked a cigar. In his years as bishop he seems to have been always very aware of the coming judgment, personal and general, but nevertheless was unafraid of death.

The two major disappointments of his mature life were his treatment by his spiritual father, Archbishop Purcell, when embarking as bishop of the new diocese; and the financial failure of his seminary in Columbus. His two major failures as bishop were his poor relationship with the Dominican Sisters (though this was, of course, a two-way street) and the debt of some $200,000 he left for his diocese. Had God given him a longer life, both of these might have been resolved. His successor, Bishop Watterson, got along well with the Sisters and his next successor, Bishop Moeller, when the effort finally was made, eliminated the debt within a few years.

We will give Bishop Foley the final words:

> Born and educated in the midst of the people over whom Divine Providence placed him as spiritual ruler, he was a man after his subjects' own heart. He understood them, they corresponded with him. Though his years of usefulness amongst them was limited to half a score, still that life is long which answers life's great end, and when the soul of Bishop Rosecrans sank to rest on the 21st of October, 1878, he was greeted with the Heavenly salutation: "Well done, thou good and faithful servant, enter thou into the joys of thy Lord."[11]
>
> Amen.

*The tomb of Bishop Rosecrans,
under the sanctuary of St. Joseph Cathedral*

Sources and Notes

Frequently Cited Sources

Brown County: *Fifty Years in a Brown County Convent*, Cincinnati: McDonald & Co., 1895

Burton, Katherine, *Make the Way Known, The History of the Dominican Congregation of St. Mary of the Springs*, New York: Farrar, Straus & Cudahy, 1959

Columbian: *The Catholic Columbian*, newspaper of the Diocese of Columbus

CRSB: *Bulletin* of the Catholic Record Society-Diocese of Columbus.

Hartley, Rt. Rev. James J., *Diocese of Columbus: The History of Fifty Years, 1868-1918*, Columbus: 1918.

In Memoriam. Rt. Rev. S. H. Rosecrans, D.D., First Bishop of Columbus, Columbus: Catholic Columbian, 1878. (36 page booklet)

Journal: "The Journal of Sylvester H. Rosecrans," extracts from the manuscript, appeared in the *Bulletin* of the Catholic Record Society - Diocese of Columbus in nine of the twelve issues of Vol. 1 (1975). The Journal entries are dated Dec. 21, 1847 to June 4, 1852, but some entries are retrospective. The original manuscript is in possession of the University of Notre Dame Archives. From a letter in the diocesan archives, it appears likely that the manuscript was loaned out by the diocese late in the 19th century and never was returned.

K&K: Michael J. Kelly and James M. Kirwin, *History of Mt. St. Mary's Seminary of the West, Cincinnati, Ohio*; Cincinnati:

Keating & Co., 1894 (A biographical sketch of Bishop Rosecrans appears on pages 234-240.)

Kenneally, Finbar, *United States documents in the Propaganda Fide archives; a calendar* (later volumes by other editors.; Washington: 1966-1987

Lamers, William M., *The Edge of Glory, A Biography of General William S. Rosecrans, U.S.A.*, New York: Harcourt, Brace, 1961

Lee, Alfred E., *History of the City of Columbus, Capital of Ohio*, New York and Chicago: Munsell & Co., 1892 (two vols).

Longley, Max, *For the Union and the Catholic Church, Four Converts in the Civil War*, Jefferson, N.C.: McFarland & Company, 2015

Mulhane, L. W., *Memorial of Major-General William Stark Rosecrans*; Mt. Vernon, 1898

Mullay, Camilla, O.P., *A Place of Springs, A History of the Dominican Sisters of St. Mary of the Springs, 1830-1970*, Columbus: Dominican Sisters of St. Mary of the Springs, 2005.

Norviel, Rebekah, *St. Joseph Cathedral and the American Gothic*, An Honors Thesis, Ball State University, Muncie, Indiana, December 2013.

O'Daniel, Victor F., *The Dominican Province of St. Joseph, Historico-Biographical Studies*, New York: Holy Name Society, 1942

O'Daniel & Coffey: Victor F. O'Daniel and James Reginald Coffey, *The First Two Dominican Priories in the United States*, New York: Holy Name Society, 1947

Sketch: Bishop Rosecrans' 1872 *Sketch of St. Joseph's Cathedral*, published as a small pamphlet.

Studer, Jacob H., *Columbus, Ohio: Its History, Resources, and Progress*, Columbus: 1873

Telegraph: *The Catholic Telegraph and Advocate*, newspaper of the Archdiocese of Cincinnati

UCLA: The Rosecrans Collection, Department of Special Collections, The Library, UCLA (letters from Sylvester to his brother William and other materials)

UNDA: University of Notre Dame Archives

Chapter 1 - Youth, Conversion, and Education

1. *Telegraph* Jan. 28, 1854.
2. CRSB, March 1981, "The Rosecrans Family at Homer, Licking County."
3. Journal, Jan. 27, 1848. Lamers pp 8-11. When the question of General Rosecrans's ancestry and Catholicism came up in public, during the Civil War, the Catholic Telegraph proclaimed on "the highest authority" that the maternal grandmother of the Rosecrans brothers was an O'Keefe. No such name can be found in the Rosecrans ancestry. It seems likely that Father Edward Purcell and Father Rosecrans discussed their ancestry while co-editors of the Telegraph. Purcell's mother was born Johanna Keefe and Father Rosecrans may have made some remark in jest that the same was his grandmother's name. But Father Purcell ran the statement twice, on November 5, 1862 and Feb. 11, 1863, after Father Rosecrans had left the editorial staff.
4. *Telegraph* May 1, 1858.
5. Kelly & Kirwin p 234.
6. CRSB, April 1979, p 403 Msgr. Herman E. Mattingly, "Father Fidelis of the Cross, C.P., The Rosecrans Family, Kenyon College—Some Observations," quoting Dr. Thomas A. Greenslade, archivist at the college.
7. Letter from General Rosecrans, *Columbian*, Dec. 5, 1878.
8. Journal, Feb. 5 and July 15, 1848.
9. Kelly & Kirwin p 234.
10. Journal, July 15, 1848.
11. CRSB March 1981 from Rosecrans Collection, UCLA Library.
12. Journal, July 15, 1848.
13. *Columbian* Nov. 21, 1878.
14. Journal, July 15, 1848.
15. Letter of W. S. Rosecrans to Rev. L. W. Mulhane, Dec. 11, 1886, in Mulhane's *Memorial of Major-General William Stark Rosecrans*; Mt. Vernon, 1898, pp 48-50. Code's *Dictionary of the American Hierarchy* gives the date of his baptism as May 10. Other secondary sources say it took place in 1845, but certainly it was 1846. The latter is the year given by William and was the year Sylvester left

Kenyon for St. John's. In addition, in a letter to William dated Gambier, Jan. 26, 1846 Sylvester wrote that he expected to be baptized as soon as possible. (Letter to William, Department of Special Collections, The Library, UCLA.)
16. Letter from Gen. Rosecrans, *Columbian*, Dec. 5, 1878.
17. *Columbian* Nov. 21, 1878.
18. Journal, July 15, 1848.
19. ibid.
20. So he wrote in his journal in 1848, but it seems that in his later years he smoked cigars at least occasionally.
21. Journal, July 15, 1848.
22. *The Freeman's Journal and Catholic Register* July 31, 1847.
23. Journal, July 15, 1848
24. Kelly & Kirwin p 235.
25. ibid. Letter to William, Sept. 25, 1847, Department of Special Collections, The Library, UCLA.
26. Letter to William, Oct. 12, 1847, Department of Special Collections, The Library, UCLA.
27. Letter to William, Oct. 22, 1847, Department of Special Collections, The Library, UCLA.
28. John Gilmary Shea, *History of the Catholic Church in the United States, 1844-1866* (Vol. IV) 1892, p. 550. Code 1940 p 14. *Telegraph* Nov. 4, 1847.
29. Letter to William, Nov. 13, 1847, Department of Special Collections, The Library, UCLA.
30. Kelly & Kirwin p 235.
31. *Telegraph* Jan. 19, 1853 and Aug. 18, 1860. K&K 235.
32. Max Longley, *For the Union and the Catholic Church*, chapter 3, places Sylvester at Frascati, twelve miles southeast of Rome, for most of 1848. This seems to be a mistake. Sylvester was in Rome at least through June. He was in Frascati on September 13 and on September 30 noted that his stay there was half over, so this may have been a visit of only a few weeks. He definitely was in Rome again by December 11. (Journal entries)
33. Journal, Apr. 24, 1849.
33. *Telegraph* Nov. 5, 1853. Journal, May 9 and June 14, 1849.
34. *Telegraph* Nov. 30, 1861 and Apr. 17, 1858.

Notes - Chapter II

35. Letter to William, February 26, 1850, Department of Special Collections, The Library, UCLA.
36. Kinneally VII/828.
37. F. Tanconi, Rector, Propaganda Fide College, to Prefect of Prop. Fide, Sept. 3-Oct. 28, 1859.
38. Purcell's sermon at The Month's Mind for Rosecrans, held in Cincinnati, Nov. 26, 1878 in *Columbian*, Dec. 5, 1878.
39. Journal, Palm Sunday, 1851.
40. Letter to William, July 17, 1851, Department of Special Collections, The Library, UCLA.
41. *Telegraph* Nov. 29, 1851.
42. Journal. *Telegraph* July 31, 1852.
43. Kinneally VII/1020. F. Tanconi, Rector, Propaganda Fide College, to Prefect of Prop. Fide, Sept. 3-Oct. 28, 1859.
44. *Telegraph* Oct. 16, 1852.

Chapter II - Cincinnati Clergyman

1. Kinneally IV/1494, PF to Cardinal Wiseman, Archbishop of Westminster, 1852 July 27, Rome.
2. Rosecrans to Orestes Brownson, Oct. 25, 1853, UNDA.
3. Kinneally II/601, SHR to PF, 1852 Nov. 17.
4. John H. LaMotte, *History of the Archdiocese of Cincinnati, 1821-1921*, New York and Cincinnati: Frederick Pustet Co., 1921, p 133, based on the *Telegraph*, Nov. 20, 1852 and Jan. 1, 1853. *Telegraph* Feb. 26, 1853.
5. Kinneally II/807, SHR to PF, 1854 Aug. 17.
6. ibid. Kinneally II/601, SHR to PF, 1852 Nov. 17.
7. Kelly & Kirwin p 235.
8. Hartley p 29, quoting Msgr. John B. Murray.
9. Kinneally II/601, SHR to PF, 1852 Nov. 17.
10. *Telegraph* Jan. 8, 1861.
11. *Telegraph* June 25, 1859.
12. *Telegraph* Dec. 10, 1859.
13. *Telegraph* March 19, 1862. SHR to JBP, June 15, 1868, UNDA.
14. *Telegraph* Jan. 15, 1862.
15. Kelly & Kirwin, p 236.
16. See for example the *Grand River Times*, Jan. 4, 1854 for the telegraph report; and the full account in the *Cincinnati*

Gazette, printed in the Wheeling *Daily Intelligencer*, Dec. 30, 1853. *Telegraph*, Dec. 31, 1853.
17. *Telegraph* Jan. 7, 1854.
18. *Telegraph* Jan. 21, 1854.
19. Hartley pp 27-28.
20. Letter to William, July 20, 1855, Department of Special Collections, The Library, UCLA. *Telegraph* July 30, 1859. Brown County p 110.
21. *Telegraph* April 18, 1857.
22. *Brown County* p 115.
23. Msgr. John B. Murray, quoted in Hartley p 29. M. Edmund Hussey, *A History of the Seminaries of the Archdiocese of Cincinnati, 1829-1979*, Norwood, Ohio: Mt. St. Mary's Seminary of the West, 1979, p 19. Oct 26, 1863, Macleod to Purcell, UNDA. *Telegraph* July 10, 1858.
24. Kinneally II/1036, 1856 Oct. 24 SHR to PF.
25. *Telegraph* July 10, 1858.
26. *Telegraph* Aug. 21, 1858, reprinting a column from the *Commercial*.
27. Kelly & Kirwin p 205.
28. Hussey, op. cit.
29. John J. Cosgrove, *Most Reverend John Lancaster Spalding, first Bishop of Peoria, Mendota*, 1960, pp 9 and 28. See also David F. Sweeney's biography of Spalding. *Telegraph*, Sept. 18, 1858 and July 9, 1859.
30. Spalding to Purcell, July 12, 1859, UNDA. Kinneally VI/860 and II/1503. Rev. Francis J. Pabish, in Rome, to Purcell, 1859 Nov. 20, UNDA.
31. *Telegraph* June 29, 1861. Kinneally VI/686.
32. Kinneally V/666, VI/1615, & 1616. *Telegraph* February 19, 1862.
33. Kinneally VI/1976.
34. Brown County p 129.
35. *Telegraph* Mar. 26, 1862.
36. Kelly & Kirwin 200-201.
37. Kinneally III/393.

Chapter III - Auxiliary Bishop

1. *Telegraph* May 4, 1861.
2. *Telegraph* May 11, 1861.
3. David Spalding, "Martin John Spalding's 'Dissertation on the American Civil War'" *Catholic Historical Review* 52 No. 1 (April 1966) 66-85. Cf pp 82 and 83.
4. Spalding, op. cit., pages 68-69, citing APF, Ser. rif., A.C., Vol. 20, fols. 725r-728r, Spalding to Barnabò, n.p., March 8, 1864.
5. Wheeling *Daily Intelligencer* Nov. 11, 1863.
6. Lewisburg, Pa., *Union County Star and Lewisburg Chronicle* Nov. 3, 1863.
7. See for example the *Fremont Journal*, Fremont, Ohio, Oct. 30, 1863.
8. *The Alleghanian*, Ebensburg, Pa., Nov. 12, 1863, reprinting a report from the *Cincinnati Commercial* of Nov. 2.
9. Rt. Rev. S.H. Rosecrans, Cincinnati, to Prop. Fide, Mar. 7, 1864, UNDA Microfilms, MPRF: Catholic Church. Congregatio de Propaganda Fide, Reel 67.
10. Oswego *Commercial Times* Jan 14, 1863.
11. *Telegraph* April 8 and 15, 1863.
12. UNDA, SOR_1-87_004.
13. *Lockport Daily Journal* (New York) Aug. 21, 1863.
14. *The Chicago Tribune* Aug. 18, 1863. *The Urbana Union* Aug. 19, 1863.
15. Young to Purcell, Aug. 10 and 16, 1862, UNDA.
16. *Cleveland Morning Leader* July 20, 1863, quoted in Zanca, Kenneth J., *American Catholics and Slavery, 1789-1866: An Anthology of Primary Documents*, University Press of America, 1994, p. 282.
17. Garraghan, Gilbert J., *The Jesuits of the Middle United States*, Chicago: Loyola U. Press, 1983, II/161. Based on letters from Rev. Ferdinand Coosemans to Rev. Peter Becks, the General of the Order, Jan. 15 and May 18, 1864, in the General Archives, Society of Jesus, Rome.
18. P. Fishe Reed, *Incidents of the War; or, the Romance and Realities of Soldier Life*, Asher & Co., 1862, p 39.
19. *Telegraph* April 15 and 29, 1863. Spalding to Purcell, Apr. 21, 1863, UNDA.

20. Louisville *Weekly Journal* April 16, 1863.
21. *History of the Seventy-Third Regiment of Illinois Infantry Volunteers, Regimental Reunion Association of Survivors of the 73d Illinois Infantry Volunteers*, 1890, at page 163, quoted in Wm. F. Drake, *Little Phil: The Story of General Philip Henry Sheridan*; Prospect, Ct.: Biographical Publishing Co., 2005, p 126.
22. *Telegraph* Feb. 4, Apr. 1, June 10, and Aug. 26, 1854 and Dec. 16, 1863.
23. *Telegraph* June 10, 1863.
24. *Telegraph* Dec. 27, 1865. Kelly & Kirwin p 237. *Columbian* Nov. 7, 1878. Brown County p 142.
25. *Columbian* Nov. 21, 1878.
26. M. Chatard to Purcell, Mar. 17, 1866 UNDA.
27. *Telegraph* Nov. 14, 1866 and Dec. 12, 1866.
28. *Columbian* Nov. 7, 1878.
29. *Telegraph* Mar. 24, 1870.
30. *In Memoriam* p 9. *Columbian* Oct. 24, 1878. Ohio State Journal Oct. 22, 1878.
31. *Stark County Democrat* July 13, 1870. Urbana Union June 3, 1863.
32. *Telegraph* May 28 and June 4, 1859.
33. *Telegraph* July 23, 1859, from the *N.Y. Freeman*. *Telegraph* July 30, 1859.
34. *Telegraph* Mar. 24 and 31, 1860.
35. *Telegraph* Jan. 14 and 28 and Feb. 4, 11, 18, and 25, 1863.
36. *Telegraph* June 17 and July 1, 1863. *The Urbana Union*, June 3, also announced it.
37. *Telegraph* Aug. 19, 1863 and the *Urbana Union* Aug. 19, 1863.
38. *Telegraph* Nov. 16, 1864.
39. *Telegraph* Nov. 30, 1864.
40. *Telegraph* Feb. 8, 1865.
41. *Telegraph* Jan. 31 and Feb. 28, 1866.
42. *Telegraph* Feb. 21, 1866.
43. *Telegraph* Apr. 25, 1866.
44. *Telegraph* Nov. 6, 1867.
45. *Telegraph* Jan. 29 and Feb. 5, 1868.
46. *Telegraph* Mar. 4, 1868.

Notes - Chapter IV

47. *Pittsburgh Catholic* reprinted in *Telegraph* June 25, 1862.
48. *Boston Pilot* June 28, 1862 and *Telegraph* July 2, 1862.
49. *Telegraph* July 20, 1864 and Jan. 11, 1865.
50. 1865, June 23, Rosecrans to Purcell, UNDA
51. *Telegraph* Aug. 1, 1866.
52. *Sermons Delivered during the Second Plenary Council of Baltimore*, Baltimore: Kelly & Piet, 1866, pp 29-37. Letter to Mary L. (Maime) Rosecrans, Department of Special Collections, The Library, UCLA.

Chapter IV - New Diocesan Ordinary

1. Kinneally VII/1488, undated [1866 October], Baltimore.
2. Kinneally VII/334, JBP to PF, 1866 Dec. 12; and VII/1537.
3. Archives of the College of Mt. St. Joseph, Delhi, O.
4. *Telegraph* Jan. 16 and 23, 1867.
5. Kiefer, Sister Monica, O.P., *Dominican Sisters St. Mary of the Springs, A History*, Historiette Four, "At the Springs," [Columbus: nd] p 11.
6. SHR to JBP, March 4, 1867, UNDA.
7. SHR to JBP, March 16 but dated March 26, 1867, UNDA.
8. *Telegraph* Apr. 3, 1867. *Columbian* Oct. 24, 1878.
9. SHR to JBP, Mar. 4 and Mar. 16, 1867, UNDA. *Telegraph* May 8, 1867.
10. *Telegraph* May 29, 1867.
11. *Telegraph* May 22, 1867.
12. Kinneally VIII/1540 and 1544 and 1545. *National Republican* (Washington, D.C.) July 30, 1867.
13. SHR statement, July 3, 1867, Rome, UNDA. Daily Ohio Statesman July 23, 1867.
14. Sr. Mary Agnes McCann, *Archbishop Purcell and the Archdiocese of Cincinnati*, dissertation, Catholic University of America, 1918, p 86, quoting from a letter of July 10, 1867 to Mother Regina, Archives, Mt. St. Joseph-on-the-Ohio.
15. *Daily Ohio Statesman* Apr. 18, 1868. *Telegraph* Sept. 18, 1867.
16. Kinneally IX/49, 1232, 1271, 1272 and X2186 and 2187. *Telegraph* Feb. 19, 1868. SHR to JBP, Mar. 2, 1868, UNDA.

17. SHR to JBP, Mar. 29, 1867 and Apr. __, 1868; and Bishop John Quinlan to Purcell, July 11, 1868, UNDA.
18. SHR to JBP, Apr. 30, 1868 and May 7, 1868, UNDA.
19. *Columbian* Oct. 16, 1878. Bishop Foley, sermon at Rosecrans's funeral, *Columbian*, Oct. 24, 1878.
20. *Freeman's Journal* May 12, 1877.
21. *In Memoriam* p 9.
22. *Columbian* Nov. 7, 1878.
23. *Telegraph*, reprinted in *Columbian*, as well as other articles, Nov. 7, 1878. *In Memoriam* p 10.
24. *Columbian* Nov. 1, 1878.
25. *Columbian* Mar. 27, 1879 and special edition, Apr. 10, 1925 p 29.
26. Kinnneally VII/495, 1867 Oct. 21, anonymous to Propaganda Fide.
27. Biographical sketch by Father Daniel B. Cull, *Ohio State Journal* Oct. 22, 1878.
28. *Telegraph* Jan. 14, 1863, June 29 and Aug. 3, 1864, and July 11, 1866.
29. These figures differ slightly from those in the 1869 Catholic Directory, printed in Hartley pp 18-24; that list omitted many of the mission churches.
30. *Columbian* Nov. 7, 1878.
31. CRSB June 1977 pp 227-228, quoting the *Freeman's Journal and Catholic Register*, Dec. 27, 1873.
32. June 8, 1871 letter of Louis Cartuyvels to the Holy Father, Kinneally IX/1041. O'Daniel, p 365.
33. SHR to JBP, Mar. 2, Apr. 16, 18, 22, and 30 and May 7, 1868, UNDA.
34. SHR to JBP, Aug. __, 20, 25, and Sept. 5, 1870, UNDA.
35. CRSB Feb. 2007. See also CRSB July 1985. Unpublished history of St. Francis de Sales Parish, 1844-1977, by the late Rev. Msgr. William E. Kappes (Catholic Record Society files).
36. Kinneally: IX/1040, 1041, 1043, 1076, 1077, 1078, 1079, 1080, 1081, and 1083, and X/1, 2, 3, 4, 5, 6, 7, 30, 98, 99, 100, 676,681, 716, 752, 763, 829, 937, and 1083. SHR to JBP, Jan. 3, and 22, 1872, UNDA.
37. Report of Rev. Louis DeCailly on the Newark investigation,

Notes - Chapter V

June 5, 1872, Archives, Diocese of Columbus.
38. Mullay p 128.

Chapter V - Clergy, Journeys, and the Rosecrans Family

1. *In Memoriam* p 10.
2. *Columbian* Jan. 2, 1879.
3. *Columbian* Oct. 24, 1878.
4. CRSB Oct. 2014 p 276, "Rev. Christopher L. Pindar (1842-1906)."
5. CRSB Jan. 2015, conclusion of "The Early Years of St. Sylvester Parish, Zaleski."
6. 18 documents in Kinneally Vol. 10 and one in Vol. 13.
7. SHR to PF, Aug. 17, 1854, (referred to at Kinnealy II/807).
8. CRSB April 2011, "A Priestly Life of no 'Light Trials' Rev. William O'Reilly (1843-1890)."
9. CRSB May and July 2009, "Rev. Jeremiah A. Murray (1844-1924)."
10. O'Daniel & Coffey p 229.
11. The Catholic Directory lists Father Sheehy, but see O'Daniel & Coffey p 221.
12. *The New Lexington Democratic Herald*, December 5, 1872. In *The American Dominicans*, (New York: Saint Martin de Porres Guild, 1970) Dominican Father Reginald Coffey mischaracterized this transfer. He wrote that the Dominican visitator, Father Burke, turned over to the bishop all the Dominican parishes and missions in in the diocese except St. Joseph's; Holy Trinity, Somerset; and St. Thomas, Zanesville. He wrote that the properties, though of considerable value, were transferred to the bishop without cost to the Diocese of Columbus. (page 437) Even setting aside the fact that that the Dominicans had little or no investment in the properties, for the lands had been donated or purchased by the congregations and the churches built by the efforts of the people, this was not a fair characterization. The church lot in New Lexington was not transferred until 1887, to Bishop Watterson of Columbus. The 3 1/2 acres at McLuney were not transferred to Bishop Watterson until 1896, after the church had been closed and abandoned. The one acre at

South Fork was held in the name of the Literary Society of St. Joseph until Bishop Griffin, in the Society's name, transferred it to the township trustees in 2001. It is not clear that the Dominicans ever had legal title to St. Patrick's, Junction City, for if Alexander Clark gave them a deed for the property they neglected to have it recorded at the court house. The county records to this day do not list an owner of the original four acres at that site.

13. O'Daniel and Coffey p 226.
14. O'Daniel p 365. SHR to JBP, Jan. 22, 1872, UNDA. Hartley p 150. Kinneally IX/420, 1653, and 1640.
15. Based on the funeral sermon by Rt. Rev. Thomas Foley, *In Memoriam* p 25. Kinneally IX/389 and Archives, Diocese of Columbus. *Telegraph* June 2, 1869.
16. *Telegraph* Jan. 13, 1870. *New Orleans Morning Star and Catholic Messenger* Mar. 13, 1870. James J. Hennesey, *The First Council of the Vatican*...[New York]: Herder and Herder, 1963, pp 24-25. *Telegraph*, April 28, 1870. Archives of the College of Mt. St. Joseph, Delhi, O. *Telegraph* Apr. 21, 1870, from the *New Orleans Morning Star.*
17. *Telegraph* Mar. 31, 1870.
18. Hennesey, op. cit., pp 24 and 31. Hecker to Orestes Brownson, June 18, 1869, UNDA.
19. John Farina, *An American Experience of God*, New York: Paulist Press, 1981, p 138. John Farina, ed., *Hecker Studies*, New York: Paulist Press, 1983, p 27.
20. SHR to JBP, Aug. 16, 1870, UNDA, Purcell Papers.
21. SHR to JBP, Aug. 25, 1870, UNDA, Purcell Papers. Hennesey, op. cit., pp 302-303.
22. *Columbian* special edition, Apr. 10, 1925, p 29.
23. *New Orleans Morning Star and Catholic Messenger* Aug. 30, 1868. See account from *Telegraph* in Brown County p 162.
24. *Stark County Democrat* July 6 and 13, 1870. *Telegraph* July 7, 1870.
25. A page of notes, apparently from newspaper clippings, perhaps from the *Freemans Journal* - Department of Special Collections, The Library, UCLA. *Nashville Union and American* May 26, 1872. Joseph McSorley, *Father

Hecker and his Friends, St. Louis & London: B. Herder, 1953. General Rosecrans Papers, Special Collection No. 663, UCLA Research Library, Los Angeles, Box 107, Folder 8; cited by HEM in CRSB Apr. 1979 p 405.
26. *Saratoga Sentinel* Sept. 3, 1874. Why Bishop Rosecrans was asked to officiate at Lake George is a mystery. The only remote connection that has been found is that the deceased pastor of Saratoga Springs, some 30 miles to the south, had been Rev. Daniel B. Cull (c. 1813-1873., uncle of Rev. Daniel B. Cull (1848-1888. of the Diocese of Columbus.
27. *Columbian* May 22, 1875.
28. *Columbian* May 27, 1876. *Brown County* pp 201-208ff.
29. *New York Tribune* June 27, 1878.
30. Lily Rosecrans Toole, "*In Memoriam.* Anita Dolores Rosecrans." *Contributions to the Historical Society Of Montana*, Volume 5 (Helena, 1904).
31. Lamers 45. *Personal Memoirs of Major-General D. S. Stanley, U. S. A.* Cambridge: Harvard University Press, 1917, p 158.
32. A biographical sketch of Father Rosecrans appears in Joseph McSorley, *Father Hecker and His Friends*; St. Louis and London: B. Herder, 1953, pp 143 ff.
33. Letter from New York, Nov. 2, 1878 in *The Catholic Columbian*, Nov. 7, 1878. A longer and more involved account of this incident from the General appears in *In Memoriam*, p 33. According to the latter account, the bishop was writing not an article but a pamphlet.
34. A page of notes, apparently from newspaper clippings, Department of Special Collections, The Library, UCLA; *Columbian*, Dec. 25, 1875. *Brown County* pp 192-201 and 213. *The Cambria Freeman* Aug. 24, 1877, and others.
35. *Columbian* Apr. 4 and Sept. 12, 1878.
36. See CRSB 1993, pp 246-249, 252-252, 275, and 277.
37. *Brown County* p 186.

Chapter VI - Academies for Young Women
1. Funeral Sermon, *In Memoriam* pp 26-27.
2. *Telegraph* Aug. 20, 1862.
3. *Telegraph* Oct. 23, 1867.

4. Mullay pp 65-68 and 133.
5. Burton p 86.
6. *Telegraph* May 27 and July 1, 1868.
7. Burton pp 92-93.
8. SHR to Miss Eva Watkins, Sept. 11, 1872 and Jan. 3, 1873 and note "To Rose" Leonard, dated May 18, 1872, UNDA. Poem for Eva Watkins Mooney, 1872, published later in *Grail* magazine.
9. Kiefer, *At the Springs* pp 30 and 39.
10. Mullay p 110.
11. *Columbian* Nov. 7, 1878.
12. CRSB, Vol. XVIII No. 8, Aug. 1993, "The Dominican Sisters of the Sacred Heart and Sacred Heart Academy", part 3.
13. Mullay p 113.
14. Burton pp 112-113.
15. Mullay p 114.
16. *Columbian* July 8, 1876 and June 27, 1878, per Feth 68 and 71.
17. Sr. Vincent Feth, S.N.D. de N., *A History of the Sisters of Notre Dame in Columbus, The First Fifty Years, 1855-1905*, Thesis, Xavier University. "The Early Years in Columbus of the Sisters of Notre Dame de Namur," information taken from the same, in CRSB, July and August 1980.
18. Hartley p 579. CRSB, Oct. 1983, "The Early Years of St. Aloysius Academy, New Lexington."
19. The Sisters paid Father Eis back many years later. This and others of his actions caused complications that plagued relations between Father Eis and Bishops Watterson and Moeller many years into the future. See the "Rev. John B. Eis, Intractable Rector of Columbus Sacred Heart," CRSB Jan. Feb., Apr. and June 1987.

Chapter VII - Institutions and New Parishes

1. See CRSB July/August 1983, "The Early Days of St. Francis Hospital in Columbus" by Donald M. Schlegel.
2. Hartley 593-595
3. Kelly & Kirwin p 238.
4. CRSB, Jan., Feb., Mar. 1981, "Saint Aloysius Seminary, Columbus, 1871-1876."

Notes - Chapter VIII

5. *Telegraph* Mar. 31, 1869.
6. Hartley pp 583-590. CRSB Oct. 2002, "A Suggestion from Heaven: How the Sisters of St. Francis of Penance and Christian Charity came to the Diocese of Columbus."
7. *Columbian* Aug. 28 and Sept. 4, 1875 and May 16, 1878. Hartley p 585.
8. Per a newspaper tribute of sometime after 1912. The 1977 Holy Family Parish centennial booklet names Sister Mary Paul, Sister Stanislaus, Sister Teresa, and Sister Agnes as as the parish school's first teachers, not those of the earlier boys' school.
9. Rev. Andrew Arnold Lambing, *Brief Biographical Sketches of the Deceased Bishops and Priests who Labored in the Diocese of Pittsburgh...*, Pittsburgh: Republic Bank Note Co., 1914.
10. "Holy Family Columbus Ohio" manuscript by Mother Genevieve Ryan, page 2; courtesy of Kathleen M. Washy, Archivist, Sisters of St. Joseph of Baden.
11. *Columbus Evening Dispatch* quoted in the *Cambria Freeman* of May 4, 1877.
12. *Ohio State Journal* Nov. 3, 1874. CRSB June 1979, "Mt. Calvary Cemetery, Columbus, Early History and Early Records."
13. Franklin Co. Incorporation Record I/253. Lee I/444.
14. Reprinted in the *Columbian*, Nov. 7, 1878.
15. *The Vinton Record* Dec. 16, 1869.
16. *Telegraph* Sept. 9, 1868.
17. *Telegraph* Dec. 9, 1868.
18. *Telegraph* Apr. 28 and June 30, 1870.
19. *Columbus Dispatch* July 1, 1871.
20. *Telegraph* Nov. 9, 1871. *Columbian* Oct. 7 and 14, 1876.
21. *Columbian* June 28, 1878.

Chapter VIII - St. Joseph Cathedral,

1. Lee II/648.
2. CRSB Jan. 2012, "How Bishop Moeller Wiped out the 'Nightmare' Debt of the Diocese—or Did He?" pp 1-2. In Bishop Rosecrans's 1872 Sketch of St. Joseph's Cathedral, discussing the cost of the building, a pledged amount of

$24,868 is mentioned. The difference of $12,132, with rounding of the $37,000 figure, seems to adequately represent the cost of the lots.
3. CRSB May 2015, "The Works of Michael Harding (1823-1895), Columbus Contractor and Architect." Norviel.
5. John R. Grabb, *St. Mary's Parish—150 Years in Chillicothe, Ohio, 1837-1987*, Chillicothe: St. Mary's Church, 1986, p 13, citing the Scioto Gazette of Aug. 25, 1869.
6. *Daily Ohio Statesman* June 14, 1866.
7. Lee II/649, section on the Catholic Church written by Rev. Dennis A. Clarke.
8. Rosecrans to Purcell, Mar. 29, 1867, UNDA.
9. Ohio State Journal July 15, 1868.
10. Brooks was arrested in November 1867, charged with fraud in connection with the embezzlement of lumber and brick from the state project by the asylum's main architect. The charges against Brooks were dropped in December 1867 for "insufficiency of the affidavit." (*Daily Ohio Statesman* Nov. 21, Dec. 12, Dec. 19, 1867, May 16, June 22, 1868) But hearings held by the State Legislature brought out evidence that clearly indicated his involvement. (*Official Report of the Proceedings and Debates of the Third Constitutional Convention of Ohio* (1873), Vol. 1, pp 282-285 ff; quoting a *Report of the Select Committee of the House relative to frauds in the erection of the new Deaf and Dumb Asylum*) *Architecture Columbus*, p 82. *Ohio-An Architectural Portrait*; West Summit Press, 1973, p 252. Yet he continued to work on the local scene for a time. He was architect of the Sessions Block at Long and High, built in 1868. (Studer p 551) He was architect for the Columbus City Hall on State Street, built from May of 1869 to March, 1872, and for Towers Hall at Otterbein University in Westerville, built from 1870 to 1872.
11. *Sketch*.
12. Norviel.
13. Studer p 173. Norviel.
14. Norviel. Brooks' design of the Columbus City Hall, completed in 1868, included no such buttress and left room for a large, central window in the third story of the facade

Notes - Chapter IX

to light the public hall. The city hall design was not a clean one, combining Gothic, Second Empire, Renaissance, and a touch of Romanesque style. By the early 1900s it was being decried as the ugliest building in town. (Bill Arter, *Columbus Vignettes*, III/72, Columbus: Nida-Eckstein, 1969).

15. *Columbian* Jan. 20, 1906.
16. Mullay p 90, based on a manuscript prepared by Sr. Evangela Schilder.
17. M. M. Meara, *Columbian*, Jan. 20, 1906. Mr. Fahy died on January 12, 1906 and is buried with his family in Mt. Calvary Cemetery Cathedral section, 111-B.
18. Hartley p 149, based on Studer.
19. *Telegraph* Jan. 15, 1868.
20. Cf. note 2.
21. Studer p 172.
22. *Sketch*
23. SHR to Eva Watkins (probably) Jan. 3, 1873, St. Mary's of the Springs, typescript of letter in UNDA.
24. *Sketch*
25. Lee II/651-652.
26. *Ohio State Journal* Oct. 21, 1878.
27. Kelly and Kirwin place Bishop William McCloskey of Louisville in the sanctuary and omit Kain. But Kain and not McCloskey was at Rosecrans's funeral, per the *Columbian*.
28. Cf note 25
29. Kelly & Kirwin p 239.
30. *Ohio State Journal* Oct. 21, 1878.
31. This and the following excerpts and statements are from Lee II/651-653 and *In Memoriam* p 13.

Chapter IX - This Life's End

1. *In Memoriam* p 12.
2. *The Cambria Freeman* Aug. 24, 1877. *Philadelphia Enquirer* before August 29, 1877.
3. *Brown County* pp 213-214.
4. *Columbian* Aug. 22, 1878.
5. Letter, SHR to WSR, Department of Special Collections, The

Library, UCLA.
6. *Telegraph*, reprinted in *Columbian*, Nov. 1, 1878.
7. *Columbian* Oct. 24, 1878.
8. *In Memoriam* p 12 with additions.
9. Account in the *Ohio State Journal*, corrected as necessary and reprinted in the *Columbian*, Oct. 24, 1878. *In Memoriam* pp 13-15.
10. Full account in *The Catholic Columbian*. Lee II/653-4. *In Memoriam* pp 16-32.
11. *In Memoriam* p 11.

Selected Public Words of Bishop Rosecrans

The folowing is a sample of the 613 items that comprise the known public words of Bishop Rosecrans. They have been chosen to illustrate some of the major points of the wide range of subjects on which he spoke and wrote and the styles of his sermons, lectures, and editorials. It is hoped that the entire corpus will be made available in digital form. Each item is identified as to type of work, source, and date. Editorial titles enclosed in brackets [ ] have been supplied for those originally published without title. Sermon Books 1 and 2 are bound volumes of manuscripts in the Archives, Diocese of Columbus.

Sermon, Book 1, No. 17
Charity and the Last Judgment
The coming of the last day, although known only to God, will be preceded by many signs in the material world. First there will be terrible earthquakes, wars, famines and pestilences, such as were never witnessed before, which shall fill society with fright and confusion. Next signs shall appear in the Heavens, the stars disappearing from their places in space and making the nights strangely and unnaturally dark. After that the sun shall be suddenly darkened and the moon will cease to give her light, leaving the nations with failing hearts, and wild foreboding, shrouded in rayless gloom. Then a fire shall break forth on the earth and, directed by God's almighty power, will run all over the earth and consume all its cities and fields, its houses and ships, its forests, its money, its merchandize, dry up its lakes and rivers, and reduce it to a heap of cinders and ashes. Then, at last, the

trumpet of the Archangel shall sound, that is, the command of God will be given in the twinkling of an eye, the dead will rise each in his own body and appear in the valley. The world has been compared to a great field of death, a vast cemetery holding in its bosom the dead of a thousand generations, for every single man that walks living on its surface. This vast cemetery shall suddenly swarm with life. The ashes that were scattered ages ago shall be gathered together; bone shall be fitted to bone joint to joint, and all the generations shall live again. They shall come from the four winds of Heaven, from the sea whose angry waves buried them in storms, from the bowels of the earth in which they were swallowed by earthquakes, from the grave in the quiet churchyard in which they were laid by mourning friend, from the pit into which they were thrust on the battlefield. They of old times and they of modern times shall meet together. The king shall stand cowering by the peasant; the master will be of the same rank with the servant; the philosopher and the fool shall await their turn side by side; all the children of Adam of all colors, ranks, ages, sexes, qualities, mingled in one undistinguishable shuddering mass, shall stand together in the valley looking out with sadness on the ashes of the desolated earth, and with trembling on the shining countenance of their Judge.

Brethren, you and I will be there together in that crowd. You and I will be there to witness the desolation of the world, there to see the vindication of God's Justice, the triumphant assertion of his supreme dominion over all creatures, to have recounted to our shame our evil thoughts, words, and deeds. Our eyes shall see that great multitude of men and Angels; our hearts shall sink in the presence of that awful majesty; in our flesh we shall see God. There we shall stand, how long hence I know not, but one day, together, on the verge of two lives, the one finished, the other commencing, stripped of our wealth, learning, dignity, reputation, leveled with the poorest, having brought with us through the wrecks of the burnt up world only the burthen of the deeds we have done in the body, awaiting the decision that will settle, without appeal, whether we shall go to the left hand into an eternity of pain or the right into an eternity of rest. There we shall stand, in the valley, Hell open

Charity and the Last Judgment

beneath us, Heaven glowing with light above us, on either side of us the unnumerable multitude of men and angels, before us in midair the Cross planted, the Throne set, the Book open, and the great God in the garments of his awful glory seated to judge.

In that day of wrath, of calamity, of confusion and terror, what, beloved friends, shall we have to console us a little in our unutterable agony, to prevent us from crying out in our shame and remorse, to the mountains to fall upon us and to the hills to cover us and hide us from the awful presence of the majesty our sins have outraged? I fear we shall find no consolation in the memory of our lives on earth. From the first dawning of the light of reason in our souls, to the end of our lives, we ought to have spent all our time and talents, our influence, every thought, word, action in giving glory to God. The knowledge of this standard of our duties will be written on our souls then in characters of light. And as we remember all the days of our life on earth, days in which we forgot God, to think only of money and pleasure and reputation, our time lost in vanity, our actions vicious, our words profane, obscene and idle, our thoughts selfish, vain, ambitious, impure, and contrast what we have done with what we should have done, remorse will seize upon us and terror will overwhelm us. Alas, who, in the confidence of innocence, shall face the living God, in whose eyes even the angels are not pure? In what then may we hope? Only in the cross, only in the mercy of Jesus Christ. How shall we cling to the Cross, how shall we hope in the mercy? How can we effect, that from his awful eye will descend on us the beam of pity and not the lightning flash of wrath? Ah! if that eye in singling us out in the midst of the multitude can recognize in us one who in the days of his sorrow on earth comforted, who in the person of his poor fed him, clothed him, visited him, one who used the perished treasures of earth for his on honor and according to his will, its sternness will relax and a smile of benignity like a gleam of sunshine darting athwart an angry winter sky will illuminate his divine countenance.

He has declared long ago that Charity to the poor was the test virtue by which He was going to judge all men. He has told us that those who are kind to the poor, who feed them when they are hungry, clothe them when they are naked, visit them when they are sick and in prison, shall be taken by him into a kingdom prepared for them from the foundation of the world; and that on the contrary, those who have been hard hearted to the poor shall be driven from his presence, accursed, into everlasting fire.

Beloved friends, we have lost our baptismal innocence and our only chance of salvation is in sincere repentance. But sincere penance [repentance] cannot exist where there is no charity. We cannot be forgiven much unless we love much. Our salvation therefore depends upon our right performance of the duty of Charity.

Let not any of you be startled at hearing charity called a duty. Let no one wonder that I assert that in contributing today, bountifully, for the relief of the poor of your city, he is not doing an unnecessary act of generosity but one of strict obligation, and that if he refused to give out of his abundance, he would violate the law of God.

Duty is, unfortunately, a cold, harsh word and I fear that in appealing to your charity on the ground of obligation I do no service to the poor who are waiting for the returns of your generosity. I fear that many cares for the future, many pretexts of worldly prudence may arise in your mind to withhold the gift, which cares and pretexts would have been forgotten, in the glow of awakened tenderness, and excited compassion. Still, sorry as I am that the poor should suffer through my want of prudence and tact, I should be sorrier still to have you give anything under the false impression that you were doing thereby a work of supererogation, an action with you discretionary, and even profusion. Sorry as I should be if the widow and the orphan must sigh unrelieved, the sick still pine for want of nourishment, attendance, or medicine, I would regret much more if through any neglect or human respect of mine you should go to the Judgment Seat to learn that almsgiving is a duty.

There, according to the testimony of our Lord in His Gospel, some shall be told to go away into everlasting fire, for not having given help and consolation to the distressed and miserable. Now the most merciful and just Lord cannot be capable of punishing with eternal fire, any one for not having done that which he was not bound to do. It is certain therefore that to give alms is a duty, and to refuse them to the needy is a crime.

If it were not, how could the Providence of God be vindicated, how could the equality of men be established, the hopeless misery in which some by birth, sickness, misfortune, circumstances beyond their control, be reconciled with the equal love God bears to all? We are told by our religion that we are all children of the same Father, bought by the blood of the same Redeemer, stewards of the same Master as we shall be culprits before the same Judge. From the fact, therefore, that some are born poor and needy and others are given much worldly goods, it follows necessarily that the rich must practice liberality towards the poor, must relieve out of their abundance the wants of the indigent. In the world no family is called poor, until all the members of it are reduced to distress. So the great human family is never poor so long as there are rich people, who might relieve the wants of the poor out of their superabundance. The bond of brotherhood has to be cemented by the spontaneous care which the strong and the wealthy exercise over the feeble and poverty-stricken.

I do not advocate agrarian laws and a leveling of the rich in order to establish fraternity among men. That fraternity must begin in the heart, and not on the statute book. It must be the fruit of faith, and not the effect of robbery and disorder. The world has mistaken its character and is searching for it now in reforms and benevolent projects for people away off, instead of looking for it in the hearts of men for miseries at home.

Our age is emphatically an age of inconsistency and hypocrisy, of magnificent theories and revolting practice. The world has borrowed the doctrines of the Church, and taking away from them the spirit of Charity, has made them its own, retaining at the same [time] in practice all its native selfishness and meanness. Hence in theory the world proclaims the equality of men, in practice it crouches to and fawns upon the rich and powerful, and avoiding the poor, tells them roughly to remain within their own sphere.

In theory, the world [has] not only Charity but affection and veneration for the laboring classes; in practice it forces those laboring classes to toil on from year's end to year's end, from daylight till long after dark, in damp mines, in suffocating furnace rooms, and pest laden factories, for a pittance that scarcely supports life.

In theory the world weeps over and appoints committees to investigate into the grievances of the needy and distressed, in practice it treats the pauper as a criminal and considers itself over-bountiful in providing him prison room in a poor house. In theory the world denounces every species of servitude as injustice and sin, and is affected to tears in thinking of the romantic sufferings of the Negro race; in practice, the great ones of the world exact a servitude from their dependents, as abject as the wildest freak of tyranny could invent.

In theory, the world advocates fraternity and favors socialism; in practice it pays no alms but in the shape of taxes, it sends Jesus Christ cold and hungry and naked from the door, and afterward gives him a forced relief through the hands of the tax collector.

Yet even the world was not always thus mean and vile and hypocritical. There have been times in which the Catholic Church was the guardian of the poor and the dispenser of every nation's charity. In the times called the Dark Ages, public opinion on this subject was but the expression of religion. Then by the side of the noble cathedral in which the thoughts of men were raised up to Heaven by the grandeur of the edifice, the vast hospital was seen and it was loved because its inmates were the poor, and there was no contumely, no rich man's mockery to pain the hearts of its beneficiaries, because he who entered saw in the object which moved his pity another Christ and all who ministered thought they were sympathizing with the Redeemer. And though these holy ages have gone by, for a time to teach us the folly and tyranny of human wisdom, we have yet surviving in us the spark of faith, to light in us the flame of charity. We ought to feel a sympathy uniting us to the older time and as we pass through the ruins of other ages, where we can still trace amongst them memorials which enable us to conjecture, though fancy cannot equal the reality, the grandeur of the structure ere the Spoiler in his vain attempts to exterminate the builders, expended his rage on the consecrated places which virtue has hallowed as her own and to which religion still points with sorrowing but proud affection; we can see that enough survives to animate us to the duty of Catholic charity, to call upon us to forget the world and to imitate the zeal of our ancestors; and to you my friends, a voice comes forth from the buried past, a voice that pierces through the silence of centuries, a voice which is heard in every Catholic heart today, calling upon you to give glorious testimony to the Charity which wrought such miracles of old, which hung such garlands on the shrines of faith, which covered with perennial flowers the institutions of religion, flowers whose fragrance is not yet extinct and whose beauty casts a glow of brightness over the dark pages of European history.

You are here, from many climes; remember now, what the land of your forefathers did for the poor. Call to mind the monastery, the hospital though now decayed at which the traveler was refreshed, the sick restored to health; wander in spirit by the fountains where the poor were healed by the saints whose memory has consecrated their waters, and to which the pious pilgrim yet resorts, and ask yourselves if with all these endearing recollections thronging upon you, you would not incur a fearful guilt, by an uncatholic heartlessness, if you did not exclaim, by the memory of those times of faith, by the tie of brotherhood that associates me with the men whose Charity originated those might institutions, gorgeous in their very ruins, I will forget my selfishness, my cares for the future today, and when I give with joy my offering to the poor I will think that faith has conquered, that the monastery is restored, that the poor are again welcomed to the gates of the Abbey, that all live again in beauty as in the middle ages, that the vision of sorrow is passed away forever, that the ruins are replaced by a thousand altars sparkling in peace and clouded with incense; and I will exult in the thought that the glory, of which my Charity makes me a participant, is a glory that shall not pale even in the presence of the Sun of Justice, but like the light of morning shall go on from brightness to brightness unfading forever!

Those were times in which, whatever be said of their political institutions, the doctrine of the equality of men, of the fraternity of our race was not expressed in cold soulless words, written in pamphlets and newspapers, but in the hearts of men; the sentiment of respect for and sympathy with the poor was not the hollow catchword of the demagogue, the sounding brass on which the sanguinary Revolutionist beats the shrill tocsin of civil war, and robbery and arson, but the deep, sincere, heart-felt feeling of faith that made the rich sacrifice their possessions to relieve the poor, that caused kings and popes to doff their purple and wash the feet of the penniless travelers and to minister to the wants of the children of poverty as they would have ministered to the wants of Christ.

In those days men showed their affection for the poor not by getting them to subscribe revolutionary and Reformation funds, but by giving them money and service that cost sacrifice and did not win popularity. Those were times when Charity was Charity, when it came pure from selfish taint gushing from the depths of the faithful self-sacrificing heart that made the relief of the poor not a measure of political economy, not a suggestion of public decency, but a sacred duty, enjoined by Christ, fraught with the promise of eternal rewards.

Those times, beloved friends, will rise in judgment against us, if recreant to the spirit we acquiesce in the world's doctrine, that not God but fortune has given us an abundance of worldly goods, that we can therefore spend what we possess in our pleasures, our luxuries, the gratification of our caprices, that what we bestow on the poor is a gratuitous bounty to be rid of disagreeable importunities, or to be in fashion with our charitable neighbors.

If, forgetful of the teachings of faith, we spend our superabundance in building elegant houses, in purchasing costly furniture, in dressing richly and faring sumptuously, leaving meanwhile the poor to pine in hunger and want, we shall be confronted face to face with thousands of those who have given not only their superfluity but their all to the poor, and be covered with shame in their presence.

If, imbued with the maxims of a shallow conventionalism, we imagine that it does not become us to be seen in the dwelling of the poor, or that our nerves will not bear the shock of contact with the diseased and suffering in filthy garrets and dark cellars, we shall be undeceived with remorse, in the day of Judgment, by a host of men and women, more highly born and more delicately nurtured than we, who will step forth from the crowd and point to the steps they have taken, the sacrifices they have made, the disgusts endured, the wounds they have dressed, the sicknesses they have nursed, now shining like gems in the crown that shall bind their brows forever, to demonstrate to us that the pretext on which we indulged our self-love and sloth was vain and frivolous.

If we take up with the common idea of the day and consider the demands of charity satisfied by poor-houses and city hospitals, where the needy are imprisoned and made to feel at every step that they are a burthen on the public; if we persuade ourselves that this cold ministration to material want, accompanied as it is with the crushing of self respect and the annihilation of every delicate sensibility, is all that is required of us, the founders of abbey, the humble laborers in the hospitals and monasteries, the pious confraternities, the popes and cardinals and kings, who have washed the feet of the poor and served the table at which beggars were eating, the noble men and women who like St. Elizabeth of Hungary and St. Camillus of Lellis, who spent their lives in working among the sick and destitute, will rise up in long array against us and exclaim, "So the heartless philanthropy that gives prison hospitality to the penniless traveler, sending him up as a vagrant, that from the luxurious parlor pays a pittance for a hireling to nurse the sick, that deals grudgingly out the contumelious bread bought by taxation, is not enough to satisfy the heart that burns with the Charity of Jesus Christ and that Charity pants to be among the poor, to nurse them console them, feel for them, bear with them, give them, nay sacrifice all for them for the sake of their Redeemer and lover Jesus Christ," and as they so speak, how will the memory of sensual, selfish, useless, frivolous lives, which despite of the teaching of your faith we led, fill us with sorrow and remorse!

Regard therefore almsgiving as a duty and whatever you give, give it not with the thought that you are performing an unnecessary work that shows your generosity to men and ensures you acceptance with God, but in the full firm Catholic belief that in giving to the poor you are but rendering to Jesus Christ what is His own, that even after you have given, you are still but unprofitable servants, having done that which it was your duty to do, that you are still far from perfection, not having as yet gone and sold all you had and given it to the poor, to follow Jesus.

But while you give in a spirit of humility, as the fulfillment of your duty in imitation of your glorious Catholic ancestors, I would not have you, beloved friends, ignorant or forgetful of the great reward that awaits your alms. It is precisely the fulfillment of duties that our Lord delights to reward. I would have you remember with consolation the kingdom prepared from the foundations of the world, for those who practice the corporal works of mercy, and be animated by the thought of the last day to fulfill this duty with joy.

Every good work we perform has annexed to it the promise of eternal life. Every prayer we breathe, every step we take for the love of God, every word we utter that suggests good thoughts in others is set down by the record and in the Judgment day will appear before us in sweet consoling array; but foremost in the ranks of these will appear our works of mercy to the poor. They shall sparkle before us like gems about to be set by our Divine Judge in the crown of glory that shall bind our brows forever, its bright and most splendid ornaments, both because Charity is the virtue dearest to the heart of God and because Charity, like light, piercing and pervading all, makes ours the merits of others.

Who that has reflected but for a moment on the ways of God as revealed by religion does not know that the virtue he most prizes is Charity? "I came to put fire on the earth," said Jesus Christ; and the fire He came on the earth to enkindle was the fire of Charity. He was putting fire on the earth, when He was born in stable for love of us, when He lived a life of mortification and poverty among the poor, teaching them, healing their sick, raising their dead to life, whispering hope of a better life, guiding them to obtain it. He was kindling fire on the earth when, stripped of this world's goods, of His honor among men, in the midst of the buffets and mocking of savage enemies, He was nailed to the cross and lifted up to die for love of us.

The fire was kindled there on Calvary and it burned in the hearts of his Apostles and Martyrs, when they braved the wit of philosophers, the satire of poets, the cruelty of emperors, the fury of mobs, to die for His name; it burned in the hearts of his Saints and confessors ever since, and its holy flame, flashing and gleaming through the thick darkness of the world's impurities, from a few holy hearts, is all that the earth now contains to delight the eye of God, is all that stays the outstretched arm of his Justice, and prevents him from permitting the awful Judgment to begin today.

Charity therefore being the virtue dearest to the heart of God, with what joy will he welcome to his bosom those who upon earth have practiced it with zeal.

"Come, ye blessed of my Father," He will say to those who according to their mercy have always honored the unfortunate. "Come, inherit the kingdom prepared for you from the foundation of the world. It was not in vain that I taught you the precept of charity by word and by example; it was not in vain that I told you to consider the poor as our brethren, entitled to your respect and veneration on the very grounds for which the world avoids them. It was not in vain that my ministers repeated to you to look upon the goods of this world as given to you to buy the treasures in heaven, through the hands of the poor. It was not in vain that I purchased for you, at the price of my Blood, the grace to be lifted up far above all, all worldly considerations and to love your neighbor as yourself with a supernatural love. You have done well. Fear not. There is no judgment for you but only heaven. Put off your anxiety, raise up your eyes, and see beyond those ranks upon ranks of holy angels, shining in the light of Heaven. Those heavenly palaces, those houses not made with hands, in those fields of brightness afar, there amid those floods of glory will dazzle your eyes, where there is no poverty, nor wrong, nor suffering, nor temptation, nor want, nor sadness, nor weeping, there in peace, in tranquility, in security, inebriated with torrents of delight, every desire content, every craving satisfied in the

Devotion to Truth

midst of the citizens of Heaven, you shall reign forever. Come ye blessed of my Father etc. etc."

Oh my brethren, shall we not do today what is necessary in order that these consoling words be addressed to us, in that awful day? Jesus Christ is cold and hungry and sick and in prison in our midst today. He is cold and hungry in the person of the poor mendicant just from the old country, whose ragged and filthy [clothes] scarcely cover, much less protect his shivering limbs and who cannot stop long enough to warm himself in any respectable shop lest customers should be driven away by disgust at this appearance. He is hungry in the person of the poor widow with her little ones who, wan with fasting and haggard with vigils, after having sold the last trinket that reminded her of happier days to buy food for her orphans, is at last reduced to the necessity of applying for relief to the priests, or to the sisters. He is sick in the person of those who are lying parched with fever in garrets and cellars, more consumed by neglect and bad air, than by disease, [who] are waiting to see if after today the Bishop will not be able to help to buy medicine and restore them to health.

Jesus Christ is in our midst in the person of the abandoned, desolate poor, cold, hungry, sick. Shall we clothe him, feed him, nurse him into health?

Beloved friends it is for you to answer by the generosity with which you contribute to the collection for their support, this day.

Nor is the reward which Jesus Christ holds out to those who are kind to His poor, in direct recompense, the only fruit of generosity to the distressed. Charity stands not like other good works alone, upon its own merits.

It is a queen among virtues; and like a queen must always have its train. Charity diffused through the heart and poured out upon our neighbors returns to us freighted with all the holiness of other [?]. Like the bee among the opening flowers of spring, it contrives to gather sweet from every rose and make honey in every bower, though hedged with thorns. Whatever there is good in the heart is evoked by gratitude. And when we give, there is a God bless you that wells up from the heart, so fervent that even though it be the first prayer for years, it is of priceless value. We are saved by prayer; and as our prayers are short and imperfect and full of distractions, oh how much of our salvation may depend upon the prayers of others.

Our charity for the poor will go to purchase for us petitions more fervent, more earnest, than any we can offer.

Editorial, *The Catholic Telegraph and Advocate*, October 29, 1853

The Sifting of the Wheat

In the old fashion of winnowing grain we have often noticed the energy with which the winnower hurled the chaff and grain together into the air. From his manner you would judge that he intended to cast away from him entirely and leave to the mercy of the winds the whole mass. Yet his only object was to cast it far up into the air in order that the wind may sweep away all the chaff, and the effect of his action was a more thorough cleaning of the wheat the more furiously it was tossed.—Such, it seems to us, is the providence of God, in the calamities with which He visits His Church. He casts far from Him, as it were in wrath, both the evil and the good. He hurls far away into the winds of adversity, both those who "worship Him in spirit and in truth," and those who by a bad practice belie the sanctity of their belief. But, like the winnower, He has no intention of losing the wheat. He knows the strength of the gale and that it will only bear away the chaff, leaving the wheat to be "gathered into the garners." And so, when the adversity is over we find the good and the evil separated. The good are chastened and purified and elevated above earthly things; the bad are carried by the gale into the barren deserts of infidelity, or open heresy.

In the hour of her prosperity the Church is courted by worldlings. Aspirants to power fawn upon her in order to acquire place, and Judases creep into the very sanctuary in search of gold. Fashion kneels before her altars with assumed devotion; and Pleasure makes the sign of the cross at the beginning of voluptuous revels. But when adversity comes, the good and the earnest are left alone. The ambitious seek distinction in the ranks of her enemies; the avaricious aim at the pay of champions against her. The vain win applause by flippantly decrying her; and the sensual stifle their remorse of conscience by insulting her in the midst of their beastly orgies. So God purifies His Church; so from time to time during the ages He places the world, the flesh and the devil outside the walls of His holy city. He allows her to lose credit with the world, influence, power, wealth; and forthwith the place seekers, the gold-hunters, the fashion-courters—an unclean herd—like the swine mentioned in the Gospel, as constrained "to run violently into the sea," issue tumultuously and in hot haste from her midst, and rush into the ocean of unbelief.

This we have seen and do see, every day. What a herd of impure wretches, who had drawn a sacrilegious subsistence from the sanctuary, were unmasked in the late misfortune of the Church in Italy! See the terrible career of those men who, had no political convulsion ever taken place in Italy, to reduce ecclesiastical wealth and dignity, would have hidden their wickedness from their acquaintances, and lived and died in the outward communion of the Church! Without adversity the Church would yet have ministering at her altars (frightful thought!) such men as Achilli and Gavazzi; and participating of the sacrament of love, such ministers of hate as Mamiani and Cicerowhaichio.

So in this country, we are indebted to adversity that our Catholics are so fervent and earnest, and so little afflicted by the sight of scandals in their midst. The Church in America is exposed on every side to attacks, as the oak on the mountain's brow has to buffet with every wind of heaven. And as that oak is stripped of its withered leaves, and has its sapless twigs carried away as fast as they decay, so the Church is cleansed by adverse circumstances from the contact of the unprincipled and [is] preserved from the profanation of hypocrites.

Editorial, *The Catholic Columbian*, May 1, 1875

May.

All that is belongs to the Son of Mary. Fire, hail, snow, frost, dew, with all the other forces and phenomena of nature do His will. As when one sees a standard waving he looks for the standard-bearer; or, as one hearing the report of a gun looks under the smoke for him who discharged it, so we, in witnessing all the changes in sky, earth, and air, as the seasons follow each other, ought to be led to think of Him whose power and wisdom effect those changes, in time and measure. Winter He has chosen for the season in which we ought to remember Himself—the little helpless babe of Bethlehem—and had he not chosen to be born in the cold, the bleak skies, the howling winds, the ice-fettered waters, and the fierce storms might have suggested to us His anger and our impenitence, and the terrible ruin awaiting all who die at enmity with Him. As it is we remember nothing but our misery and His compassion, and the sweet work of showing mercy to His poor.

But when May comes the ice-fetters are broken, the skies are serene, the breezes are balmy, the fields and forests put on their verdure, and the bright flowers everywhere gladden the sight. How natural at this season to think of the author of all beauty, and her whom He has chosen for its Queen!

She is the only one of the daughters of Eve who is all beautiful in the eyes of God. Chosen to be His mother, she is, by that, raised above all the ranks of the Saints and all the choirs of the Angels, and her loveliness is made to accord with her exalted rank. She holds throughout eternity the same relation to Him as when in the Temple she said, "Son, why hast thou done this?" or when at the marriage feast she said, "They have no wine;" or when, standing at the foot of the cross, her soul was pierced by the spear that gashed His side. "What He once took He never put away." His human nature and all that belong to it remain His, evermore. What she can ask therefore He will never refuse to grant.

What graces, therefore, may we not hope for during the Jubilee this month. Let us ask them without fear and continually, for ourselves and for those we love. It would be a very good thing if the confraternities, during this month, would beg the grace of conversion for those who are staying away from the Sacraments in their respective congregations, and also for those outside the Church. There are so many upright and sincere people whose lives seem to plead for them, that who knows how great a number may be moved to take the one step needed to place them inside the Church of Jesus Christ, if we only pray for them.

But our lives must accord with our words, in order to make our prayers acceptable and efficacious. Let each one do what he can to put the vices of drunkenness, cursing, impurity and uncharitableness away from all Catholic people. Let each one remember to adorn the altar and to be present always at the devotions and instructions and to hear Mass every day in May. We fly to thy patronage, O holy Mother of God.

Sermon at the consecration of Rt. Rev. John L. Spalding as first Bishop of Peoria, May 1, 1877, in St. Patrick's Cathedral, New York, New York, *New York Freeman's Journal and Catholic Register*, May 12, 1877

The Catholic Church a Kingdom.

Today, the Feast of the Apostles SS. Philip and James, when a new member is added to the hierarchy of that kingdom which exists throughout all time, and embraces under its sway every nation, seems a fitting occasion in which to give a simple explanation of the nature of that kingdom. There are Christians who are scandalized at calling the Church of Christ a kingdom at all. They would have it to be a kind of disjointed society—an aggregation of atoms held together only by the thread of human caprice; in fact, capable of being divided into parts, and still remaining the Church of Christ. But our Lord Himself has called it a kingdom. He has described it under many other similes, and in every one of these there is the idea of a rule, of a government. When He established it—when He commissioned the apostles, as this one is commissioned today—He prefaced that commission by saying, "All power is given thee in heaven and on earth." That is, He gave them power. He did not send them forth to preach, simply, but He sent them forth to preach and explain, to lay down the law, to define the truth, and to govern the world. It is essentially in the nature of a government that it have authority, that it have unity, that it have the power to make laws and the power to sanction laws. Now the Church of Christ has these. She represents Him under one peculiar [particular] aspect, for the reign of Christ, who is called the King of Kings, and the Lord of Lords, exists over all things. He is the Lord of nature, and

The Catholic Church a Kingdom

He rules all through nature, because He created it, and He created all causes and He shaped all effects and the forces that produced them. He reigns also in glory over the elect, where He manifests His family, and over the reprobate, where His justice is shown forth. The Church represents Him as far as He reigns by grace, for this is the third kind of kingdom that He possesses over what He has created. The Church is His person, in so far as He rules in that kingdom of grace. All that are saved out of the children of men are saved by her ministrations, and all that are lost of the children of men are lost because she has to bear witness against them. I say the Church represents Him not simply as teacher, for the teacher may be neglected; not simply as the author of morality, for the author of morality may be the bearer of another's message; but she represents Him as the Lawgiver, as the Teacher, as the Redeemer, and in all things accepted as the Judge. This Gospel is to be preached for a testimony, He says, and the Church is the bearer of this testimony. He made the Church a corporate body, an organized system, placing one at the head, and then establishing individual orders of the hierarchy. And this He did, not for the age in which He made St. Peter the Head of the Apostles, and not for the generation—or nation, rather—that understood the language which St. Peter then spoke, but He did it for all nations and for all generations.

He said so in so many words, speaking to the body of the apostles of whom He had already constituted St. Peter the head, and told them to go and teach all nations, "For," said He, "I am with you all days." The idea is plainly expressed there. By saying, "teach all nations," He indicated clearly that it was not to these eleven simply that He was speaking. By saying "all generations," He pointed out how they could increase their band by the sacrament of Holy Orders, and how they could perpetuate it through all times—this race that was to teach all nations and give the law to all men. So He made His Church self-governed, self-sustained, a power within itself and all-sufficient for itself. That is to say, the Church rules in His stead, in His name, in His person. That is what he means when He tells the apostles—for in telling them He told it to all that were to be of their order—"He that hears you hears Me; and he that despises you despises Me." Not as if there was some figure of speech in it by which He would say, "You are such good friends of mine that I will receive any insult offered you as if it were offered to myself, and I will reward any kindness or respect shown to you as if it were shown to Me." He did not mean this. He meant more than this. He meant precisely what He said: "He that hears you hears Me." Because in their teaching capacity and in their law-giving capacity the apostles are Jesus Christ. We can have no scruples, then, in calling the Church a kingdom—that is, a government; and it is the only one that will know no change. But, in order to understand it rightly, we must call to mind the entire doctrine of Christianity—I mean the fundamental doctrine of Christianity—which is expressed very perfectly by St. Paul, that in Christ Jesus neither circumcision nor uncircumcision is of any avail, but "a new creature." See what this means when applied to the Church. In the long line of Roman Pontiffs in the almost endless aggregate of holy bishops and priests and founders of religious orders we read the names and the doctrines of men eminent for their learning, for their saintliness, for their zeal, for their sincerity, for every virtue. But it is not their learning, it is not their zeal, it is not their virtue that have upheld the cause of Jesus Christ in the world. To be sure a society formed among men must be composed of human elements; but in so far as they are men, in so far as their natural capacity, their natural talents, their acquired learning or genius, are concerned they do not constitute the soul of the Church. They are nothing but the outward appearance. But that which gives life to the Church, that which vivifies the whole frame of this vast society, extending as it does in one form, or another, from the first that was saved down to the last when the trumpet shall sound, is the presence of the Holy Ghost, the indwelling of Him who is sent by Jesus Christ to be the soul and life of the Church. In Him nothing is of any worth that is of natural creation, because the whole Church is a supernatural creation. So you see this illustrated in all the sacraments of the Church. When the priest baptizes—that is when he regenerates the soul, cleansing it from the sin in which it was born—he does not pray over the child, "May this soul be cleansed as I wash its body with water," but he says, "I baptize thee in the name of the Father, Son and Holy Ghost." When in the confessional the priest, having heard the penitent accuse himself of all his sins, imparts to him the remission of those sins, he does not pray that those sins may be remitted, but he says, "I absolve thee from thy sins." You see it is not the natural man that speaks, but the new creature. It is the creature of divine grace that says these words. When the priest stands at the altar and performs that most stupendous of all miracles, the changing of the bread and wine into the body and blood of Christ, he does not beseech God that this wine may be changed into His blood, but he says, "This is My body, and this is the chalice of My blood," which would have no meaning unless he really personated Christ—unless in him spoke the living God. And this we believe—that the moment a man is lifted up by the sacrament of holy orders to sacred priesthood that moment, in all the functions that he performs about the altar, in all that he does for the salvation of men, he is no longer a man, but is the minister, the very person of Jesus Christ.

So, when we call the Church of Christ a kingdom it is only to those who are grossly misinformed or who are willfully blind and prejudiced that there is any alarm, as if we spoke of the Church coming into collision with the kingdoms of this world. She is a kingdom—but not of this world. Her power does not originate in this world. It is not as the other kingdoms of the earth are, a power built up on policy, that is built up by war, or the lover of plunder, or the feeling of nationality, or by the astuteness of those men we call statesmen, but it is built up simply by the power of God and upheld by that power. Of all the absurdities that have ever been urged against the Church by those who are determined not to understand what she is, the most absurd seems to me that of those who imagine the Church to rest on the policy, the cunning and the management of the hierarchy throughout the world; for, in the first place, there is no human power, no human wit or shrewdness that could crate that hierarchy, that could ever make a body of men so devoted to one interest as is the hierarchy of the Church. And, in the next place, there is no human policy that could maintain her power and her influence throughout the world, since she had no human arms by which to protect herself. Her doctrine now, today, is as hard to the natural heart, is as difficult to the natural reason, as it was when it was first proclaimed by the apostles, and then it was folly to the Gentiles and a stumbling block to the Jews. Her doctrine is as hard now and as repulsive to natural feelings as it was in the days when our Lord first said, "Let a man deny himself and take up his cross and follow Me." And, though widespread now throughout the world, and including the majority of men calling themselves Christians within her fold, still, so far as human influences are concerned, she is the weakest of all bodies of men—weakest because she never can take up those human arms by which the sects propagate themselves until the time comes when they perish.

But this new creation of God, the Church, can never decay. There is no power in the Church, there is no authority in the Church, there is nothing venerable in the Church which does not belong to this new creation. Of course our Lord accepts the talents of men when they devote themselves to Him; but He does not need them. He accepts the influence of nations when that influence is offered, but He does not need it. He has accepted both extremities—that of the extreme of the prejudice of the people and of the power of governments—I mean He has in His Church; and He has accepted also—experienced, also—days when it was a shame not to be called a Catholic. But in either case the passions and caprices of governments and of men are changing and shifting, quickly passing away, but the Church remains the same now as when the apostles were constituted the body of preachers and lawgivers for the entire world; and so the Church will remain; the Church will never be acknowledged as the head of the temporal power of the earth, because the world will never be worthy of it. She will always be persecuted and always triumphant. The world and its changing opinions and prejudices and governments seem like the ocean in restless moving to and fro, now here and now there; and the Church is like the rock that raises its head above the billows and remains firm forever while the waters are chafing at its base. But it is the nature of the

The Catholic Church a Kingdom

order established by our Lord that St. Peter, the head of the Church, should govern all, and his successor has the same power that he held. He had the control of everything, and he unties all things in himself. Those who were his co-laborers throughout the world, like him, always have guided men when they lacked the power of enforcing the law, and, therefore, let it be no scandal to us to call the Church a kingdom and a government. Let us not be afraid of those who say we must be disloyal to one government if we are loyal to another. We can be loyal to both, and the best and most loyal of citizens is the true Catholic.

In conclusion, let me say to the young chosen one who today has received the episcopal consecration, who goes forth on the same mission and with about the same resources as that undertaken by the apostles, that henceforth he must be alone in the world. His duties, his position, will necessarily make him without any one to lean upon; but all will expect to lean upon him. I congratulate both the Church and him on his accession to the episcopacy, but in how different a sense! The Church—that is, our brethren of the episcopacy and of the clergy—have one in him, coming, as he does, from gens a sacerdotas—a family of priests—who have supported the fabric of our religion in this country and will maintain its honor, not only among Catholics, but will defend it also among those who are not Catholics. We look, therefore, upon him as a gem, literally, in the crown of the Church in America. Our Lord invites him by this consecration* to a closer relationship in His holy family; for truly, when the gold cross is hung around his neck, then the heavy cross of sorrow, disappointment and responsibility will also be hung on his heart. He is to wear the crown of thorns, and it will press more sharply around his brows than if he had never been promoted to this high dignity. Still, as I stand here, and the memories if his boyhood, and of my fresh manhood in the priestly life cluster around me, I can see, better than I could then, reason why we should both feel consoled; for the time is so short it seems but yesterday when we were together at the college—and yet years and years have flown away. So it will be years hence; and when at our dying day we shall look back again and remember where we met, the time then also will seem as if it were but a day—and it is but a day. Oh, my brethren, let us so conduct ourselves that, in looking back upon this dream of our lives, we may never have occasion to regret, but, on the contrary, have occasion to look forward with hope and confidence to Him who is the reward of all good.

* "conversation" as printed in the Journal

Editorial, *The Catholic Columbian*, Oct. 2, 1875
[The Pope's Mission.]

Some eastern journal of high pretensions—whose name we must be excused for forgetting—lately discussed the policy of making an American Cardinal out of the Most Rev. Archbishop of New York (in a friendly way, you know). The editor took in the situation in this way: "Catholicity is on the decline in the old world; the Pope wants to make up for it, by conquests in the new. Will the creation of an American Cardinal effect this object?" He discusses the question sapiently and impartially, and concludes that the effort is vain. Catholicity is going down on both sides of the ocean, and no stroke of policy will save it from being numbered with the past.

Now, if he only knew it, the writer of all this wisdom would almost vote himself a lunatic. Imagine a person standing where he can see a cloud-shadow flitting across a valley, and gravely assuming to understand and weigh the policy of the sun in permitting the shadow to darken the landscape! The See of Peter is as far removed from political vicissitude as the sun is from the clouds and vapors of earth. Politicians can make martyrs of popes, but they can no more touch the papal office, or diminish the influence of the Catholic religion, than they can change the course of the sun. The Holy Father has no policy but to fulfill the mission of Jesus Christ: to teach His revelation and enforce His law in charity, in all lands and through all generations. This is a scandal to the Jews and folly to the Gentiles, but to the believing it is the wisdom of God.

Editorial, *The Catholic Columbian*, Sept. 11, 1875

The Decoration of Our Churches.

The ornamentation of our churches ought to be an object dear to the heart of every Catholic. Penetrated with the spirit of faith, he feels that it is for Almighty God he is doing it. It is to show love for our blessed Lord, who dwells within them, that our costly cathedrals are erected; it is for that same object that all the aesthetic skill of the artist is taxed in decorating them. Feeling as we do, that all we have is from God, we cannot do too much for Him in return. Gratitude and love are two of the noblest sentiments of man's heart. If he really feels that gratitude and love towards God, he will not stop to think of what he has done already, but will consider all that he can do as paltry in comparison with the graces and gifts which he has received. To honor Jesus Christ in the Blessed Sacrament, who deigns to come and dwell in our midst, is the motive which prompts the true Catholic, even to make sacrifices—and our cathedrals and churches stand as lasting monuments of his love and adoration of the Creator of the universe.

Editorial, *The Catholic Columbian*, July 10, 1875

[The Necessity of True Faith.]

There are some really honest men who think that what a man believes has nothing to do with his moral worth. "Creeds and dogmas are all nonsense," they have been saying, ever since David Hume. "Let a man do right, and who cares what he believes?" Now, it is true that a man [can] believe what he ought, and still be a bad man. But a man cannot, without believing as he ought, be good enough to reach salvation. He may be good enough to keep a tavern or be a congressman, but he cannot share the redemption of Jesus Christ. "Without faith it is impossible to be saved." "Unless a man be born of water and the Holy Ghost he shall not enter into the kingdom of God." "He that believeth not shall be condemned." "This is eternal life, that they know Thee, the only true God, and Whom Thou has sent, Jesus Christ."

To those with whom such plain declarations of Holy Writ have no weight, let us say that good works must begin from knowledge, and a full, clear and certain knowledge of what is good and what is evil cannot be in the mind without the light of divine faith. Therefore a man cannot do right in all things without faith. For one's "life to be right" he must have true faith and obey it!

Editorial, *The Catholic Columbian,* January 23, 1875
Devotion to the Sacred Heart.

Devotion to the Sacred Heart of Jesus is often spoken of and practiced, too, amongst us. Its object it so revive in the hearts of Catholics a personal relationship with our Redeemer. He is the true light that enlighteneth every man coming into this world. He is not only the author of our faith, revealing to us, through the Church, what we need to know of the nature and will of God, but He is the "finisher" of it.

Catholics by baptism and by general wish to be what we promise in baptism, we can not fulfill our vows without a personal acquaintance and sympathy with Him who for our sakes "endured the cross." St. Jerome tells of St. John the beloved disciple, that when asked why in his old age he had no other sermon for the people but, "Little children, love one another," he answered, "Because it is the command of the Lord." That saying is the key-note of the Christian life. We believe because He reveals. We practice because He commands. "It is the wish of the Lord."

But where can we learn His wishes, unless by meditating on His Sacred Heart, and identifying ours with His? He came to overthrow the world, its pride and its passions, its power, its science and literature. He came to found an order in which time would be subordinate to eternity, matter to mind, fashion to truth. He came to establish liberty of soul from the bondage of human respect, avarice, ambition, lust and pleasure; and we must understand and love these ends to belong to Him. We must learn of Him to be meek and humble of heart. And so our meditation must be on Him day and night.

Editorial, *The Catholic Columbian*, Sept. 11, 1875 (1)

A Career for Catholic Young Men.

There is no denying that the mass of Catholic young men fail to appreciate their vocation. After their First Communion very many of them neglect their religious duties one after another, with the necessarily damaging result of a life dragged out under the shadow of God's curse.

Here, one becomes known as a blasphemer, there, another passes down step by step into a drunkard's grave. This one suffers the mental and bodily blight wrought by impure excesses. That one loses his piety first and then his faith. On them the knowledge of God's revelation, the grace of Baptism, of Confirmation, of the Holy Eucharist, and the whole supernatural life for which the martyrs were willing to give even their blood, are lost. This is a solemn fact, attested by nearly every pastor's experience. Now what do these recreant Catholics get in exchange for the graces they squander? Darkness of understanding, remorse of conscience and the contempt of the world they foolishly fawn upon in abandoning the practice of their faith. This and nothing more. They lived in the King's palace, had the Son of God for their brother, Mary for their mother, angels for companions, God for their inheritance. Neglecting their religious duties, "becoming as the horse and mule without understanding," they abandon their proud and secure position and enter into competition with those who are "without hope and without God, in the world." Nero, Emperor of the world, earned the contempt of history because he had the ambition to compete with the horse-jockeys. Every Christian youth will earn the world's contempt, his own self-reproach and the scorn of the very demons, by postponing the goods of faith to the delusions of sense.

The career for Catholic young men is to be Catholics. Life is short. Eternity is all that is worth aiming at. Eternity alone will unravel mysteries, satiate longings, cool heartburnings, pay for sufferings, refute calumnies, adjust all wrongs, and bring perfect and enduring peace.

Editorial, *The Catholic Telegraph and Advocate*, December 25, 1858

[Conversion a Gift of God.]

The doctrine that conversion is the work of grace and must be looked for rather as the fruit of prayer, and of God's mercy, than as the effect of human effort, is singularly consonant with the dictates of reason and experience. One could almost reach the conclusion, by analyzing the act of conversion, and studying the difficulties in its way.

Every man is, in his own settled and unquestioning estimation, the centre of the world. In his view, all things are made, and events fall out, with reference to his interests and inclinations. The seasons change for his accommodation, and he reprehends the weather when it interferes with his plans. The man of state thinks the masses formed for his purposes; and the man of low degree turns the ruler to account, by gazing on the pomp and circumstance of greatness, without price. No matter what his rank, each human being measures the value of all things by their bearing on his already settled plans, so that, in his view, the world might as well be annihilated as to be without him.

Now conversion implies a complete revolution of this entire world, within the heart of man. "The mountains must be brought low and the valleys filled up." Its very beginning must be a conviction of the soul, that hitherto it has been going in a totally wrong direction. Then it must learn to love what it hated before, to honor what it despised, to strive after what it avoided. Outwardly, it must seek for new associations, new pursuits, a new estimation among men.

Conversion is a stupendous work—scarcely less than the creation of a soul, and compared most aptly by the Prophet Ezekiel—to the gathering together, and fitting joint to joint, and covering with flesh, and filling with warm blood, and new life, the scattered bones in a charnel house. Who but God alone, can do a work like this? Who but He that framed it can glide into the secret recesses of man's heart—that kingdom where his own to ego rules without a rival—and change all that lies hidden there—shatter the throne, and build up a new kingdom?

Besides the intrinsic greatness of the work, many difficulties in its way render conversion a more than human operation.

Every man is pre-occupied with his own cares and opinions, so that you cannot chain his attention to his own spiritual wants. Talk to a merchant of the loss of souls, and his fancy will wander to the insurance office; to the banker of treasures in heaven, and he begins to calculate the capital invested, the risk and per centage; to the farmer, of God's goodness and he will wonder why the season is so wet; to the young man, of the certainty of death and he will remember his grandfather's funeral; to the old man, of the terror of God's judgments, and you remind him that he has left off his flannels and may get the rheumatism. In short, your words are but a pebble thrown into the pool of thought, that sets the waves quivering all over the surface, but itself sinks to the bottom, lies still, and is forgotten.

But even supposing that you arrest the attention for a moment, and that you make an impression with a single truth. Grant, too, that the truth is logically connected with all the other truths of religion, your work is but begun. Men are not logicians, unless where they wish to be; and the conclusions of their premises are often as strange to them as revelations from the spirit world. You must arrest the attention and produce the impression, for every new truth you propose, and in the ordinary course of things, a score of generations would pass away before you could go over the twelve articles of the creed.

At last, though your subject is convinced of the truth of faith. Who, now, is to make him act according to his conviction? to make him do what he now confesses he ought to do? Let any one who has the slightest experience of mankind, who knows how powerful are whims, and what trifles lighter than air originate them, answer, and we are sure he will say—this work is not the work of man. Reason, therefore, teaches faith and faith renders infallible the conclusion of reason, that conversion is efficiently, whatever be its occasion, a work which God alone can perform on the free will.

Editorial, *The Catholic Columbian*, February 13, 1875

Gallileo.

Gallileo is a Protestant hero because he is represented to have been imprisoned for saying that the world moves. Now, he was not imprisoned for saying that the world revolves—for that had been taught more than a hundred years before him, by a Catholic priest, who was never molested for teaching it.

But Gallileo made a theological question of it; and, encountering theological opposition, he became heated to utter sentiments which his adversaries laid hold of, as contrary to faith. He was brought before the Tribunal of the Inquisition, and there the irritable old gentleman came out with sentiments which offended the sense of faith of judges so much that they sent him to prison until he should retract. He did retract, and was released. The story that, after signing the paper, he kicked the ground and exclaimed passionately, "For all that, it moves!" is not improbable, but if true, is no great credit to him. It was the same as to say in signing this paper, "I have been a cowardly liar."

The citation of this fact as an argument against Papal Infallibility is so strangely illogical that one seems, in it, to touch with his finger an instance of wisdom becoming folly when it loses its hold, even for a moment, on the Teacher of all Truth.

Editorial, *The Catholic Telegraph and Advocate*, February 23, 1861

[Revolutionizing the Government.]

An article published in the Telegraph, a few weeks ago, maintaining that to attempt to preserve the Union by fighting, is to change the nature of the government, and therefore to take away all motive for the struggle, has met with the following objection:

Granting that ours is not a government of force, still is it not a government? Has it not power to protect itself against rebellion? If not it is worthless, and was worthless from the beginning. This objection has seemed to some to be very weighty.

Revolutionizing the Government

A government of the people is just as strong as the people of the different communities under it choose to make it. It has a right to protect itself from a rebellion of a few factious and criminal men. But where whole communities comprising good and bad, learned and unlearned, repudiate its authority, that authority is by the very fact of their opposition at an end. So weak a government may seem worthless, but a government based upon the will of the people cannot easily be stronger than the people themselves. It is inconvenient to the ruling party, but to the defeated section very comforting.

But has not the majority the right to compel submission to its behests, legally expressed?

We answer, it has, with two qualifications: 1st that the behest be just; 2d that the majority be of that consolidated community where the behest is to be law.

1. The reason of the first qualification is obvious. No majority has a right to do wrong. The oppression of Catholics by the Ohio School Law, by the taxation of Orphan Asylums, and excluding of Catholic instruction and priests from the house of refuge, &c.—is not just because the majority concur in it.

2d. Every community is a moral unit, and as such has its rights. There are more votes in Cincinnati than in Covington. Yet a majority of Cincinnatians would not have a right to make laws for Covington. Now it is manifest that our Federal Government is not a consolidated government. The people of the United States are not one community but many. the Preamble to the Constitution may say "We, the People," but the consolidating policy went down hopelessly with the elder Adams, and "Federalist" has been a term of political reproach for many years. The Federal Government cannot therefore be the channel through which the people of one State can govern the people of another. Each community must govern itself. Now the question whether the seceding States complain justly or unjustly, is not to the point.

They do complain and secede. You may regret the catastrophe, but you cannot prevent it by force nor attempt to prevent it without revoluntionizing the government.

If such a government is "contemptible," the fault lies in its nature, and not in its administration.

Editorial, *The Catholic Telegraph and Advocate,* July 9, 1853

Reforming by Law.

A large class of men have in our times adopted and pertinaciously retain the idea that the world is to be set to right by legislative enactments. There are, in the first place, the European Red Republicans, who thought that if an assembly would declare Europe to be free, Europe would, forthwith, be free—forgetting that in the change of tyrants, the tyranny remains.

In the second place, there are the "manifest destiny" men of our own country, who think (regardless of the unredressed social oppression they see about them) that if the American flag but waves over a land, that land must be an elysium.

Thirdly, we have the fanatical abolitionists, who dream that if Congress should pass a law abolishing slavery, the colored race would cease to be "down trodden."

Fourthly, comes in a phalanx of Maine Liquor Law men, who speak as though a law against drinking liquor would at once banish drunkenness from the land—forgetting that there is a much drunkenness in the Eastern States since its enactment as there was before.

Besides these there is a host of other fanatics, socialists, Fourierites, women's rights people—all eager to get some favorite law passed, and shouting that should it be passed, evils are to cease and disappear.

It is wonderful how men of any logic can be deceived by such patent nonsense. No law can remedy any evil unless it be obeyed. No law will be obeyed unless its subjects have a motive for obeying it. Now the evils at which our reformers aim arise precisely from the fact that the people are not taught the sanction of laws already existing, and not for want of laws.—Thus for example, the evils of slavery would not exist were masters taught that in proportion to their power over the slave is their responsibility of preparing him for heaven by instruction and example. Again, the sentence that drunkards shall not enter into the kingdom of heaven would do away with the evils of drunkenness, could drunkards be brought to believe practically that there is a kingdom of heaven at all.

We have plenty of laws already. Right and wrong are sufficiently defined. Men need a motive for doing right and abstaining from wrong. This motive never can be a legislative enactment, nor a corporal penalty. Corporal penalties are of weight among a people who are reminded by them of the terrible and unerring justice of God. But where no thoughts of eternity are stirred up in the beholders, the sight of a man swinging between earth and heaven deters no one from crime. It may lead to greater caution in the manner of its perpetration. It may induce him to seek a darker night, a lonelier spot, a surer dagger, a subtler poison, but it gives him no horror of the crime, unless he see in the human penalty a figure of the more awful penalty to be inflicted in the other world by God.

When will quack reformers learn that reforms must commence in the individual, and not in the mass? When will they understand that laws have no weight if the moral sense of society be not correct and strong?

When Christianity overthrew the paganism of Rome, the impure worship of idols was never prohibited, until the sixth century, when the common sentiment of the masses cried out for it. The reform had been working its way through the individual mind for six centuries; and, after many fiery persecutions, had at last leavened the masses and found its expression in public statutes. So every reform must commence from the individual. The individual must be taught what is right, and why he ought to do it. And one by one the great majority of the members of society must be "reformed" before the reformation can be written in the statute books.

Suppose the Legislature of Ohio should pass the Maine Liquor Law;—would drunkenness cease? Certainly not, at least not until two conditions were fulfilled, viz.: 1st, the law should be proved just. 2nd, the people should be furnished with a conscience so tender that they could do nothing unjust. Legislation, especially in this country, may express, but it cannot control public sentiment; and it is ridiculous to expect that laws are to reform society.

Editorial, *The Catholic Columbian*, June 6, 1878
[Equality of Men Before God.]
Editor Catholic Columbian:

Why should communism be considered as something so very horrible? Have not all men equal rights: You dare not say "no" for fear of the Declaration of Independence, and Emancipation Proclamation and the American Eagle generally. Then every man has a right to live, and to the food, clothing and shelter, necessary for living, and no man has a right to more. Is not this plain? Therefore all who hoard up wealth they can never use, who live in houses built for luxury, and not shelter, who spend their time in idleness, are drones, thieves and robbers. LOGIC

Ans. Our correspondent's logic is sounder than his principles. The doctrine of equality which Christianity taught to the world means equality before God in the things necessary to secure the eternal happiness for which we are created. Every soul has from Our Lord a right to know how it can be saved, and the grace to avoid sin, and so, men are equal in their accountability before their almighty Judge. But their equality ceases in gifts of mind, body, and fortune. No two men were ever equal, or ever can be. A man who has genius is no robber of him who is dull. The athlete did not wrong the cripple when he grew into strength. The comely woman stole nothing from the wrinkled beldame. The person who inherits or earns a fortune may find his soul in danger from it, but he owes nothing for it to those less fortunate, or less successful. God disposes these gifts to suit himself, and each must be grateful for his own whether great or small. "Logic's" mistake is in taking this life as a finality, and its goods as the only goods. Every man has a right to live as long as God chooses and in the way God chooses. He has a right to all he fairly inherited or honestly earned. If he has built a roof over his head, he has not robbed the tramp who goes without one. The equality will appear when the end comes; when each one shall appear before his Judge bearing his own burthen, and rendering account of his stewardship, whether it may be over many or over few things. Short of that the equality of men is an idle fable.

Editorial, *The Catholic Columbian*, July 15, 1876
[Men are Not Equal.]

Men are free—it is a solemn truth. Men are equal—it is an absurd lie. Men are unequal in sex, age, understanding, education, power of will, influence over others—in all the minutiae of their formation and fortune. Take away the common origin and common destiny—the fact that each man is God's handiwork, steward and servant—and men are equal in nothing else. The mischief of French Communism is not preaching equality but believing Atheism. The defect of their argument is the impiety of their unbelief. All men are equally entitled to happiness. True. But happiness is being rich, eating good dinners, wearing fine clothes, riding in carriages, &c. This is the baleful proposition which Protestantism has brought into the problem of government, by rejecting the reality of Christianity and making salvation a matter of feeling and sentiment. If life is all beastly, you cannot blame men for living as beasts; and naturally the good things of the world will go where the brute force is.

Editorial, *The Catholic Columbian*, August 19, 1876 (1)
[Socialist Unbelievers.]

There are two classes of unbelievers; one class knows nothing of religion, its teachings or the grounds on which it rests its claims. The other knows what religion is, and hates it because it is good. The European socialists are of this latter class. They love darkness rather than light, because their deeds are evil. They acknowledge God to be what Christianity represents Him to be; and His only begotten Son to have done all the Church teaches He has done to save men from being ruined. They hate God for His greatness and purity as Milton's hero in Paradise Lost hated Him, or as Shelley's, when he called Him "the omnipotent Tyrant." They hate Jesus Christ because he taught that poverty was a more blessed condition than wealth. They hate monks and nuns because they try to practice angelic virtue; priests because they tell the people to be patient and look forward to eternity for the righting of wrong and the reward of suffering. Those who do not know the Church's teachings are converted with comparative ease when they happen on the knowledge of the truth. But the others are beyond the reach of everything but prayer and the all-powerful grace of God. We have never met an American Communist.

Editorial, *The Catholic Columbian*, Sept. 25, 1875 (5)
Liberalism in Religion.

Frequently we hear the assertion made by those who call themselves liberals, that it makes no difference to what religion a man belongs, provided only he lives a good moral life. We are all striving for the same destination, they say, and it makes no difference which road we take, even though it be not the most direct one, provided we finally arrive there.

The object of every religion, they argue, is to give men a moral training, and thus enable them to attain the end of their existence. Every religion is therefore good.

In answer to this, we must say, that the argument of the liberal is not only false, but absurd.

No person can admit the existence of God, the necessity of a first cause, and reasonably deny his dependence upon that first cause, and consequently the necessity of a religion of some sort.

But let us come down to the proposition of the liberal—"every religion is good." This proposition gives us the license to commit the greatest crime of which man is capable. Let us examine the meaning of it. It means simply that whatever act of idolatry man may commit, into whatever error he may fall in regard to Almighty God, it is just as pleasing in His sight as the purest act of worship. Mahometanism and Buddhaism are also religions, they too teach a code of morals. Yet they deny Jesus Christ, and their members prostrate themselves before Mahomet and Buddha. [This indicates a deficient knowledge of Islam, or possibly just of the term "Mahomet" or Muhammad, on the part of the Bishop.]

If every religion is good, then is truth an error; to adore the true and only God, or worship the devil in idols, all one and the same thing.

The Jews, before the coming of Christ, had a religion. They adored the true God; they were His chosen people. Yet Christ came down from heaven to change that religion, and to institute a new one. If what the liberal says is true, there would be no necessity for this.

But he may argue, "Well we are not talking about Jews and idolators. When I say that it makes no difference to what religion a man belongs, I mean, of course, a religion which acknowledges Jesus Christ; for the Scripture says we must believe in the Lord Jesus, if we would be saved." Suppose we limit his proposition thus far; it is none the less absurd.

Protestantism is divided into numerous sects, each one differing from the other. This difference can only be with regard to what they believe. Their very names imply a distinction and a distinction without a difference is logically an impossibility. Hence it follows that while some hold a certain truth to be revealed, others deny it altogether.

Starting out with these premises, let us bring the proposition of the liberal into play again. If every religion is good, then it would follow again that truth and falsehood would be one and the same thing. That it would be equally good, for instance, to adore the Blessed Sacrament on our altars as we Catholics do; or to believe in the Sacrament of Penance, or to look upon it as ridiculous; to hold that Christ is God as most Christians do; or to regard Him as a mere creature, as do the socinians and unitarians.

The doctrine of the liberal is therefore a false one, and is plainly making a mockery of Jesus Christ.

Our Blessed Lord came down from heaven to found a Church by means of which the merits of our redemption might be dispensed to all mankind. He made that Church the depository of His doctrines; promised His own assistance and that of the Holy Ghost, lest she should ever fall into error; confirmed His doctrines by numberless miracles and by the blood of thousands of martyrs. Yet after all this, those new-fangled teachers come forward to tell us that it makes no difference to Jesus Christ what we believe, provided only we live good and moral lives. If this is not plainly making a mockery of Him, we are greatly mistaken.

If their doctrine is true, what is the use in the preaching of Protestant ministers, since they would gain nothing if we were all to become Protestants; nor would they lose anything by all becoming Catholics, since even Catholicism is a religion and every religion is good.

But they say Catholics are so intolerant. We will not stop to answer that question today; it has been refuted so often that its upholders must be entirely blinded by prejudice not to see that it is false. But even if it were so, which we deny, have not Catholics a sort of right to be so, since we hold that what is not true is false, and consequently that one religion is not as good as another. During our late civil war we beheld the spectacle of frail women, going forth for God's sake, amid a hail of shot and shell, to tend to the wounded and dying. Today we see those same women, sacrificing home and earthly happiness, in order to tend to Catholics and Protestants alike in our hospitals. Does this look like intolerance? On the contrary how have our so-called liberals acted? Certainly not very liberally. We see those same Sisters of Charity driven out of Mexico; the Pope a prisoner in the Vatican; the bishops and priests of Germany imprisoned or driven into exile—even in our own State of Ohio we Catholics are abused for applauding liberty of conscience in our prisons. One of our own priests, in a country town not a hundred miles from Columbus, was threatened with arrest for attending a man dying of the smallpox, though no mention was made of the doctor, who visited the house a great deal oftener than the priest did.
Does this look like liberalism, or does it look like intolerance? But enough. God knows we do not wish to be otherwise than charitable, but we can scarcely open a newspaper, in which we do not find our religious convictions grossly misrepresented.

We, however, expect nothing else but persecution. The disciple is not above his master. Christ himself was persecuted in the name of religion, and so religious were His persecutors, that they would not even allow His body to hang upon the cross on the Sabbath day. We have always been persecuted, and yet we are stronger than ever. "The blood of martyrs became the seed of Christians," says Tertullian. "The gates of hell shall never prevail" against God's Church, and her wondrous vitality is a shining proof that she is not the work of man.

Truth is necessarily one. Christ has made but one revelation; whatever is not true is false. Since, therefore, such is the case, it follows that every religion is not good, for there can be but one true Church.

Lecture, *The Catholic Telegraph and Advocate*, March 14, 1866 and Sermon Book 2, No. 17
Braces { } indicate the manuscript version, where there are differences of substance.

Religion and Progress.

The religion of Christ is Catholic, in this sense: that it can be brought home to the understanding, the conduct, and spiritual life of all conditions of men. It is wider than the range of science, more comprehensive than the sphere of political or social progress. It jars with no form of just government, requires no abrogation of innocent local customs, debars no one from honorable employment, clogs no fair enterprise, fetters the mind in no kind of investigation or study. It is Catholic, or universal, filling all the earth, living on till the Day of Judgment.

In the early ages of the Church it used to be a reproach to a doctrine to say "it is new." And by that rule alone heresies were detected in the days of Tertullian, St. Augustine, and St. Athanasius. "What you preach is new," they used to say to Marcion, Arius and Pelagius, therefore not taught by Christ, therefore, false. Now the ideas of men seem to be reversed and the enemies of faith say "your Church is old, therefore false," "yours are the ideas of the men of the twelfth century, of the ages preceding the invention of printing, of the steam engine, the electric telegraph, and the sewing machine, therefore you should discard them." "It is vain," said the renowned writer Mr. Bancroft the other day, in Washington, "for the Pope to attempt to bring back the ecclesiastical institutions of the fourteenth {XVI.} century." In other words, progress is set up as the great antagonist of the Church of Christ; and conspirators against truth throughout the world have determined among themselves to make the very ideas she first taught to man, of human brotherhood, equality and liberty, and the fruits those ideas bring forth in society, the pretext of their hostility to her and a reason for her destruction.

The object of this lecture will be to examine the relations between faith and all desirable progress, and to show that no antagonism between it and the Catholic religion can exist.

Progress, according to its primary meaning, is an advance, or a movement forward. In this meaning it is not necessarily a good. If the movement is in the right direction, then each forward impulse that adds to it is good. If in the wrong direction, the more there is of it, the greater evil. Crime may progress as well as virtue, disease as well as health.

To know, therefore, what there is of desirable in modern progress, we must know in what direction modern progress is carrying us. On this point opinions are somewhat divided. Some say the direction is downward towards anarchy in government, barbarism in social life, corruption and unbelief in the individual heart, in a word, to temporal and eternal ruin.

Others maintain that we are progressing towards felicity. Each day strikes some chain from the limbs, some fetter from the mind of humanity. Each day brings us nearer the goal of our destiny. We and our fathers have been passing through the Red Sea, and lingering with worn garments and weary hearts in the desert. But the promised land will come in sight, at last, if not to us, at least, (what ought to comfort us, all the same) to posterity. And the era of happiness—whatever that may consist in—will surely dawn at last.

A solid {sober} minded thinker can not agree with either of these views. It is certain that this world will never contain either heaven or hell. "After death is the judgment." Death is the precipice over which corruption takes the final plunge in its progress to the lowest depth, and where true worth is lifted up as the water that rises in mists above a cataract, to its home on high. Therefore as there can be nothing very appalling to the heart that understands its destiny in the evils to come, so there is nothing to bring ecstasy in the good.

Whatever there has been, therefore, or whatever there is going to be in progress, it will not be anything to take the place, or remove the necessity, of religion. Individuals must die, be judged, and go to heaven or hell, according to their previous choice, whatever happens to humanity; and so individuals will need faith and prayer and the Sacraments that cleanse from sin and strengthen against temptation all the same.

But to ventilate this subject more thoroughly let us take up one by one some of the items of progress from the mouths of its advocates, and see whether any one of them conflicts with the Catholic Church.

Since the sixteenth century, they say, there has been progress in science, in civilization, in arts, and in government. Consider these one by one.

1st. Science—The attempt to bring science into antagonism with religion is made in two ways:

1st. From its assumed vastness in modern times. We know so much more now, than they knew in the twelfth century, that it would be absurd for us to believe what they believed. "As the grown man puts aside the garments of his childhood, so humanity ought to cast aside the opinions of its pupilage." But however much more than the men of the twelfth century we may know of other things, we do not know more of religion than they knew; and nothing that we know on any subject contradicts what they held, or warrants in us any claim of superiority, on that subject, over them. Confronting age with age, on the point of religious knowledge, I fear that our polished Nineteenth Century could not bear comparison with that rude time chosen to be called the Iron Age. I say nothing of ignorance among the uneducated classes, who very often have never heard the name of their Redeemer, except in curses. But even among the educated and polished classes how dense is the ignorance of the true religion all over the land! almost a majority, knowing neither what Christianity teaches nor on what grounds it rests its claims. Even if our conceited assumption of superiour knowledge were true, it would be no warrant for rejecting the faith they held, for that can never grow old.

"But science contradicts the dogmas of faith and on that ground explodes religion." This is the assertion most insisted on by recent enemies of religion, men in many instances calling themselves preachers of what they seek to discredit and undermine. Suppose, now, I recite the twelve articles of the Creed, and you name over your sciences. Which science will come into collision with what "I believe?" and which article will it conflict with?

Religion treats exclusively of the invisible. "Faith is the evidence of things not seen." But science deals exclusively with the visible. Though both were false, or both true, they never could conflict because they never meet in their teachings. What one asserts of the body can never deny what the other teaches of the soul.

A few examples of attempts made to bring science to bear as an argument against religion will serve to illustrate this statement.

Astronomy was once thought to be in contradiction to the Church's doctrines, and, as long as this idea prevailed, was studied with much eagerness. "The earth moves," said Galileo, and he began to prove it from scripture. "That is heresy," exclaimed his rivals, and the argument from scripture went on until Galileo was obliged to admit that he could not prove the earth's motion from scripture, or, in other words, retract what he had said. And "yet it moves," he persisted in saying, and by the time the controversy had passed through the Roman congregations and up as high as the Pope, all he had to say was "perhaps it does move; the Church does not teach anything to the contrary." "God made the rainbow a sign of his league with men that He would no more destroy the earth with water." "A contradiction" said the infidels. For the rainbow is but light refracted by drops of water in the air, and must have existed from the beginning, whenever light came from the sun, and water hung on the mists {of the air}. In their hurry to find a mistake they never noticed that God is not said to have first made the rainbow after the deluge, but to have it then for the first time a sign of the league between Himself and men; and so, made the mistake themselves.

2d. "The stars are much larger than the earth, and perhaps inhabited. What then becomes of the old notion that all visible things were made for man, and what probability is there, that the Son of God would, out of almost countless worlds far greater in size and in population, choose the earth for the dwelling of

His love, and human nature for the one in which to offer the Ineffable Sacrifice to His eternal Father?"

The stars are many of them larger than the earth undoubtedly, and that they are inhabited is no improbable conjecture. But this, although contrary to the opinion formerly held among men, is not contrary to any teaching of faith. Almighty God never taught astronomy. When He had occasion to speak of the sun and moon and stars, He did not explain what they were in themselves, but what they were to us—what use we were to make of them in working out our salvation. His Revelation is mysterious enough when dressed in our language. It would be utterly unintelligible were He to clothe it in His own.

We knew from scripture, long before any one conjectured the stars to be inhabited worlds, that there are nine choirs or orders of angels, each higher in excellence and, for ought we know, exceeding in number all the race of men; enough to furnish inhabitants for a million of stars, if God chooses them to dwell there.

That God should stoop to redeem man is indeed a mystery of condescension and love, above our comprehension. But then He stooped to create us, and why not to save us? That He should choose human nature rather than any other is no great difficulty, for the distance from Creator to creature is so great that it is neither here nor there what creature God comes to, after He has once decided to come to any one at all.

Geology was next invoked to oppose religion. It too exploded some old ideas but none that were of Faith. The strata marking the duration of the earth were such as to indicate indubitably an age compared to which the Biblical six thousand years were as a day to a hundred years. The philosophers clapped their hands, and cried, "The cause is finished." They did not reflect that religion never pretended to give the mechanical process of the earth's formation, but only to assert that God made it, and incidentally to mention in what order He made it, and to designate the periods, after the one which "the earth was without form and void," occupied by each step of the operation as "days" which were doubtless periods of almost countless years, as the word is used to signify, not their length, but the order in which they succeeded one another. But this order, mentioned only incidentally, agrees with the one in which geologists say the earth must have been constructed.

The Azoic Time, or time when there was no animal or vegetable life, corresponds to the scriptural time, when the earth was without form and void.

Vegetable life opens the Silurian Era or Palaeozoic time; and we read in Genesis that after making the dry land appear, God created the plants and vegetables. Next in order in Geology came the fishes and reptiles, then the animals, and last man; an order though not distinctly marked in the Biblical account, yet is in no wise contradicted by it.

Moreover, geology asserts that all the component parts of the earth were originally in a state of fusion—were all liquid. And the scripture says "darkness was on the face of the deep, and the spirit of God moved across the face of the waters."

So geology instead of contradicting, did but confirm the teachings of faith, and the philosophers soon grew tired of it, and left its study to the professors in colleges.

I might illustrate the uselessness of all efforts to bring science into collision with faith, by many other examples, as of the efforts made by the French academicians to trace back the history of the Chinese, East Indians and Egyptians to an antiquity far beyond the Mosaic era; of rationalists, and other Protestants to assail the Church through ecclesiastical history, philology and criticism. But these two must suffice to show that our age had made no progress in science which will justify any departure from the old Catholic Faith.

2d. The Arts.—In the arts which contribute to what Macauley called the aim of Baconian Philosophy, human comfort, the present is unquestionably in advance of the past. A New England writer, long ago, wrote his opinion that "They did not know everything down in Judea," and the opinion is just. We have more comfortable dwellings, better means of transportation, better clothing and food, and better patent medicines than they had in the first, or eleventh or sixteenth century. But what then? Therefore we can follow Christ without carrying a cross? Therefore we can be saved without faith, and obtain grace without the Sacraments?

We can not carry any of our inventions or comforts into eternity with us, and therefore can not make any of them an excuse for neglecting the religion by whose practice alone we can save our souls.

3d. Civilization.—As for progress in civilization, so much boasted of among us, it is hard to tell what it is. That there has been a softening down of the rudeness of public manners, a refining disposition to hide, at least, the grossness of vice, nobody can deny. It is not the fashion now to kill one's enemies with weapons that make so much noise as fire-arms, or such ugly gashes as steel. The progress seems to me to consist in this: there are certain ideas of justice and right, which Christianity introduced, and by ten centuries and more of labor, made respectable and fashionable in the world; and fashion will rule the outward conduct, though the ideas that gave it birth, may never find a lodgment in the mind.

Civilization, therefore, is but a consequence of Christianity, and it would be absurd to speak of it as superseding the Church, as absurd as to propose to let the moon do the office of illuminating the earth. When Christianity is rooted out of society in any place, civilization will go along with it. But let there be ever so much of it, civilization can never save souls. Refined, elegant, genteel people may have the stain of guilt upon their souls, may die in sin and be lost. Dives was an elegant gentleman. He dressed richly and gave faultless dinners, but for all that "he died," and, as our Divine Redeemer expressed it, with awful simplicity, "was buried in hell."

The same unjust reproach is urged against the Church in the name of freedom and just government. "The world grows freer as it recedes from the Catholic Church," was the calumny of Protestants. "The world grows freer as it recedes from Christ," is the parallel blasphemy of the atheists. Both are equally calumnies.

Have you not, in the history of the world, O, Atheist, enough of peoples and tribes, never subjected to the yoke of Christ, to put to the proof your theory of the sufficiency of unfettered humanity to find freedom and felicity on the earth? What result did you obtain in Greece and Rome of old, or in China or New Zealand of today?

Has not the experiment of Christianity without the Pope been sufficiently tried during the last three centuries in the civilized world? Yet where is your perfection of freedom in Prussia, in Sweden, Norway, and England? Facts refute the calumny, and the nature of things shows it to be clearly absurd, that any movement from the Church should be in the direction of true liberty.

For liberty, as a good, does not mean freedom from all control, a condition that belongs only to Almighty God, but freedom from illegitimate control. The soul is free when the understanding is set in truth and the free will in justice. Those only are free, indeed, whom Christ has made free.

The Church, being the infallible teacher of truth and the sole channel of grace, is the source of true liberty to the world. Those who depart from her therefore to seek liberty are like persons running into the desert after water. Error and sin are the only shackles of the soul. The great end, that which gives its value to freedom, is eternal happiness, with God in Heaven; just as eternal reprobation is what makes slavery hateful and loathsome. Personal and political freedom are fruits of the Catholic teaching, smaller, yet still precious. They follow the spiritual freedom imparted by grace as effect follows cause. In any country, true liberty is attained in proportion as justice is supreme, in proportion, that is, as government controls no more and the people obey no less, than right demands. Hence there can be no true liberty where the public conscience does not worship truth and justice as absolutely supreme. But the public conscience is the public belief. But the Church alone teaches the belief that right and justice not only ought to be, but infallibly are to be supreme. Therefore Christianity alone affords society any sure foundation for civil liberty.

If there is, as a matter of fact, oppression in Christian lands, what would there not be in those same lands, were Christianity removed? If men were not withheld from trampling upon one another's right by the fear of judgment, what measure would there be to crime were that fear taken away?

They who recede from the Church, therefore, cannot approach liberty, and there is no desirable progress that has its source outside of Jesus Christ and His immaculate bride, the Catholic Church.

Pastoral Letter, *The Catholic Telegraph and Advocate*, Sept. 1, 1870

Promulgation of the Decree on Papal Infallibility

Sylvester, by the Grace of God, and the Appointment of the Holy See, Bishop of Columbus,

to the Clergy and Laity of the Diocese.

With a glad heart, venerable brethren and beloved children, we fulfill our duty of promulgating the solemn decree of the great Vatican Council, concerning the prerogatives of the See of Peter, immediately on its reception in the very language of the Holy Father himself.

As the date shows it was announced on the 18th of July. It reached us on the 10th inst., the Feast of St. Lawrence, Deacon and Martyr. We have nothing to add to the clearness of its language; but a few words to say on the greeting it deserves from us. We accept it without questioning because it is the oracle of the Holy Ghost. It is the judgment of the successor of St. Peter by the advice of a council which has unquestionably all the mark of legitimacy in a preeminent degree, legitimately convoked by the Roman Pontiff in letters apostolic of Dec. 8, 1869. Every bishop and prelate of Christendom had knowledge of its assembling, and free access to participate in its deliberations. Presided over by the Delegate of the Holy See, every latitude of discussion and voting was allowed before the decision was reached. If the actual debate was shortened because the repetition of arguments had become irksome, both sides were cut off impartially from further speaking. The vote was taken and only two bishops were found registering their names as advising against it. In the document above-mentioned is the solemn approval of the Holy Father, which is the essential source of authority to all decisions of the Catholic Church. With regard to its reception by the bishops not in the council (though that is of little importance) there can be no doubt that the great mass of them will receive it, like ourselves, with joy.

Hence all the authority ever invoked by any theological school calling itself Catholic is in this decree: The sanction of the Holy See, which in all ages sufficed for the great mass of Catholics: The vote of a general council, and the approbation of the Church dispersed or not in council, are united in silencing forever those schools whose opinions can no longer be held by any who believe in the divine authority of the Church of Christ.

The way of faith is now made so plain that no one can be mistaken.

We know that this decision is both true and opportune because the Holy Ghost has made it. All things on earth are in the hands of God's providence, so that working what way they will, He governs the world. But the Church is not merely under His control. She is His own work. What she proclaims is His proclaiming. What she commands or forbids is His commanding and forbidding. A decision once rendered, therefore, there is no longer question of its opportuneness. This is the victory that overcomes the world—our faith.

But aside from this consideration of supernatural faith, this solemn proclamation of the ancient and cherished belief of the universal Church ought to fill us with joy.

This long and acrimonious discussion is over. The books that were written in the cause of Caesarism and national vanity, which afforded pretext to so many acts of oppression of the Church by the rulers of European nations, can now be laid aside forever. They need no further confutation. The misguided will receive the light with joy. The others who believed nothing, but employed theology to deceive the incautious and pervert the faith of the simple, will go away to their own place, and disgrace no longer the name of Catholic. The line between the believing Catholic and the politician Catholic will be drawn clear and sharp; and the Church in her struggle with atheism, infidelity, heresy, and materialism will no longer be encumbered with the dead weight of those who for the past three centuries have been trying to use religion as a means of promoting their own selfish, temporal ends.

It is now of divine faith, that the spiritual authority, or the human conscience divinely taught, is free from every trammel of human enactment, every placitum of king or cabinet, and the calumny of those who have represented the Church as opposed to true liberty, is forever silenced.

We have no fears, beloved brethren, of any defection of sincere Catholics, whether converts or by education. If any

Promulgation of the Decree on Papal Infallibility

"go away and walk no more with us" on account of this decree, their defection was a thing of long ago. The faith they held was never Catholic faith, because they never held to the divine authority of the Church. To them faith was taste, fancy, caprice, self-interest, not reality. The vineyard of the Lord of Hosts is all the better to be pruned of such dead branches.

On the world, outside the Church, this proclamation can have but one effect and that is a good one. To define where the infallibility of the Church resides, does not in the least alter her attitude toward them. But the definition has created much ignorant comment, many foolish misrepresentations, and bitter feelings among them. All this will provoke inquiry, and consequent knowledge of the truth. In a few years from now writers for public journals will blush to remember that they once confounded infallibility with impeccability, or the Pope teaching as head of the Universal Church, with the Pope expressing private opinions on local facts, or scientific theories. Above all things we have to rejoice that we have verified by divine authority the saying of St. Cyprian, "A head is constituted, that the occasion of schism may be removed." Henceforth, there is one fold under one shepherd. The Church the spouse of Christ appears before us now, with all her majestic proportions defined—a purely spiritual kingdom whose strength is from above, not from beneath. The kings of Europe have foolishly tried to resent the declaration of the independence of the spiritual authority. Austria has abolished the concordat and France has left the Holy Father to the mercy of the perfidious Italian government. Time will show that Jesus Christ is able to take care of His own—and perhaps teach a lesson to those rulers who imagined themselves not the children but the patrons of the Church.

To signalize the proclamation of this dogma we direct that in each principal Church on a day to be designated by the pastor, a Te Deum be sung and benediction of the Blessed Sacrament given after the reading of the decree, and this pastoral letter, with such observations as the pastor may see fit to make.

In view of the fact that the council is no longer in session, and that the Holy Father is menaced by grave perils, we direct also that the prayer *de Spiritu Sancto* be discontinued, and the prayer *Deus Omnium Fidelium* be placed in its stead in every Mass whose rank allows the recitation.

+ SILVESTER H. ROSECRANS
BISHOP OF COLUMBUS.

Given at the pro Cathedral of St. Patrick's, Columbus, August 13, 1870.

Editorial, *The Catholic Columbian*, January 29, 1876 (2)

[The Editor-Bishop is Found Out.]

Saturday's Cincinnati Enquirer condescends to say: "Bishop Rosecrans, of Columbus, has a fool to write the editorials for his organ."

We did not expect to be found out so soon. But if the Divine Author of our Faith will deign "to use the foolish things of the world to confound the wise," and bring all into subjection to Him, we shall be content with our motley.

What the courteous editor adds, indicating his intention to assist in "keeping the Catholic Church in Ohio in 'hot water,'" does not take us by surprise. All the elements of mischief in society will work against her whenever it seems to be their interest to do so.

Index

Adams, Leo Rev. O.P. 69,108, 111
Ahern, M. J. Rev. 26,67,69, 110,131
Ahrens, Gerhard H. Rev. 56-58, 67,100,109
Albrinck, John C. Rev. 16,28,51
Anderson, Henry Rev. 128,129
Anderson, Peter O.P. 13
Anthony, St. John 109
Archer's Settlement, St. Michael 75,109
Athens, St. Paul 109,114
Badin, Stephen Rev. 12
Baltimore, Second Plenary Council 48,49
Banchet, —— Rev. 28
Barnabo, Alessandro Cdl. 63,73,74
Barrett, William Rev. 17
Barry, William J. Rev. 24,25
Batesville, St. Mary 75,109,126
Bayley, James Rt. Rev. 52
Bazin, Stephen Rt. Rev. 13
Bedini, Cajetan Most Rev. 20-22
Bellaire, St. John 75,105,109
Bergin, Thomas 115,118,129
Bigelow, William T. Rev. 26,67,111,112
Blanc, —— Rt. Rev. 13

Boeker, W. Rev. 29
Bokel, J. V. Rev. O.P. 58
Bokel, John A. V. Rev. O.P. 72
Bolivar, St. Martin 109
Bonner, —— Dr. 41
Borgess, Caspar H. Rt. Rev. 28, 51,73,92,140
Bouche, —— Rev. 28
Boyle, Peyton 52
Boyle, S. S. 126
Brady, Bernard Rev. O.P. 70,111
Brennan, Edward 63
Brent, Julius Rev. 67,111
Brexel, Gonzaga O.S.F. 94
Brogard, Joseph Rev. 67,109
Brooks, Robert T. 119,121,122,124
Brothers of St. Francis 103
Brough, John 34
Brown Co., St. Martin's 22-23, 31,40,76,80,81,131
Brown, Catherine O.P. 88,91,92
Brownsville, St. Michael 109
Brummer, John W. Rev. 67,110
Bryant, William C. 47
Buerck, George 118
Bunker Hill, St. Francis de Sales 46,47

Burke, Nicholas T. Rev. O.P. 70
Burke, Thomas J. 118
Byrne, Luke G. 106
Byrne, Stephen Rev. O.P. 71
Cady, Thomas Rev. O.P. 70,111
Calmoutier, Ste. Genevieve 76,109
Campbell, Francis J. Rev. 51,65,68, 131
Canal Dover, St. Joseph 75,109
Canton, St. John 77
Cardington, St. Joseph 109,112
Caren, John 115,118
Carrell, George A. Rt. Rev. 28
Cartuyvels, Louis Rev. 58,62-64,67, 111,119
Cassella, John A. Rev. 101
Cathedral School of the Sacred Heart, Columbus 89
Catholic Columbian 106-107
Challoner, Richard 4
Chapel Hill, St. Francis 109
Chatard, Silas Rt. Rev. 129,131,133,134,140
Chatfield, Julia O.S.U. 22,23,135-136
Chauncey, Seven Dolors 109
Chillicothe, St. Mary 117
Christy, Richard C. Rev. 104,113,13+A210
Churchtown, St. John 109
Cincinnati, Mt. St. Mary's College 26-30
Cincinnati, St. Augustine 17
Cincinnati, St. Philomena 73
Cincinnati, St. Thomas 17
Circleville, St. Joseph 66,75,109
Clarke, Dennis A. Rev. 106,139
Clarke, John D. 115,116,129
Clarke, William J. 139

Clarkson, Sydney A. Rev. O.P. 86
Clements, Francis X. S.C. 62
Clinton Furnace 109
Coll, Peter C. V. Rev. O.P. 72
Collins, John Rev. O.P. 70,111
Columbus, Catholic Cemetery 105
Columbus, Good Shepherd Convent 51,98-99,101,104
Columbus, Hannah Neil Mission 100-101
Columbus, Holy Cross 51,75,92,105,108,109,118,125
Columbus, Holy Family 105,113
Columbus, Mt. Calvary Cemetery 105-106,119
Columbus, Naughten Hall 71,115, 125,128
Columbus, Pontifical College Josephinum 104
Columbus, Sacred Heart 95,96
Columbus, Sacred Heart Academy 81,89-92,101,112-113,129,133
Columbus, St. Aloysius Seminary 71,99-100,102
Columbus, St. Ann's Infant Asyl. 96
Columbus, St. Charles Seminary 96
Columbus, St. Francis Hospital 97-98,109,119
Columbus, St. Joseph Academy 92-94
Columbus, St. Joseph Cathedral 50-52,58,61,71,72,89,91,115-134
Columbus, St. Joseph's Orphan Asylum 104,105
Columbus, St. Joseph's Seminary 104-105
Columbus, St. Mary 76,108,109
Columbus, St. Mary's of the Springs 64,86-92,125,136

Index

Columbus, St. Patrick 46,50,60,71, 74,75,92,93,105,109, 112, 115,116, 118,119,125
Columbus, St. Rita's Home for Working Girls 96
Columbus, St. Therese's Shrine 96
Columbus, St. Vincent's Orphan Asylum 94,95,100-103
Conahan, John 115
Conway, —— Rev. 60
Coppinger, T. J. J. Rev. 29
Corcoran, —— Rev. 28
Corcoran, E. P. Rev. 29
Coshocton, St. George 63,109,126
Crane's Nest, Ss. Peter and Paul 109
Cull, Daniel B. Rev. 27,51,58,60,65, 68,131
Curran, Ellen 100
Curran, Jane 100
Dailey, George R. Rev. O.P. 72
Daly, Patrick J. Rev. 67,111,119
Danville, St. Luke 109,126
Darr, Francis Gen. 80
De Cantillon, Edward Rev. O.P. 72
De Goesbriand, Louis Rt. Rev. 46
De Saint-Palais, James Rt. Rev. 28
Deavertown, St. Michael 109
DeCailly, Louis Rev. 64,127
Delaware, St. Mary 51,66,118,126
Dennison, Immaculate Conception 113
Diocese of Columbus 49,52
  - consecration to Sacred Heart 57
  -early statistics 55-56
  -synods 58-59,126,127
Dix, —— Gen. 47
Dolan, Thomas 9
Domenec, Michael Rt. Rev. 51
Dominican Fathers 69-73

Donahoe, J. Rev. 131
Donahue, N. Rev. 28
Donahue, P. B. Rev. 28
Donnelly, Owen 94
Dover -- see Canal Dover
Downing, Agnes S.S.J. 104
Dresden, St. Matthew 109
Driscoll, C. Rev. 28
Dues, Henry Rev. 51,65,68,131
Duffy, John 115
Duffy, John D. Rev. 29
Duffy, Mary 129
Duggan, James Rt. Rev. 73
Dunn, Joseph F. V. Rev. O.P. 69,70, 72,136
Dunn, Patrick 118
Durbin Church, St. James 109
Durkin, John A. Rev. O.P. 72,134, 136
Dwenger, Joseph Rt. Rev. 26,28,29, 130,131,132,140
Edelin, James V. Rev. O.P. 69,85,111
Eis, John B. Rev. 58,94-96,102,112, 127,131,139
Ely, —— Rev. Dr. 47
English, John C. 140
Eppinck, Magnus Rev. 67,109
Ewing family 22
Fahey, Joanna 129
Fahey, Julia 129
Fahey, Mary 129
Fahey, Michael 124-125,129
Fehlings, Henry Rev. 66,67,109,112
Ferneding, H. Rev. 28
Ferneding, W. Rev. 29
Finck, William E. 84
Fischer, Herman Rev. 67,110
Fitzgerald, —— 59
Fitzgerald, —— Rt. Rev. 20

Fitzgerald, Edward M. Rt. Rev. 29, 50,98,115,117,119,140
Fitzgerald, Joseph Rev. 60
Fitzgerald, Richard J. Rev. 68
Fladung, Edward L. Rev. 27,51,60, 68,108
Foley, Thomas Rt. Rev. 27,59,73,76, 140,141
Fox Settlement, St. Patrick 75,109
Franklin Twp., St. Nicholas 109
Fulda, Immaculate Conception 75,109
Gallagher, Nicholas A. Rt. Rev. 27, 51,58,59-60,68,91,99,112,128, 131,139
Gallipolis, St. Louis 110
Galveston, Holy Rosary School 81
Galvin, Michael 115
Garibaldi 13
Garvey, John H. Rev. O.P. 72
Garvey, P. Rev. 28,29
Gels, B. Rev. 29
Geneva, Sacred Heart 110
Gerts, A. Rev. 29
Gibbons, James Rt. Rev. 74
Gilmour, Richard Rt. Rev. 28,29,46, 129,132,140
Glasgow, St. Joseph 113
Glendale 45
Glenmont, SS. Peter and Paul 76, 110
Gockeln, F. W. Rev. 5
Godwin, Parke 47
Goesbriand, Louis Rt. Rev. 46
Goetz, F. J. Rev. 29
Goldschmidt, John C. Rev. 60,65, 68,94,95,103
Good Hope, O.L. of Good Hope 110

Griffin, Cecilia S.C. 62
Grimmer, Charles L. Rev. 60,68
Groveport, St. Mary 112
Guilfoyle, ―― Rev. 28
Gundersheimer, ―― 129
Halley, W. J. Rev. 28,29
Hamilton, John W. Dr. 97,138,139
Hammondsville, St. James 112
Hanging Rock 110
Harding, Michael 115-117,122,125
Harrietsville, St. Henry 75,108,110
Hartley, James J. Rt. Rev. 21-22
Hartman, Joseph E. 121,123,124
Hartman, Michael 115
Hartnedy, M. M. A. Rev. 65,68,114, 131
Hawe, William T. Rev. 113
Hecker, Isaac Rev. C.S.P. 74
Heery, Patrick M. Rev. 68
Hegeman, Annie 5-6,77
Heimo, Joseph A. Rev. 67,109
Heisser, ―― 60
Hemsteger, J. B. Rev. 29,51,56,57, 65,67,94,102,109,113,119,126, 127,132,138
Hemsteger, Mary Ligouri S.N.D. de N. 93
Henge, ―― Rev. 28
Hengehold, ―― Rev. 28
Hennaert, Peter V. Rev. 31
Hessian Hills, St. Peter 110
Higgins, Arthur Rev. O.P. 72
Hillebrand, Bernard Rev. 67,69,119
Hoban, James D. Rev. O.P. 72
Hopkins, Jemima 1,2,5,7,11
Hopkins, Stephen 1
Hopkins, Timothy 1
Howard, John 118
Ironton, St. Joseph 75,110,126

Index

Ironton, St. Lawrence 75,87,88, 110,126
Jackson, Holy Name 110,126
Jacquet, John M. Rev. 63,67,109
Jandel, Alexander V. Most Rev. O.P. 71
Jersey, St. Joseph 110
Jessing, Joseph Rev. 60,61,68,103-104,131
Jones, John L. L. 123
Joyce, ⸻ 139
Joyce, James 118
Joyce, John 115
Joyce, Mary E. 129,131,140
Juncker, Henry D. Rt. Rev. 51
Junction City — see Perry Co.
Junior Furnace 110
Kain, John J. Rt. Rev. 77,130,132, 134,140
Kalenberg, John F. Rev. 67,69,111
Karge, Francis Rev. 67,69,111
Kelly, ⸻ Rev. 28
Kelly, D. Rev. 29
Kenmert, P. Rev. 131
Kennedy, John J. Rev. 59,60
Kenrick, Francis P. Most Rev. 27
Kenrick, Peter R. Most Rev. 27,75
Kenton 45,51
Keogh, ⸻ Rev. Dr. 44
Keogh, Patrick Rev. O.P. 69,111
Killbuck, St. Elizabeth 110
Kimble, ⸻ 7
Klueber, Damian J. Rev. 67,108,109
Know-Nothings 39
Laffan, Joseph Rev. 112
Lake George, N.Y., Sacred Heart 77
Lamy, Jean Rev. 11,62
Lancaster, ⸻ Rev. Mr. 52
Lancaster, O. 22,37,50

Lancaster, St. Mary 75,87,110,126
Lane, Thomas J. Rev. 68,139
Lawson, ⸻ Mrs. 7
Leatherwood, St. Patrick 110
Legouais, Thomas Rev. 8
Lenders, Aloysia O.S.F. 101
Leonard, Theodore 86,115
Lewis Center, St. Aloysius 110
Lick Run, St. Peter 75,110
Lilly, Frances O.P. 92
Lilly, Hugh F. V. Rev. O.P. 72,136
Lilly, St. John 75
Linahan, William F. Rev. O.P. 72
Lincoln, Abraham 43
Little Hocking, St. Mary 113
Little Scioto, St. John 110
Lodi (Malvern), St. Francis X. 75-76,110
Logan, St. John 75,110,112
London, St. Patrick 76,116,118
Long Bottom 110
Loretto, St. Francis Monastery 46
Loving, Starling 97
Luers, John H. Rt. Rev. 28,
Luken, ⸻ Capt. 21
Lynch, John J. Rt. Rev. 50
Lynch, Rose O.P. 87-89,91,93
Macheboeuf, Projectus Rt. Rev. 62, 77
MacLeod, Xavier D. 24,25,28,29
Magevney, Eugene 87
Magevney, Mary Agnes O.P. 87-91, 93,139
Mallon, Francis C. Rev. 60,67,69, 109,119
Malvern -- see Lodi
Marges, Immaculate Conception 75,110
Marietta, St. Mary 110

Marion, Marion 45,66
Marion, Ohio 51
Martins Ferry 110
Marysville 75
Mattingly Settlement, Nativity of the B.V.M. 110
Mayrose, Herman H. Rev. 26,67,110
McArthur, St. Francis Evangelization Center 96
McCabe, John 115,129
McCarron, P. 9
McCloskey, John Most Rev. 51
McCloskey, William G. Rt. Rev. 27,129
McGarvey, John R. Rev. O.P. 72
McGuire, Agatha S.C. 62
McLuney, St. Dominic 70,110
McMillan, William Dr. 97
McNally, Bernard 115
McSweeney, John E. Rev. 66,67,111
Meagher, James Rev. 92
Meara, John Rev. 65,68
Meara, Michael M. Rev. 51,65,68, 102,106,125,129
Meara, Stephen 129
Meigs Creek, St. James 110
Menge, B. Rev. 29
Menge, J. J. Rev. 29
Meschenmoser, Philip Rev. 95,108
Metzger, Charles V. Rev. O.P. 72
Miller, Sallie 140
Miller, Thomas 86
Millersburg, St. Peter 76,113
Miltonsburg, St. John 110
Minerton, St. Mary 110,126
Moeller, Most Rev. Henry 127
Moitrier, Francis Rev. 94,108,131
Monday Creek, St. Peter 110
Monroe Furnace 110

Monroe, James 3
Montag, John G. Rev. 68
Morrogh, W. P. Rev. 28
Morrough, —— Rev. Dr. 44
Mt. Vernon, St. Vincent de Paul 111,126
Mulhane, Lawrence W. Rev. 131
Murphy, —— Rt. Rev. 15
Murphy, Patrick 118
Murray City, St. Philip Outreach 96
Murray, Jeremiah A. Rev. 60,65,68, 69,125,128
Murray, John B. Rev. 69,119
Nagel, Charles 129
Naghten, William 115,118
Nativism 20
Naughton, James 115,129
Nesbit, Phoebe 2
Nevill, J. C. 118
New Lexington, St. Aloysius Academy 94-96,108
New Lexington, St. Rose 70,94,95, 108,111
New Straitsville, St. Augustine 112
New York, St. Patrick 77,80
Newark, Ohio 51
Newark, St. Francis de Sales 45,61- 64,71,75,87,111,118
Newark, St. Francis de Sales Academy 62
Noon, Dominic Rev. O.P. 69,111
Nordmeyer, John Rev. 66,67,109
Nothnagel, —— Prov. 132
O'Boylan, Bernard M. Rev. 65,68
O'Brian, —— Rev. O.P. 85,136
O'Brien, Margaret 125
O'Brien, Matthew A., O.P. 11
O'Brien, William F. Rev. 57
O'Carroll, William V. Rev. O.P. 71

Index

O'Dea, —— 59
O'Donoghue, James Rev. 29
O'Donoghue, Philip J. Rev. 66,67, 110
O'Donohue, J. B. Rev. 29
O'Donohue, Michael Rev. 29
O'Leary, Charles M.D. 24,25
O'Mahoney, Jeremiah Rev. O.P. 72
O'Reilly, —— Rev. 119
O'Reilly, William Rev. 66,68
O'Shea, T. Rev. 29
Pabish, Francis Rev. 24
Patriz, Constantino Cdl. 16
Pecoraro, Christina O.S.F. 96
Perche, Napoleon Rt. Rev. 74
Perry Co., St. Patrick 69-70,75,86, 126
Peter, Sarah Worthington 97
Phalen, —— 7
Philips Church, St. Joseph 111
Pilger, Nicholas Rev. 60,67,110
Pindar, Christopher Rev. 66,67,109
Pine Grove, St. Mary 75,111,126
Piqua 45,51
Pius IX 13,15,20,27,73
Pomeroy, Sacred Heart 64,103,111, 126
Pomeroy, St. Joseph's Orphan Asylum 103
Pond Creek, Holy Trinity 111
Portsmouth, Holy Redeemer 64,75, 87,111
Portsmouth, St. Mary 75,111
Postlewaite, —— 11
Price, —— Gen. 37-38
Purcell, Edward V. Rev. 11,18-19, 27, 28,30,31,34,61,64
Purcell, Johanna 22
Purcell, John B. Rt. Rev. and Most Rev. 11,12,15-17,21,22,27,28,32, 34,35,42,43,46,49-52,56,59-64,66, 69,74-75,77,92,115,117,124,129, 131-133,139
Quantrill, William 35
Quinlan, John Rt. Rev. 24,25,51
Quinn, William Rev. O.P. 72
Rainbow Creek, Ave Maria 111
Rappe, Amadeus Rt. Rev. 37
Rauck, John J. 67,111
Red Republicans 13ff,20,39
Riches, William 115,118,124
Rochford, John A. Rev. O.P. 58,70, 71,111,115,128,136
Rosecrans, Annie — see Hegeman
Rosecrans, Annie (Anita) 54,78,81
Rosecrans, Charles W. 2,81
Rosecrans, Chauncey 2
Rosecrans, Crandall 1,2,5,7,9,11
Rosecrans, Daniel Capt. 1
Rosecrans, Daniel Dr. 1
Rosecrans, Henry C. 2,81
Rosecrans, Jemima — see Hopkins
Rosecrans, Lily 77,78,82
Rosecrans, Louis Adrian Rev. C.S.P. 74,77,78-80
Rosecrans, Mamie (Mary Louise) 48,54,80-81
Rosecrans, Mary (Sr. Imelda) 81-82, 140
Rosecrans, Parmenus 12
Rosecrans, Sylvester
 birth 2
 at Kenyon College 3-5
 conversion 5-7
 Baptism 7
 First Communion 8
 Confirmation 9
 vocation 9-10

at St. John's College
7-10,45,47,77
journey to Rome 12-13
in Rome 13-16
Ordination 14,17-18
minor orders 15
subdeaconate 16
Doctor of Theology 16
pastor at St. Thomas, Cin'ti 17
professor of theology 17-18,29,
39,50,51
editor of *The Catholic
Telegraph* 18-20,32-34
the Bedini incident 22-25
president of Mt. St. Mary's
College 23-27,77
auxiliary bishop 27
consecration 27-30
and the Civil War 31-39
school examiner 39
shot in the leg 39-42
episcopal acts a auxiliary 42-43
his humility 42
as lecturer 43-46
his book 44
at Second Plenary Council 48
pastor of St. Patrick, Columbus
50-51
Assistant to the Pontifical
Throne 52
appointed Bishop of Columbus
52
character as bishop 54-55
first pastoral letter 56
seal 57
crozier 57
controversies with Archbishop
Purcell 59-64
problem clergy 66

relations with Dominican
Fathers 69-73
avoids the Vatican Council 73-75
papal infallibility 74-75,205-208
relations with Dominican Sisters
84-92
residence at Sacred Heart
Academy 90
editor of *The Catholic
Columbian* 107,208
pastoral letter on the cathedral
debt 127
and costly churches 128,183
illness 135ff
devotion to St. Joseph 137-138
death 139-140
tomb 140,142
Rosecrans, William S. 1,2,4-10,21-
22, 25,32,35,37,38, 41,47,76-81,
104,124,125,137
Ross, Charles 42
Rudolph, Francis R. Rev. 67,69,110
Ryan, Michael J. D. Rev. 26,67,110
Ryan, Patrick J. Rev. 51
Sandusky, Sts. Peter and Paul 47
Saunders, George W. 124
Scallon, Thomas A. Rev. O.P. 72
Scammon, Ezekiel P. J. 24-25,41,79
Scannell, Patrick J. Rev. O.P. 72
Schelhamer, Charles Rev. 26
Schmitt, John B. Rev. 95,131
Sheehan, P. Rev. 29
Sheehy, J. D. V. Rev. O.P. 72,111
Shiff, J. Rev. 29
Sisters of Charity of Cin'ti 61-64
Sisters of Notre Dame de Namur
51,89
Sisters of Our Lady of Charity of
the Good Shepherd 98,102,113

Index

Sisters of St. Dominic 64,81,84-92
Sisters of St. Francis of Penance and Christian Charity 94-96,100-103,113
Sisters of St. Joseph 104-105
Sisters of the Poor of St. Francis 97-98,101
Skinner, —— 60
Slevin, James J. Rev. 60,68
Smith, —— Rector 4
Smith, Andrew J. 9
Sofge, Henry 25
Somerset, Holy Trinity 70,71,84-85,111
Somerset, Sacred Heart Academy 81,91
Somerset, St. Joseph 69,70-72,75, 85,111,136
Somerset, St. Joseph's College 22, 70,85
Somerset, St. Mary's Academy 75, 84-86
Soprania, —— Rev. S.J. 28
Sorin, Edward Rev. 36
South Fork, St. Pius 70,111
Spalding, John L. Rt. Rev. 26,53, 77,130,132
Spalding, Martin J. Rt. Rev. 27,28, 32,38,48,51,74
Specht, F. X. Rev. 26,51,67,108, 119,127,131
Spitznagel, Genevieve S.C. 62
Springfield 45
Springfield, St. Raphael 41
St. Mary's, Indiana 47
Stambaugh, —— 60
Steubenville, St. Peter 64,75,111, 112,126
Steyle, Philip Rev. 68

Stockport, St. James 111
Stoehle, —— Rev. 28
Stone, James K. Rev. C.S.P. 77
Sullivan, P. J. 140
Sweeney, Teresa S.S.J. 104
Syracuse 111
Taggart, Rose O.P. 86
Tancioni, Philip Dr. 27
Taylorstown 111
Tello, Hortense S.S.J. 104
Thebaud, Augustus J., S.J. 10
Thienpont, Emmanuel Rev. 67,110, 112
Thisse, J. N. Rev. 28,29
Thurheimer, P. Rev. 131
Timon, John, Rt. Rev. 51
Toebbe, August M. Rt. Rev. 28,29, 51,73,129,132,140
Toole, Joseph K. Gov. 81,82
Tuohy, Joseph Rev. 65,68
Tuomey, Thomas Rev. 65,68
Turney, Owen T. 106
Ullrich, Anthony 59
Urbana 45
Ursuline Sisters 78
Valandingham, Clement 34,35
Vatican Council 73
Victor Emmanuel 52
Vilanis, Felix Rev. 6-7
Vogt, —— Rev. 28
Wachten, —— Rev. 28
Walker, Augustine O. Rev. 67,111, 126
Wall, William 115,129
Walshe, —— Rev. 28
Washington Furnace 111
Watterson, John A. Rt. Rev. 91,106
Weisinger, Simon P. Rev. 68
Whalen, James Rt. Rev. O.P. 72-73

Whalen, Martin 115
Wheeling 77
Whittler, Joseph Rev. 29
Whytler, —— Rev. 28
Wieser, —— 95
Wilcox, Thankful 1,2
Wilder, —— 39
Williams, Sylvester S.C. 62
Wills Creek, St. Ann 111
Wills Creek, St. Joseph 111
Wiseman, —— Cdl. 17
Wismann, B. Rev. 26,67,109,126
Woesman, Francis M. Rev. 68
Wolfe, Zita S.S.J. 104
Wolke, Thomas 78
Wood, James Most Rev. 15,27,44, 52
Woodsfield, St. Sylvester 111
Worthington 111
Young, Josue Rt. Rev. 37
Young, Raymond N. Rev. O.P. 85
Zaleski, St. Sylvester 66,108,111,126
Zanesville, St. Columba's Academy 87-88
Zanesville, St. Nicholas 75,111
Zanesville, St. Thomas Aquinas 70, 72,75,87,111
Zettler, Louis 102,104